Darra Goldstein's interest in Russian cookery began in her childhood when her grandmother, an émigré, taught her various Russian recipes. As a foreign student at Leningrad State University she pursued her interest in Russian food, and as a guide for a travelling US Department of Agriculture exhibition that toured the Soviet Union, she enjoyed the hospitality of people from Alma-Ata to Odessa who shared with her their cherished family recipes.

A graduate of Vassar College and a Ph.D. from Stanford University, she is assistant professor of Russian literature at Williams College, Massachusetts.

A Taste of Russia

DARRA GOLDSTEIN

SPHERE BOOKS LIMITED

First published in Great Britain by
Robert Hale 1985
Copyright © Darra Goldstein 1983, 1985
Published by Sphere Books Ltd 1987
27 Wrights Lane, London W8 5TZ

Printed and bound in Great Britain by
Collins, Glasgow

'When you come for a visit, we'll give you melons the likes of which you've never tasted! And you'll find no better honey in any other village. Why, when we bring in the honeycomb, the scent fills the room! You can't imagine it, our honey is pure as the Tsarina's tears, or the clear crystal of her earrings. And the pies, what pies my old lady will feed you! If you only knew, they're sugar, pure sugar! and the butter brims on your lips when you bite into them! Wizards these old ladies are! Did you ever drink kvass made from pears and blackthorn berries? or vodka infused with raisins and plums? Have you eaten frumenty with milk? My friends, what glorious flavours there are in the world! Once you start eating, you can hardly stop . . . ah, sweet nectar of life! Why, only last year. . . . But what am I prattling on about? You'll just have to come and see us, come soon! We'll feed you such treats you'll tell all the world . . .'

Rudi Panko, Beekeeper, in Gogol's
Evenings on a Farm near Dikanka

To my Russian friends

Contents

Preface

My interest in Russian cuisine stems from two sources. As a student of literature, I was eager to satisfy my curiosity about the preparation of foods described in Russian novels and short stories. More deeply rooted in me, though, were memories from childhood – the dishes I first tasted from my grandmother's spoon.

My grandmother emigrated to America from White Russia in the early part of the century. We called her Baba, and whenever she came to visit, her favourite pastime (her only pastime!) was cooking and baking for her grandchildren. I could spend hours at her side in the kitchen, watching her fingers deftly rolling out the dough for my favourite jam-filled biscuits, *rogaliki*. She would let me choose the jam and spread it on, and I always opted for a mixture of plum and cherry. Baba made the cookies early in the morning so we could have them fresh for lunch. As soon as they were safely baking in the oven, she'd start preparing the evening meal. It might be *golubtsy*, 'little doves', a mixture of minced beef and rice carefully rolled up in cabbage leaves and simmered in a spicy tomato sauce, or a tender pot roast flavoured with rum, or chicken stewed for long hours with prunes and sometimes apricots. Baba never followed a recipe, but as I grew older I would ask her questions as she cooked, hoping to be able to reproduce her delicious meals once she was gone.

Later, when I began studying Russian literature, I was struck by the number of references to food in obscure tales as well as in the classics. The opulence of the aristocratic tables thrilled and enchanted me, while the descriptions of thick soups and chewy breads – the foods I had grown up on – invariably sent me running to the kitchen for a snack. Luckily, not all of my pleasure was vicarious. I was fortunate to be able to experience Russian food first-hand, as a student in Leningrad and later as a guide for a travelling exhibition which toured several Soviet cities. People from Odessa to Alma-Ata generously opened their homes to me, and my hosts were always eager to share their treasured recipes. From them, I learned how the culinary art had evolved from the nineteenth-century extravaganzas described in literature to the monumental *zakuska* buffets of today. Each new family I met asserted that *theirs* was the best kvass, *theirs* the best cabbage-rolls. And when I think of the friends behind each recipe, they do seem like the best to me.

Other recipes in this book were given to me by émigré friends, and I combed old Russian cookbooks for the interesting and the unusual. I wanted to share my love of the Russian people and their cuisine. I wanted to write a book which not only described how to prepare traditional foods, but which also painted the Russian life and culture corresponding to them.

One word of warning is in order, lest the delicacies presented cause the reader to assume that *coulibiac* and champagne-sturgeon soup are the usual fare of Russians today. The Soviet Union suffers from a chronic, and at times severe, food shortage, and Russians more often dine on kasha, canned peas and cabbage soup than on a cut of meat. Food distribution is based on a system of hierarchies, in which Moscow, most prominent and visible to Western eyes, receives priority over all other Soviet cities. Next on the ladder come the capitals of the larger republics, along with the military and scientific centres, and so on down the rungs, until the smallest rural villages receive their meagre allocations, which provide for only the barest necessities. A common sight on the Moscow metro are peasant women, laden with sacks of produce and sausage, heading home to their villages after buying up food for their families, friends and neighbours. Muscovites blame their shortages on the hordes of peasants who arrive daily and buy up the stock.

Even within these city allocations, there exists a hierarchy of privileged positions and special stores. The system is a complicated one, but the point is that some people are able to eat much better than others. And the reason is not simply a matter of money, as in Western society, but rather of influence, 'pull', or *blat*, as it is called in Russian. In Moscow particularly, there are special stores closed to the general public which sell everything from fresh caviar to Heinz ketchup. The food in these stores is purchased with coupons, not money, and very few people have access to the coupons. In addition, there are foreign currency stores which stock imported delicacies – but of course it's illegal for a Soviet citizen to possess foreign currency.

Yet the Russians are nothing if not resourceful, and even the average citizen knows how to obtain good food. There exists an extensive system of barter. If, for example, Natalia Fyodorovna works at a meat shop, she can reserve for her friends the minced beef that has just arrived. Her friend Sofia Pavlovna, who works in the dairy, returns the favour, and when good butter comes in she sets it aside. Virtually any foodstuffs can be had in this manner, trading what one can get for what one cannot; it is simply a matter of knowing the right people, cultivating good connections. When I lived in the Soviet Union, I didn't immediately understand why the shops had nothing at all on the shelves while I was served all kinds of meat and fish at people's homes. The reason is simple: most of the food exchange goes on *under* the counter, not across it. Even the vocabulary is expressive of this fact of Russian life. Most products cannot simply be 'bought' (*kupit'*), but they *can* be 'obtained' (*dostat'*).

This business of getting food is a complicated game one must learn in order to survive, but it can be learned only by experience. In Kishinev I was invited to spend New Year's Eve with some friends. A few weeks earlier I'd been served a sumptuous feast in their home, and so I ate lightly all day, anticipating the celebration and the endless parade of courses. The night was bitterly cold, and by the time I reached their flat, I craved hot food. But the table that greeted me was virtually bare: one hunk of cheese sat in the centre, surrounded by bottles of cheap wine and vodka and a few boxes of confectionery. My friends apologised, complaining that Kishinev's allocation was poor, and all the food in the city had been bought up within a few hours in anticipation of the New Year. As we thought-fully munched our sweets (called, ironically, *ptich'ye moloko* or 'bird's milk': that which is so divine it cannot be had), I began to under-stand why women stood for hours in queues, waiting in sub-zero temperatures for the fruit someone had said was about to appear: if they didn't get there first, they might get nothing at all. Soon I too found myself buying up anything new that appeared in the shops, hoarding against the time when there might be nothing at all.

So although it is possible to eat relatively well in the Soviet Union today, one mustn't forget the extremes of inconvenience, conni-vance and expense people are often driven to for items as basic as a few oranges, sausages, or even milk. The effort of shopping is enormous, making the Russians' hospitality all the more generous. One wonders how many Western families would regale guests so lavishly if they had to go to even half the trouble.

Yet in spite of all the difficulties, the Russians still take great pleasure in preparing a good meal. Even if ingredients are often near impossible to obtain, even if meals at State-controlled restaurants are at best uncertain, the art of Russian cooking is still thriving.

Apart from Russian friends who helped (immeasurably!) in the creation of this book, I would also like to acknowledge the aid of the following people: Brett Singer, for that initial elbow in my side; Elaine Markson, my kind and enterprising agent; Jill Norman and Anne Freedgood, my wise and discerning editors; George Curth, for his help at every stage, Helen Haft and Irving Goldstein, my parents, for their endless encouragement and cheerful labours in the kitchen; and my husband, Dean Crawford, for his unflagging support, ideas, and *mots justes* – and for staying with me despite all that beetroot.

Introduction

There is an old Russian saying which goes something like this: 'You can rack your brains, but you can't beat hospitality!' Odd as this saying may be, it does capture the Russian sentiment towards guests, whom they love to regale with food and drink. As an American living in the Soviet Union, I was invited to countless homes. In most cases I hardly knew my hosts, but the moment I entered their flat I became their *dorogoi gost'*, their 'dear guest', and was treated to all they could lavish upon me throughout the evening. Their hospitality extended beyond the offering of physical sustenance. The Russians love to bestow gifts, and the uninitiated had better beware openly admiring anything in a Russian home: within a matter of minutes it will be quietly offered along with the food. The gift of hospitality is felt all the more keenly in the Soviet Union of today, where obtaining even a good piece of meat is a considerable feat. Yet somehow the Russians manage, and it is their greatest joy to present a well-laden table to their guests, especially to those who have come from afar.

Hospitality is a long-standing tradition in Russian culture. The reader of Russian literature is apt to find his mouth watering at the abundant feasts and simple peasant meals so richly described by classic Russian authors. At least one favourite character, Oblomov, of Goncharov's novel of the same name, does nothing in almost five hundred pages but lounge in bed, daydream, and eat sumptuous meals. Unfortunately, being so lethargic, Oblomov rarely entertains; thus he neglects the Russian custom of sharing one's larder with guests both anticipated and unexpected, and suffers accordingly. A prescribed etiquette exists for sharing food with guests. In Gogol's *Ivan Fyodorovich Shponka and His Aunt*, Shponka drops in on his neighbours unexpectedly. The hostess asks him if he'd like some vodka, for which she is severely rebuked by her son: 'You're not yourself, Mother!' cries Grigory Grigorevich. 'Whoever asks a visitor whether he wants anything? You just give it to him, that's all.' An old Russian saying affirms that only the ailing should be asked if they want to eat, because undoubtedly the healthy will want to! In Russian and Soviet society it is not thought impolite to drop in unannounced at a neighbour's or friend's flat, even at suppertime – the host can then take delight in begging the visitor to stay and share the evening meal. The presence of a guest is still considered an honour: it is the host who should thank his guests for coming, not the other way round.

There are many customs and superstitions regarding the receiving and entertaining of guests: greetings must take place either within the apartment or outside in the hall, since it is unlucky to shake hands or embrace over the threshold; at the table, wine must be poured from the bottle in a certain way in order not to tempt ill fate; unmarried women should never take the last morsel of food from a platter, lest they become old maids; a cigarette should never be lit from a candle flame; and before embarking on a journey, family and friends must gather and sit down in silence, wishing the traveller godspeed. The Russians love ritual – it is a large part of their daily lives even today – and hospitality is the foremost ritual in which standards of perfection must be met.

The Russian word for hospitality, *khlebosol'stvo*, is formed from two words, *khleb* 'bread' and *sol'* 'salt'. Together the words mean 'regaling with bread and salt'. To offer one's bread is to honour one's guest, and no Russian meal is complete without several richly-flavoured loaves. In old Russia it was the custom to present the guest with a loaf of freshly-baked bread (usually rye), lavishly decorated with cut-out bits of dough. This loaf, the *karavai*, often grew to an immense size. A wooden dish of salt was offered along with the bread. Sometimes the salt dish was even placed in a special indentation in the centre of the loaf. As soon as the guests appeared, the ornate *karavai* was brought to the table, and the guest cut the first thick slice of bread to dip in the salt, saying '*Khleb da sol'!*', 'Bread and salt!' or, less literally, '*Bon appétit!*' This ritual of sharing bread and salt at table came to be synonymous with the Russian concept of hospitality; hence the word *khlebosol'stvo*. To this day the Russians are capable of eating an astounding amount of bread: a family of four easily consumes two to three loaves a day, and if guests are coming, the number substantially increases. But this should come as no surprise. Russian bread is among the best in the world.

The old Russian ritual of hospitality was not confined to just bread and salt, however. A *samovar* or urn for hot water was kept always heated, ready for the arrival of unexpected guests. Guests were always accorded the best and most comfortable seats in the house. Here a distinction must be made between the pre-revolutionary gentry and nobility, and the peasantry.

The gentry usually received guests in the drawing room, in the Western manner. From there the party would move on to another chamber, where they could feast on *zakuski*, an elaborate array of hors d'œuvres, until the servants announced that dinner was ready in the dining hall. The origins of the *zakuska* table can be traced back to Scandinavia through the dynasty of Rurik, who came to rule the heathen Slavic tribes in the ninth century AD. The *zakuska* table proved well suited to the practical needs of the Russian way of life. Due to bad weather and poor roads, house guests invariably arrived late. With a large *zakuska* table set and ready at all times, the cold and hungry guests could refresh themselves immediately after their journey and dinner was not jeopardised by standing around too long.

It was a different matter in the homes of the peasantry. Peasant cottages often consisted of only one room, most of which was taken up by the marvellously versatile Russian stove, the *pech'*. The stove had two ovens: one for slow simmering and one for quick baking. It was enormous, occupying up to a third of the entire living area, because not only was the stove used for heating and all kinds of cooking and baking, it was also equipped with a sleeping ledge, the cosiest spot in the cottage. The ledge was usually reserved for old grandmothers with aching bones, but lazy children loved to scramble up on to it and try to loll away the day there undetected. Russian fairytales abound in stories of evil step-mothers who lie around on the stove all day while their long-suffering step-daughters work. Noble estates also housed large stoves with sleeping space, but the ledge was relegated to the maidservants, as the gentry themselves preferred the luxury of goosedown mattresses and comforters on a wooden bedstead.

The guest in the peasant cottage was invited to make himself comfortable in one of two honoured spots: on top of the stove or in the icon corner. The icon corner was usually situated opposite the stove and at least one icon hung there – often more, depending on the family's affluence – along with a constantly burning lamp. Beneath the icons stood the only table in the cottage, and there the guests were most often invited to sit. This corner was known as the *krasnoye mesto*, the 'beautiful spot'. The Russian language has a rich storehouse of sayings to describe these places of honour for guests. A typical greeting was 'Welcome to our cottage! Our beautiful spot is for our beautiful guest.' Or 'Make yourself at home! Climb up on to the stove!' And once a guest actually had clambered up on to the stove, he was considered one of the family.

Food in Russian literature

These rituals of hospitality were all preliminaries leading up to the main attraction, the meal itself. This meal could range from a simple, yet thoroughly satisfying bowl of *borshch* (beetroot soup), served with black bread and home-cured pickles, to a lavish feast of many courses, including such delicacies as *ryabchik* (partridge) in a sour cherry sauce, or the roe of sturgeon, better known as caviar.

Obviously the gentry ate a great variety of foods and enjoyed all kinds of delicacies, while the peasantry knew little other than their repertoire of hearty soups and *pirogi* (pies). Russian literature is rich in descriptions of food because to a Russian, cooking and eating are vital concerns. Great moments in literature often coincide with an account of what is being – or about to be – consumed. This practice extends to even the most spiritual of Russian writers. In the chapter entitled 'A Scandal' of *The Brothers Karamazov*, by Dostoevsky, Fyodor Pavlovich Karamazov has been invited to the Father Superior's room at the monastery. The initial description of the room focuses on a lavishly set table, dazzling the eye:

. . . but the main splendour at the moment was the luxuriously set table: the cloth sparkled, the china shone. There were three kinds of superbly baked breads, two bottles of wine and two of the monastery's own wonderful *kvas*, renowned throughout the region. There was no vodka. . . . Five courses were prepared for dinner: *ukha* with sterlet and *pirozhki* with fish; poached fish, prepared in a special, delicious way; salmon cutlets; ice cream and compote; and finally a fruit pudding, like blancmange.

The Russian Orthodox monasteries enforced an injunction against eating game killed by snare, so no wild fowl was served. And since no meat is featured at the Father Superior's table, we realise that this is a Lenten menu. Still, the food is tempting, in spite of the religious proscriptions; but true to Dostoevskian form, the meal remains untouched, because Fyodor Pavlovich makes a scene, the 'scandal' of the chapter heading: the visitors eventually leave without ever having sat down to table.

Many of the gentry emulated foreign mannerisms and foreign food, and entire meals were prepared *à la française* or *à l'anglaise*. When, in Tolstoy's *Anna Karenina*, Oblongsky invites Levin to dine at one of Moscow's most fashionable restaurants, he displays his refined taste by ordering a totally French meal: *soupe printanière, turbot, sauce Beaumarchais, poularde à l'estragon, macédoine de fruits*. Levin, very much a Tolstoyan character, would rather eat a simple bowl of overwhelmingly Russian *shchi* (cabbage soup) and *grechnevaya kasha* (buckwheat groats). The dichotomy between the two men, and between the two opposing camps in Russia – the Westernisers and the Slavophiles – is dramatised throughout the passage by the food they order. Even at 'French' meals, however, the service remained traditionally Russian. The various courses were brought to table separately; only desserts and flowers were allowed to remain on the table throughout the meal. These desserts were often sculpted and used as centrepieces.

It is ironic that the nineteenth-century Russian gentry worked so hard at being worldly: the French meanwhile were adapting to the idea of dining *à la russe*! French society first became enthralled with Russian culture around 1811, when Tsar Alexander I sent one of his court favourites to Paris as ambassador. This ambassador was a renowned epicure, and since Napoleon and his troops marched on Russia shortly thereafter, it can be surmised that the ambassador was more skilled in gustatory than diplomatic affairs. In spite of the hostilities, however, the Russian gastronomic romance with all things French reached its zenith under this same Alexander I, when the great Carême was invited, at Prince Bagration's request, to serve as the Tsar's personal chef. Carême served well, if condescendingly, but after being forced to prepare the victory banquet celebrating Napoleon's defeat by the Russian army, he refused to cook for the Tsar any longer. His personal legacy to Russian cuisine is the *sharlotka*, better known under its French name as *charlotte russe*.

As mentioned earlier, Russian service differed from the French in that each course was brought to table separately, the second not appearing until the first had been cleared away, and so on throughout the meal. At formal dinners even the china and cutlery were replaced as the meal progressed. Service *à la russe* ensured steaming hot soups, juicy roasts, and refreshingly chilled puddings. The diner could thus enjoy each course in turn and anticipate the next, without the distraction of having to face it on the table before him, cooling and congealing in its own gravy. French service, by contrast, relied on a feast for the eye: as the diners entered the hall, they were struck by an abundantly laden table – the myriad foods, displayed with beauty and grace, eliciting sighs and salivations, and designed to dazzle. Unfortunately, all too often, such awesome arrays of food had been sitting out for some time, and what tempted the eye was likely to disappoint the palate. The Russians, of course, deemed their service superior, especially since their copious *zakuska* table also fulfilled the function of the French *joie pour les yeux*. Gradually Russian service took hold, and by the late 1850s much of fashionable Europe was dining *à la russe*. Charles Dickens, an innovator in gastronomy as in literature, entertained in the Russian style, offering his critics a chance to censure him for more than his tales. The Russian table, once considered uncouth – even barbaric – by the 'civilised' Europeans, soon became the dominant mode; our modern-day table service, although modified, is its direct descendant.

It must be stressed that only the Russian upper class dined so extravagantly. Many aristocrats either did not know the riches of their own native cuisine, or else eschewed them, leaving the exploration of simpler food to those who did not affect French manners – the petty landowners who ran small estates in the backwoods of Russia and the Ukraine. This class of Russians also knew how to dine well. The management of their estates occupied their lives: they kept kitchen gardens; dried, salted and preserved fruits and vegetables; planted, reaped and laid up stores against the bitter Russian winter. Two such typical landowners, husband and wife, provide the theme for Gogol's story, *Old-World Landowners*. In the story the couple's lives revolve around food. It is the panacea for all complaints, real or imagined, so long as they have each other. Gogol's tale captures the essence of rural life in Russia and the Ukraine: one can almost smell the curd pies sizzling in freshly-churned butter; the sour aroma of cabbage put up in large oaken barrels lined with black-currant leaves; the spicy scent of wood grouse roasting in the oven, its garnish of gooseberries imparting a tartness to the air. The tale's heroine is the lady of the house, Pulkheria Ivanovna.

For Pulkheria Ivanovna, housekeeping meant continually locking and un-locking the pantry, salting, drying and preserving an endless number of fruits and vegetables. Her house was like a chemical laboratory. A fire was constantly tended under the apple tree; and the kettle or copper vat – filled with jam, jelly, or confections made with honey, and sugar, and I can hardly remember what else – was almost never removed from its iron tripod. Under another tree, in a copper cauldron, the coachman was forever distilling vodka with peach leaves, with bird-cherry blossoms, with cen-taury or cherry stones, and by the end of the process he was in no condition even to lift his tongue, muttering such nonsense that Pulkheria Ivanovna couldn't understand a thing. Then he'd always head for the kitchen to sleep it off. Pulkheria Ivanovna always liked to prepare more than was needed, to have some on hand, and so much stuff was preserved, salted and dried, that it would have buried the entire estate, had not the maidservants eaten a good half of it, sneaking into the pantry and stuffing themselves to such an extent that for the rest of the day they'd groan and complain about their stomachs.

As Gogol's narrator states, 'Both of the old people, in the time-honoured tradition of old-world landowners, loved to eat.' The story goes on to describe a typical day of eating: an early breakfast with coffee; a mid-morning snack of lard biscuits, poppy seed pies and salted mushrooms; a late-morning snack of vodka, more mushrooms and dried fish; a dinner at noon of various porridges and stews, their juices tightly sealed in earthenware pots; an early afternoon snack of watermelon and pears; a mid-afternoon snack of fruit dumplings with berries; a late-afternoon snack of yet other delicacies from the larder; supper at half-past nine; and finally, long after they'd retired to bed, a midnight snack of sour milk and stewed dried pears, calculated to relieve the stomachache brought on by the excesses of the day. Other characters in Gogol face the same problems: the narrator in *A Bewitched Place* boasts that 'sometimes we'd eat so many cucumbers, melons, turnips, onions and peas, that I swear you'd have thought there were cocks crowing in our stomachs.' No detail is overlooked in describing the foods these typical landowners enjoyed, foods not at all influenced by the French mode of the time. It was hard work being the mistress of an estate, and those who managed it well were highly regarded and, of course, well-fed.

For an accurate sense of the social importance of food and the extent of Russian hospitality, one need only read almost any nineteenth-century classic of Russian literature. Taken as a whole, the books cover a broad spectrum of Russian life. Tolstoy describes magnificent repasts in the French style among the nobility. Chekhov takes us into the sitting rooms of the gentry where elegant teas are served. Gogol's narrator, speaking of the old-world landowners, relates: 'But the old couple seemed most interesting to me when they had guests. Then everything in their house took on a new air. One might say that these kind people lived for their guests. They brought out the best of all they had and vied with one another in regaling you with everything their household produced.'

In *Gulag Archipelago*, Solzhenitsyn adds another lament to the already unbearable lives of political prisoners caught in a 'Catch-22' situation: they craved books to read, yet if they managed to get hold of a Gogol or Chekhov, their position often became even harder to endure: 'And it was harder still to be betrayed by an author whose books you'd loved – if he started drooling over food in great detail, then away with him! Get away from me, Gogol! The same with you, Chekhov! Both of them had just too much food in their books.'

Regional specialities

The state of the culinary art in Russia remained virtually the same from the time of Carême until the 1917 Revolution. Then, in gastronomy, as in all other aspects of life, things changed suddenly and radically. There were no more gentry to lazily pass long summer days directing servants in the art of preserving. Most women began to work outside the home, and little time remained for complicated culinary endeavours. The peasantry thronged to the cities, where they found housing in cramped apartments, often sharing one small kitchen with several other families. There were no large pantries, no Russian stoves to simmer stews or bake the hearty breads. People stopped eating the way they once had, but interest in food hardly diminished. Instead, the Russians began to adapt to the new conditions by developing a less complex cuisine. One favourable result was that yearly trips to the spa to 'cure' the liver from an overdose of rich food became less frequent. The contemporary visitor to Russia will still find chicken Kiev on most restaurant menus, but in a Soviet home one is more likely to be served chicken stew or spicy meatballs.

As if to compensate for the diminishing treasures of their own cuisine, the Russians have eagerly adopted regional specialities from the other republics. Technically speaking, Russia is only one of the fifteen republics that comprise the Soviet Union; just over half of the Soviet Union's total population is ethnically Russian, and each republic has maintained its own culinary tradition. The Soviet cuisine is varied indeed when one considers that the republics extend from the Baltic Sea (where food is rich in butter, cream and eggs) to the mountains bordering China (where standard fare is fermented mare's milk and exotic lamb stews) to the Sea of Okhotsk (where local delicacies include *balyk* and *vesiga* – the dried and salted fillet and backbone of the sturgeon) to the far north beyond the Arctic Circle (where they feast on *stroganina* – frozen raw fish).

The Russians especially love the cookery of Georgia, a southern republic in the Caucasus mountains, where fresh fruits grow all year round – a source of wonder and longing to the Russians trapped for long months in frost and ice. Ever since the early nineteenth century, when Lermontov romanticised the Caucasus in his poetry and prose, the Russians have felt a deep attraction to the dark-eyed Georgian people with their fiery tempers and fiery food. The blander Russian cuisine has eagerly adopted many spicy southern specialities such as *shashlyk* (skewered lamb) with pomegranate sauce, chicken *tabaka* (pressed and grilled chicken) and *kharcho* (a soup spiced with coriander), as well as other exotic dishes. One of the finest restaurants in Moscow, the *Aragvi* on Gorky Street, serves exclusively Georgian food. The whole restaurant bespeaks bygone elegance: the walls and ceilings are decorated with ornate eastern patterns; marble columns gleam ivory and pink; a small balcony alcove reveals a band of dark-eyed musicians who delight the diners with gay Georgian melodies. The *Aragvi* kitchens bake a special soft Georgian bread daily, and knowing Muscovites flock there to buy it hot from the oven. Because the demand for good food is so great in Moscow, it is almost impossible to get into the *Aragvi*. A crowd of people can always be seen milling outside the entrance, hoping the doorman might relent and let them in after all.

The Georgians are famed not only for their culinary expertise, but for their business acumen as well. They are notorious entrepreneurs, lacking neither the goods – fresh lemons, tangerines, pomegranates, dates – nor the market. Snowbound Russians are willing to pay almost any price and stand in queues of almost any length, to buy even a single lemon to brighten the grey winter skies and perk up the ubiquitous cabbage soup. Each Soviet city has a large central market place, and even far north of the Caucasus range it is not uncommon to see the ferocious-looking Georgian farmers, with their long moustaches and high, conical Astrakhan hats, selling fruit out of the cotton string bags used to transport it in. These bags crowd the aisles of aeroplanes and trains, holding the promise of fast fortune for the farmers. I can remember lemons in December selling two for 2 roubles 50 kopecks, or almost £1.50 apiece, in the Moldavian capital of Kishinev. Further north they command even higher prices.

Entertaining Russian-style

As in the days of the Tsar, the Russians still love to entertain, and the centre of any home is still the table, which stands in the largest room of the apartment, often in the middle of the floor. The Russians have a great knack for seating a large number of people around a small table. No one minds bumping elbows or knees: there is an intensity and excitement in such close contact. The table is spread with a clean linen cloth and small plates are set at each place. Most of the table is taken up by bottles and glasses. Each setting requires a small *ryumochka* (shot glass) for vodka and another for cognac, a goblet for wine or champagne, and a glass for juice, kvass (home-brewed beer) or mineral water. Bottles of each of these libations are placed directly on the table and remain there throughout the meal. All of the bottles are opened before the meal even begins – an impossible amount to imbibe, it would seem. But Russian meals last for hours on end, and invariably, by the end of the meal, all the bottles are empty, some even replaced.

The table is also laden with an assortment of five to ten *zakuski*, both hot and cold, accompanied by the mandatory loaves of bread. There is usually a choice of rye or white. Russians consider the white bread finer and more suitable for guests, but I always chose the rye, finding the blander white bread fit only for heaping with fresh caviar, where it does not compete with the subtle flavour of the roe. As part of the *zakuska* there are often several salads drenched with sour cream, composed of cucumbers and radishes in the winter, tomatoes and spring onions in the summer. Crystal dishes hold pickled tomatoes and marinated wild mushrooms. Several varieties of fish are offered: canned sardines or mackerel in oil; herring in various sauces; hot-smoked and cold-smoked sturgeon fillets, the likes of which I have never tasted since. There are prepared dishes such as vegetable caviars and piping-hot *pirozhki* with meat or vegetable fillings, baked or deep-fried. It is very important (and very hard) for the novice at Russian dining to bear in mind that this is only the *zakuska* spread, that the main meal has not yet arrived. Still the temptation is too great to leave anything untasted, and the hostess will invariably press second helpings, saying '*Esh'te, esh'te na zdorov'ye!*' 'Eat, eat to your health!'

Eating always starts off with a round of vodka or, out of deference to more timid guests, cognac. The *ryumochki* are filled almost to overflowing, and the host proposes the first toast – usually to his guests. Then everyone clinks glasses and downs the vodka *zalpom*, in a single gulp. This is no place for cowards! To survive the toasting and remain alert at least until the main course, one must do as the Russians do: immediately grab a *buterbrod* (bread spread with sweet cream butter and topped with smoked fish) and eat it. At the very least reach for a slice of bread and a pickle. By eating something after every gulp of vodka, one can drink a great deal without getting drunk, or at least before realising one's true condition. With the first toast, the meal has formally begun, and the *zakuski* are assaulted in earnest. Next comes the *vtoroye* or main course, for which meat, poultry or fish may be served. Russians particularly like to serve chicken to guests, because for them it's a luxury. There might be a regional speciality such as *pel'meni* (Siberian dumplings) or *plov* (rice pilaf). Soup is served at midday and rarely, if ever, at the evening meal. It goes without saying that more drinking accompanies the main meal. I was dismayed to find that even when excellent Georgian wines are served, they are knocked back Russian-style, like vodka.

But no matter how fast one drinks, one must try to eat slowly, because once one's plate is empty, it will be heaped again with more food before one has a chance to protest. The Russians still equate a large belly with good health. They say: 'If you want to be well-fed, sit next to the hostess; if you want to get drunk, sit next to the host.' Both host and hostess are compulsive about refilling glasses and plates, and each time a glass is refilled, a new toast must be raised. A full glass calls for a new toast, and each toast justifies a new glass, so either way the final outcome is inevitable. A guest's foolish smile and lethargic gait at the end of the evening indicate to his hosts that they have served him well.

Following the main course, the table is cleared of everything save bottles and glasses, but this is often a delayed process. Since there is no living room *per se* in Russian apartments, the whole evening is spent around the table. Often neighbours from upstairs or down the hall will drop in, and room is always made for them, chairs are always found. The hostess busies herself in the kitchen preparing tea, or sometimes coffee, though the Russian tea is far better. Many homes have small electric samovars to set on the table (the old-fashioned coal-heated samovar has long since disappeared from Russian homes, except as an ornament). Along with the tea, an assortment of pies, cakes, sweet breads and chocolates is presented. There are rarely fewer than three desserts to choose from, and usually one must taste a little of each. Although the Russians are great tea-drinkers, often they will have only one cup before continuing to work on the vodka, wine or cognac still standing on the table. Or they will bring out a treasured liqueur – a home-made cordial or a hard-to-obtain distillation such as Riga's famed *Balsam*, with the scent and flavour of pine resin.

The Russians love to entertain at home, but sometimes they go out to restaurants, often in large parties, placing their orders in advance. When they arrive, the tables are already set with *zakuski*, artistically displayed, as well as with a range of sparkling bottles and glasses. After the marvellous *zakuski*, restaurant second courses always disappointed me, as did the inevitable restaurant atmosphere, for the Soviet idea of a chic restaurant is the opposite of ours. A live band playing Western pop music at ear-splitting levels is invariably offered as the evening's entertainment, making conversation almost impossible, and judging by Soviet reaction, the louder the music, the more chic the restaurant.

Shopping for food

The centre of activity in any Soviet city is the market place. The market opens around six in the morning, when women on their way to work will stop and buy fresh produce for the evening meal. Later in the day the old grandmothers, the *babushki*, appear for their shopping. Knowing Soviet citizens carry an expandable string bag at all times. The bag is jocularly referred to as an *avos'ka*, a 'just-in-case' – just in case something good should appear at the market or on the street that day. The market is lined with rows of stalls manned by country folk selling the vegetables they have grown on the tiny private plots allotted them by the State. Selling at the market is lucrative for them, since their goods command a high price and most shoppers still prefer the expensive market to the cheaper State-run stores, where produce is often elderly and of poor quality.

At the market old men sit behind large canvas sacks bursting with sunflower seeds (the Russians chew these seeds all day: the floors of buses and public buildings are littered with the hulls). There are mounds of freshly-ground spices: paprika in graduated degrees of piquancy and colour; *khmeli-suneli*, a wonderfully fragrant Georgian spice mixture with coriander, dill and pepper; aromatic nutmeg and cinnamon for baking pies and breads. Bunches of fresh parsley, dill and coriander splay randomly along the counters. Green onions, cucumbers, cabbages and root vegetables create a medley of colour and form. Honey glistens golden in the comb or in crystals; it can also be had boiled if one brings one's own jar. Live geese and ducks lie with feet bound to prevent their escape; pig's heads and pig's feet startle the casual shopper. Fresh sour cream and curd cheese lend a heady smell to the air, along with salted cucumbers and mushrooms and soused apples soaked in their own juice. Springtime is the best season at the market place: the air is redolent with the blossoms of thousands of lilacs, peonies and carnations.

Since Russians have very little storage space and only tiny refrigerators, they go to market almost every day. They buy bread daily, too; it never lasts long enough to grow stale. Recently, self-service grocery stores have appeared in the Soviet Union, considerably easing the burden of food shopping, but the majority of groceries or *gastronomy* still require laborious shopping. The system is such that one must wait in several long queues to buy even a single item: first, to see what's available; next, to pay the cashier; and finally, to relinquish the cash receipt to the salesgirl in exchange for the purchase. Sometimes it's easier to seek out a *kulinariya* where one can buy a few ready-made products like risen dough ready for baking, prepared beetroot and potato salads, and frozen *pel'meni* all ready for the pot.

If one feels like eating during the day there are innumerable street stands to satisfy all sorts of cravings, the most popular being the ice-cream ones. Even in the dead of winter, when the temperature drops well below zero, bare hands eagerly clasp *trubochki* or *batonchi-ki* and icy lips happily lick the delicious frozen mass. After being chilled by a cone, frozen fingers can be warmed on a steaming hot *pirozhok* from another stand. The *pirozhki* on the streets are juicy fried morsels of minced meat wrapped in dough – often greasy, but nonetheless satisfying in the icy air. There are kiosks selling all kinds of biscuits and rusks, and kiosks selling chocolates, caramels and bonbons. I always found it amusing to watch the sweet-seller weigh out my purchase: if the scale registered 210 grams instead of the 200 I'd asked for, she'd simply lop off a corner of one of the sweets, wrapper and all, to make the weight exact. I never minded this, as it gave me an excuse to eat the damaged piece right away.

My favourite outdoor stand in Moscow was opposite the Kursk Railway Station. (Sadly, it was replaced by a more international 'Pepsi' stand for the 1980 Olympics.) When the kiosk was open and the vats in operation, a cloud of hot steam rose up into the cold air, beckoning from a good distance away. Here they made the best doughnuts or *ponchiki* in Moscow: piping hot balls dripping with fat and liberally sprinkled with powdered sugar. The vendor filled a paper cone with doughnuts and offered a hot coffee drink. High tables are still set in the ground in front of the kiosk, but one can no longer stand there and eat doughnuts to one's heart's content.

Passing through the countryside and the seasons, one is well advised to arrive in Kiev in summertime. There, old women in brightly-coloured scarves that almost hide their creased faces display home-made *medivnyk* or honey cake. The cakes are so rich in honey that a swarm of bees always surrounds them. One takes a slight risk in reaching for a slice – but it's well worth it! Finally, as in every city, rows of automated machines dispense *gazirovannaya voda*, carbonated water, a favourite Russian refresher. A glass of plain soda water costs only one kopeck, but for three kopecks the machine mixes in some flavoured syrup. Unfortunately, the machines have only one glass. After inserting money in the slot, one must hold the glass upside-down over a brush which ostensibly washes the rim of the glass – with cold water. No one *seems* to suffer (at least not on the spot), although I have encountered prudent old women who carry their own glasses around with them. With luck one can find a *babushka*, instead of a machine, selling the *gazirovannaya voda*, and it is much tastier when she prepares it.

The *Zakuska* Table

To a Russian, dinner is unthinkable without *zakuski*, those imaginative 'little bites' which make up the first course of the meal.

The range of *zakuski* is almost infinite, from simple smoked sprats on black bread to the grey pearl of the Caspian, Beluga caviar; from sliced beetroot vinaigrette to button mushrooms drenched in a spicy marinade. Olivier salad, savoury stuffed eggs, shimmering pork brawn, kidneys in Madeira, aubergine 'caviar' with its pungent tang – all these delights belong to the diversity of the *zakuska* spread.

This first course may have only a few modest dishes to whet the appetite, or it may feature a stunning array of twenty or more, both hot and cold, each designed to complement, not overwhelm, its neighbour. *Zakuski* may be as straightforward as bread spread with herb butter or as complicated as cold fish in aspic. But whether humble or grand, *zakuski* are an integral part of the spirit of Russian dining.

In any discussion of Russian hors d'œuvres, what first comes to mind is caviar, the near-legendary roe of the sturgeon. Fresh caviar is indeed sumptuous enough to serve alone, and should one wish to dine in the style of the tsars, it is still very nearly possible to do so. First, one must procure the freshest available caviar, preferably the large-grained grey Beluga. (The tsars themselves dined on a rare variety of golden caviar from the prized Volga sterlet, but as this great waterway has since been polluted and the fish stocks depleted, we must substitute the hardly less exquisite Beluga.)

Caviar should be served with a silver spoon in a crystal or silver bowl over ice – any other metal will interfere with the delicate taste of the roe. Next to the caviar place rounds of French bread, the nearest approximation to the Russian *kalach* or fine, ring-shaped loaf, and a small pot of unsalted butter should also be provided. (True *aficionados* scorn the lemon, chopped onion and egg which often accompany the lesser grades.)

Now this royal *zakuska* is almost complete, needing only a suitable drink to complement the slightly salty taste of the roe. And what could be more fitting than champagne? Here, we are in luck, for the firm that once purveyed champagne to the tsars now makes it available to the western world, and Louis Roederer's 'Cristal' is said by many to be the finest in the world. While most champagne comes in tinted green bottles, with a punt or indentation in the bottom to catch the sediment, Roederer's bottle is crystal clear with a flat bottom. According to one account, Roederer developed his unusual bottle especially for Tsar Alexander III, who was ever fearful for his life after his father's assassination. Alexander wanted his favourite champagne to be immediately recognisable, lest someone try to poison him. Hence Roederer's clear crystal bottle (alas, now made of glass). But the punt also caused some worry: an anarchist might slip a home made bomb into the depression, and the champagne, wrapped in a linen napkin for serving, would still look innocuous. And so the flat bottom was born. Following the Revolution, Roederer stopped supplying the Russians because they failed to pay their bills, but he continued to produce his original bottles. Today, the Soviets produce a very limited supply of an exceptional champagne (their *zolotoye* or 'golden') in clear glass bottles with completely flat bottoms.

For those of us without the wealth of a tsar, however, there are other less expensive caviars and Russian vodka to accompany them. One step down from the Beluga is the black Osetrova caviar, smaller-grained, but with a magnificent taste. The Osyotr sturgeon itself is smaller, weighing on the average 700 lb (some 300 kg), while the Beluga can weigh up to several thousand and yield 200 lb (90 kg) of roe. Osetrova caviar is followed in grade by Sevryuga, which comes from the smallest sturgeon, the stellate, and hence has the smallest grains of all the fine caviars.

One can also find *payusnaya*, highly thought of in the Soviet Union, though less appreciated in the West. This pressed caviar is made from damaged eggs which are crushed into a rather sticky paste, less subtle in flavour than the undamaged roe. *Payusnaya* caviar has traditionally served as soldiers' rations during their long stints at the front, as it is much less perishable, and consequently less expensive, than the fresh.

Some roe-lovers prefer the brightly-coloured eggs of the salmon, ranging in hue from deep orange to soft red. While black caviar calls for white bread, salmon roe tastes best on black, and a little chopped onion and lemon juice here are no crime. Russians living in Scandinavia enjoy the tiny golden *löjrom* from whitefish, which they mix with fresh cream and serve on toast. It is unfortunate that the dyed lumpfish roe mainly produced in Iceland is so often substituted for the real thing, as the taste of lumpfish roe is in no way comparable to that of fresh caviar. Sadly, even in the Soviet Union, caviar is becoming more and more scarce. (It is ironic that the seventeenth-century nobility found it so plentiful that they often boiled it in vinegar or poppy seed milk for a change.) One hopeful sign is the development of a caviar industry in western America, which promises to make real caviar more accessible to all.

If caviar comes to mind first for getting a Russian meal off to a good start, then vodka is not far behind, and when a liberal amount of this potent stuff is supplied to guests, the meal will not only be off to a fast start, but to a rollicking one as well. Russians love their vodka, a fact apparent in the word itself, for *vodka* is an affectionate diminutive of *voda* or 'water', the most elemental substance of all.

Strong drink has always been important to the Russian people, even as far back as the tenth century AD, when Great Prince Vladimir, the first ruler of a unified Russia, was searching for a religion under which to govern his still heathen land. Vladimir called in representatives of the Islamic and Christian faiths for consultation and was all set to accept Islam as the new faith of Rus' when he learned that religious law forbade the consumption of alcoholic drinks. Vladimir was appalled. Almost without hesitation, he declared in favour of Christianity, proclaiming, 'Drinking is the joy of Rus'!' Little has changed since those ancient days: drinking is still Russia's joy, as well as its bane. Recently factories have begun installing samovars to encourage the drinking of tea instead of vodka, but it does little good. Once a Russian is drunk, his only recourse, by popular belief, is to cure himself with the hair of the dog that bit him, which leads only to more drinking . . .

But vodka should not be blamed. It is an excellent beverage and, taken in moderation, provides the perfect balance to the salty titbits of the *zakuska* table. A proper *zakuska* course should offer several different varieties of well-chilled flavoured vodkas. Many of these are easy to prepare at home by infusing a good-quality plain vodka with fresh herbs or citrus peel, or with strands of saffron or crushed cherry stones. Less common are such specialities as a dusky, mauve vodka made from litmus (a lichen extract), or garnet *ryabinovka*, infused with the autumnal berries of the mountain ash. Some connoisseurs prefer pale-blue cornflower vodka, others *kedrovka* with its startling essence of cedar. In Gogol's food-heavy tale, *Old-World Landowners*, Pulkheria Ivanovna presents her own array of health-giving vodkas at the *zakuska* table.

Pulkheria Ivanovna was most entertaining when she led her guests to the *zakuska* table. 'Now this,' she would say, removing the stopper from a flask, 'is vodka infused with St John's wort and sage. If the small of your back or your shoulder blade aches, it really hits the spot. This vodka over here is made with centaury. If you've got a ringing in your ears or shingles on your face, it's just the thing. And this one's distilled from peach stones – here, take a glass, what a wonderful smell! If you've bumped your head against the corner of a cupboard or the table when getting out of bed, and a lump's sprung up on your forehead, then all you have to do is drink a glassful before dinner. The minute you take your hand away, the lump will disappear, as if it had never been there at all . . .'

While not all vodkas are guaranteed to heal, it is true that they take the pain away. Of the clear vodkas, the best is *pshenichnaya*, distilled from grain rather than potatoes, with a taste as pure as liquid crystal. Unfortunately, this is rarely found outside the Soviet Union, but other good Russian or Polish vodkas make excellent substitutes. Russian vodka is only drunk straight, *never* mixed with other beverages – unless one is intent upon getting drunk fast and opts for the old Russian *yorsh*, a blending of vodka and beer designed to make one's hair stand on end (in imitation, no doubt, of the fish of the same name with protruding spines on its fins).

Vodka should be kept in the freezer at all times, ready for the unexpected guest. Its high alcohol content keeps it from freezing, while the liquid turns delightfully viscous. (The sensation of thick, icy-cold vodka surging down one's throat is not soon forgotten.) Besides being drunk very cold, vodka is customarily gulped down in a single swallow, the liquid tossed far back into the mouth. The reason is a practical one: if vodka is sipped, one inhales the fumes, and the fumes cause drunkenness faster than the drink itself. Or so the Russians claim. In a Chekhov story, *The Siren*, the court chronicler explains the proper way to approach vodka:

. . . when you sit down you should immediately put a napkin around your neck and then, very slowly, reach for the carafe of vodka. Now you don't pour the dear stuff into any old glass . . . oh no! You must pour it into an antediluvian glass made of silver, one which belonged to your grandfather, or into a pot-bellied glass bearing the inscription 'Even Monks Imbibe!' And you don't drink the vodka down right away. No, sir. First you take a deep breath, wipe your hands, and glance up at the ceiling to demonstrate your indifference. Only then do you raise that vodka slowly to your lips and suddenly – sparks! They fly from your stomach to the furthest reaches of your body . . .

There are many rituals associated with the drinking of vodka. Traditionally, on the eve of his wedding, a Russian bridegroom was made to drink vodka from full glasses spelling out the name of his sweetheart. Woe to him if her name was Apollinaria! In Fyodor Sologub's novel, *The Petty Demon*, guests of the wily host Skuchaev find themselves participating in a strange game called 'Pour and Drink Up', in which Skuchaev serves his unwitting guests vodka from glasses whose bases have been sharpened to a narrow point, so that it is impossible to set them down without their toppling over. As long as the guest holds an empty glass (as he inevitably does, since the vodka is downed in a single swig), hospitality demands that it be refilled, and so Skuchaev has come up with a sure way to get his guests drunk.

In literature the most famous *zakuska* table is no doubt the one set by the Chief of Police in Gogol's *Dead Souls*. Intended to impress, the meal is ordered on the spur of the moment, and impress is exactly what it does. The spread includes several varieties of fresh sturgeon, including Beluga, also smoked salmon, freshly salted caviar and pressed caviar, herring, all sorts of cheeses, smoked tongue and salt-dried sturgeon fillets, an amazing fish pie made from the head and cheeks of a 325 lb (146 kg) sturgeon, and another pie stuffed with choice wild mushrooms. This menu more than reflects the Russian love of fish; today it would be balanced by more meat and vegetable dishes. But if one gets the impression that the 'small bite' of the *zakuska* is often a feast in itself, that's not incorrect. Indeed a delightful way to entertain like the Russians is to set up a large *zakuska* table around which guests can circulate freely before heading into the dining room for the main course.

There are a few basic rules to follow in laying a *zakuska* table, not the least of which concerns the shape of the table itself. It should be oval or round and placed away from the wall, so that all foods are accessible to all guests at all times. Small plates, forks and napkins are arranged at opposite ends of the table so that service may start simultaneously from both sides. Along the outer edges of the table are placed the various *zakuski*, hot along one side, cold on the other. Beyond the *zakuski*, towards the centre of the table, are baskets or plates piled high with bread, both black and white, and mounds of unsalted butter moulded in fancy shapes. In the very centre of the table stand carafes of flavoured vodka surrounded by small glasses or *ryumochki*. Cognac may also be provided for more timid guests.

The recipes in this chapter cover a wide range of *zakuski* which may be served singly as the opening to a simple meal, in pairs, or as part of a more impressive spread. But they are just a small sample of all the possibilities for *zakuska*, as the range of this first course is limited only by one's imagination. And while such dishes as lark pâté and wild boar's jaws *en gelée* are no longer required, a superb selection may be made by using recipes from this book. For an even grander display, the home-made *zakuski* may be supplemented by prepared specialities from the delicatessen. Here are a few suggestions:

cured fish and meats of all kinds, particularly hot-smoked and cold-smoked sturgeon; smoked eel layered with lemon slices; thin wafers of smoked salmon; sardines in oil and in various sauces; kippered herrings; Norwegian anchovies (*kilki*); sliced tongue; cured ham (Polish or Westphalian); smoked turkey; roast beef or chicken in thin rolls; brawn or potted meat; various salamis and sausages

marinated vegetables, such as pickled beetroot; pickled green tomatoes; green olives and black olives; pickled hot peppers

hard cheeses of all sorts, sliced very thinly

fresh seafood, such as oysters on the half shell; crab claws with mayonnaise; prawns with home-made tartare sauce

cocktail meatballs (*tefteli*) in tomato sauce

freshly boiled potatoes tossed with dill

In addition, the following recipes from other chapters make excellent dishes for the *zakuska* table:

Armenian Flat Bread	Fresh Ham Cooked	Radishes in Soured
Beetroot Salad	with Hay	Cream
Black Bread	Georgian Cheese Pie	Rye Bread
Blini	Georgian Kidney	Salted Mushrooms
Carrot Salad	Beans	Sauerkraut
Celeriac Salad	Kasha (Buckwheat	Savoury Pirozhki
Cold Stuffed	Groats) with	Sour Cabbage
Aubergine	Mushrooms and	Sourdough White
Cranberry-	Cream	Bread
Horseradish Relish	Kulebyaka	Soused Apples
Cucumbers in	Mushrooms in	Spiced Pickled
Soured Cream	Soured Cream	Cherries
Dill Pickles	Pickled Aubergine	Stuffed Cabbage
Dried Fish	Pot Cheese Tartlets	Leaves
Estonian Potato	Prepared	Wine Bowl
Salad	Horseradish	

Flavoured Vodkas

The ones that follow are simple to prepare at home. After infusing, keep them in the freezer.

Aniseed vodka Anisovaya

Place 2 teaspoons whole aniseed in ¾ pint (450 ml) plain vodka and infuse at room temperature for 24 hours. Strain.

Apricot vodka Abrikosovaya

Place 12 apricot kernels in ¾ pint (450 ml) plain vodka and infuse at room temperature for 24 hours. Strain.

Black-currant bud vodka Smorodinovka

Pick the buds of black-currants when still sticky. Place a handful in ¾ pint (450 ml) plain vodka and infuse at room temperature for 24 hours. Strain. Alternatively, make a very strong infusion in only ¼ pint (150 ml) vodka and then add 10 to 12 drops of this essence to a standard bottle of plain vodka.

Cherry vodka Vishnyovka

Crush 36 cherry stones and place them in ¾ pint (450 ml) plain vodka. Infuse at room temperature for 24 hours. Strain.

Coriander vodka Koriandrovaya

Place 2 teaspoons coriander seed, slightly crushed, in ¾ pint (450 ml) plain vodka and infuse at room temperature for 24 hours. Strain.

Garlic and dill vodka Chesnochnaya

Place 1 clove garlic, slightly crushed, 1 sprig of fresh dill, and 3 white peppercorns in ¾ pint (450 ml) plain vodka. Infuse at room temperature for 24 hours. Strain. A small sprig of dill may be left in the vodka, if desired.

Herb vodka Travnik

Place a few sprigs of a favourite herb such as tarragon or basil in ¾ pint (450 ml) plain vodka and infuse at room temperature for 24 hours. Strain. A small sprig of the herb may be left in the vodka.

Lemon or orange vodka Limonovka

Remove the rind from ½ large lemon or from 1 orange in a single strip, taking care to avoid the bitter white pith. Infuse in ¾ pint (450 ml) plain vodka at room temperature for 24 hours. (Do not leave the peel in longer or the vodka will turn bitter.)

Pepper vodka Pertsovka

Place 30 black peppercorns plus 30 white peppercorns in ¾ pint (450 ml) plain vodka and infuse at room temperature for 24 hours. Strain.

Saffron vodka Shafrannaya

Place ¼ teaspoon saffron threads in ¾ pint (450 ml) plain vodka and infuse at room temperature for 24 hours. Strain.

Tea-flavoured vodka Chainaya

Place 4 teaspoons black tea leaves (preferably fruit-scented) in ¾ pint (450 ml) plain vodka and infuse at room temperature for 24 hours. Strain.

Buffalo grass vodka Zubrovka

Place 8 blades of buffalo grass in ¾ pint (450 ml) plain vodka and infuse at room temperature for 24 hours. One blade of grass may be left in the vodka after straining.

Fresh Salmon Roe Caviar Krasnaya ikra

This recipe has travelled the globe. It was given to me by Alla
Avisov, a charming Russian woman who came to America by way
of Germany and Venezuela. Alla loves to cook and has a file full of
recipes gleaned from family and friends. Every year during the
salmon spawning season, Alla and her husband delight their guests
with this fresh caviar made from salmon roe. Now you can try it,
too.

1 sac fresh salmon roe	2 tablespoons salt
1½ pints (900 ml) water	

Place the sac of salmon roe in a sieve, then place the sieve over a
large bowl.

Bring the water to the boil. When it boils, add the salt. The water
will foam up. Immediately pour the boiling water over the roe,
shaking the sieve as you do so (it helps to have two people to carry
out this task).

Lower the sieve into the water in the bowl, shaking it lightly from
time to time. This process causes the roe to be released from the
membranous sac enclosing it. With a wooden skewer, carefully
separate the individual eggs.

With a slotted spoon, lift the roe from the water and place it in a
jar. The caviar will keep in the refrigerator up to 1 week. If you wish
to keep it longer, rinse the roe a second time with salt solution and
pour a little vegetable oil over the top of the caviar in the jar.

Note: If fresh whitefish or sturgeon roe is available, it may be
substituted for the salmon.

Herring Selyodka

The most essential member of the *zakuska* table is herring, its
saltiness stimulating the need for ever larger doses of vodka. In
Russia, herring is prepared in many different ways. It may be
pickled or served with savoury sauces. It may be finely chopped,
then re-shaped to resemble a whole fish and garnished with a head
and tail. Or it may be fried in pieces and served with a tomato
dressing. An elaborate *zakuska* table boasts several alternatives, but
at least one is mandatory.

One of Chekhov's most delightful stories is *The Siren*, in which a
hungry court clerk tries to speed up a diligent judge's decision by
tormenting him with a mouth-watering account of a real Russian
dinner: 'The best appetiser, if you'd like to know, is herring.
Imagine you've eaten a bite of it with onion and mustard sauce. Just
imagine! . . . Then, my benefactor, while you're still feeling sparks
in your stomach, you must immediately eat some caviar, either plain

or, if you prefer, with lemon; and then some radishes with salt, then some more herring . . .' droning on and on until the poor judge, now ravenous, can bear no more and troops off to dinner, leaving his work undone.

The recipes which follow are intended for salt herring, which must be soaked overnight before using. If you have fresh herring, by all means use it; it needs no soaking.

Pickled Herring Selyodka marinovannaya

2 lb (900 g) herring, salt or fresh (see below)	4–6 hot dried peppers
¾ pint (450 ml) cider vinegar	4 bay leaves
8 fluid oz (225 ml) water	1½ teaspoons mustard seed
6 oz (170 g) sugar	2 teaspoons coriander seed
1 large onion, thinly sliced	24 black peppercorns
1 large carrot, scraped and cut into rounds	3 oz (85 g) black olives

If using salt herring, soak it overnight in milk or buttermilk to cover; the next day rinse and pat it dry. Cut off the head and remove the fins. Slice the herring down the belly and open it flat. Remove the backbone and cut the fish on the diagonal into 1 in (2.5 cm) slices.

In a saucepan bring the marinade ingredients (the vinegar, water and sugar) to the boil. Cook until the sugar dissolves, then set aside.

In two large preserving jars, layer the remaining ingredients with the slices of herring, making sure that the spices are evenly distributed. Pour the vinegar marinade over all. Seal the jars tightly and leave the herring to mature in the refrigerator for at least 5 days before serving.

To serve, place the herring in bowls and garnish with the onion slices, olives, and a little of the marinade.

Serves 10 to 12 as *zakuska*.

Herring in Soured Cream Selyodka v smetane

1 recipe Pickled Herring, drained	8 fluid oz (225 ml) soured cream olives and onion slices to
4 tablespoons liquid from the herring	garnish

Arrange the pickled herring on a dish. Mix together the soured cream and the pickling liquid, then pour this over the herring and garnish with olives and onion slices.

Serves 10 to 12 as *zakuska*.

Herring in Dill Sauce Selyodka pod ukropnym sousom

1 lb (450 g) herring, pickled	2 tablespoons snipped fresh
¼ pint (150 ml) olive oil	dill *or* 2 teaspoons dried dill
4 tablespoons red wine vinegar	2 teaspoons sugar

Prepare the herring, cutting it diagonally into 1 in (2.5cm) slices. Mix together the remaining ingredients and pour the sauce over the herring slices. Chill for several hours before serving.

Serves 6 as a first course, more as a *zakuska*.

Herring in Mustard Sauce Selyodka s gorchichnoi pripravoi

1 lb (450 g) herring, pickled	3 tablespoons soured cream
6 tablespoons olive oil	2 teaspoons capers, drained
3 tablespoons made mustard	(reserve a few for garnish)

Prepare the herring, cutting it diagonally into 1 in (2.5 cm) slices. Mix together the olive oil and mustard. Stir in the soured cream and capers, then pour the sauce over the prepared herring and chill for several hours before serving.

Serves 6 as a first course; more as *zakuska*.

Marinated Smoked Salmon Syomga marinovannaya

Marinating such delectable (and expensive) fish may seem like sacrilege, but the result need only be tasted to prove its worth.

8 oz (225 g) smoked salmon,	8 tablespoons olive oil
in slices	8 tablespoons vegetable oil
1 large mild onion, sliced and	8 tablespoons white
separated into rings	wine vinegar
½ teaspoon peppercorns	2 cloves garlic, crushed
1 large bay leaf, crushed	1 teaspoon salt
¼ teaspoon mustard seed	

In a 1½ pint (900 ml) jar alternate layers of smoked salmon, onion rings, peppercorns, bay leaf and mustard seed.

In a small bowl, thoroughly mix together the oils, vinegar, garlic and salt. Pour the dressing over the salmon layers. Seal the jar and store it in the refrigerator for at least 1 week before serving. Have plenty of black bread on hand to serve with the salmon.

Serves 8 as *zakuska*.

Smoked Salmon Canapés Buterbrod s syomgoi

Black beads of caviar are highlighted against the brilliant pink of smoked salmon in these lovely hors d'œuvres, which take only minutes to prepare. They may be kept in the refrigerator for several hours, covered, before serving.

6 pieces thinly-sliced black bread, cut into quarters	¼ lb (120 g) sliced smoked salmon
4 tablespoons double cream, whipped	2–3 tablespoons soured cream
1 tablespoon prepared horseradish (see p. 170)	4 teaspoons black caviar parsley

Whip the double cream until it forms soft peaks, and fold in the horseradish. Spread each quarter of bread with some of this mixture, then top with a thin slice of smoked salmon.

Top each slice of salmon in turn with a dab of soured cream, and then sprinkle a little caviar over, pressing down lightly so it will stay in place.

Tuck a tiny piece of parsley into the whipped cream on each square. Chill.

Makes 2 dozen canapés.

Smelts in Tomato Sauce Koryushki v tomatnom souse

The slightly sweet tomato sauce masking these fried smelts provides a nice balance for a *zakuska* table laden with pickled fish and vegetables. If frozen smelts are available, they may be used directly from the freezer. This is an excellent appetiser.

1 egg	8 tablespoons tomato paste
1 tablespoon cold water	½ pint (300 ml) chicken stock
½ lb (225 g) smelts	1 teaspoon salt
4 tablespoons fine dry breadcrumbs	1 oz (30 g) Barbados sugar
6 tablespoons olive oil	4 tablespoons red wine vinegar
2 medium onions, very thinly sliced	8 thin slices of lemon
2 medium carrots, scraped and sliced into ¼ in (6 mm) thick rounds	parsley

Beat together the egg and the cold water. Dip the smelts in this mixture and then in the breadcrumbs until they are well coated. Heat 4 tablespoons of the olive oil in a large frying pan and fry the smelts until golden on both sides, about 5 to 6 minutes. Do not overcook.

Remove the smelts from the frying pan and set aside. Wipe the pan out and then pour in the remaining 2 tablespoons olive oil. Fry the onion and carrot in the oil until tender, about 15 minutes. Then stir in the remaining ingredients except the parsley and simmer, covered, for 15 minutes. Cool the sauce to room temperature.

After the sauce has cooled, remove the lemon slices. Arrange the smelts on a plate and pour the sauce over them, turning them once to coat. Chill for several hours before serving, garnished with parsley.

Serves 4.

Turbot in Dill Marinade   Paltus v marinade s ukropom

This is an interesting way to use up the leftover brine from a jar of dill pickles. The spicy fish may be served either plain or on squares of black bread.

2 lb (900 g) turbot fillets
salt, freshly ground black
   pepper to taste
1 onion, sliced into very thin
   rings
1 bay leaf
1 clove garlic, crushed
8 black peppercorns
¼ teaspoon crushed dried red
   pepper

⅛ teaspoon mustard seed
2 teaspoons fresh snipped dill
   or ½ teaspoon dried dill
1½ pints (900 ml) brine from a
   jar of dill pickles

lemon, thinly sliced
minced parsley
fresh dill

Preheat the oven to 180°C/350°F/Gas 4. Season the fish with salt and pepper. Lightly grease an ovenproof dish and place the fish in it. Sprinkle the onion, bay, garlic, spices and dill evenly over the fish fillets. Pour the dill brine over all.

Cover the dish. Bring the fish to a simmer over a medium heat and then transfer to the preheated oven. Poach the fish for about 15 minutes, depending on the thickness of the fillets, until the fish is flaky but still holds its shape.

Cool the fish to room temperature in its marinade and then chill overnight. The next day cut the fillets into bite-sized pieces and arrange them on a glass plate, garnished with thinly sliced lemon, minced parsley and sprigs of fresh dill.

Serves 10 as *zakuska*.

Notes: If an even spicier dish is desired, add more crushed red pepper and mustard seed accordingly.

The fish may also be served hot from the oven as a main course, in which case the fillets are left whole to make 4 servings.

Cold Fish in Aspic Ryba zalivnaya

This poached fish in aspic is a mosaic of colour and form, as though seen through the surface of a pond. A stunning addition to the *zakuska* table.

3 lb (1.4 kg) fish (any firm, white-fleshed fish will do)
2½ pints (1¼ litres) cold water
¾ pint (450 ml) dry white wine
1 onion, quartered
1 carrot, scraped
3 sprigs parsley
2 sprigs dill *or* ½ teaspoon dried dill
1 bay leaf
10 white peppercorns
1½–2 teaspoons salt

4 tablespoons dry white wine
4 teaspoons tomato paste
4 egg whites, lightly beaten
¾ oz (20 g) unflavoured gelatine
¼ pint (150 ml) cold water

lemon slices
sliced dill pickles
capers
sliced olives
pimiento

In a stockpot put the water, wine, onion, carrot, parsley, dill, bay leaf, peppercorns and salt. Bring to the boil over high heat and then simmer, covered, for 20 minutes. This is the poaching liquid (or court bouillon).

Place the fish in a poacher along with the poaching liquid, and poach until tender, about 25 minutes. Carefully remove the fish and set aside to cool. Strain the liquid.

Remove the skin, head, tail and bones from the fish. With a fork, gently separate the flesh into fairly large pieces. Do not flake it finely.

Place the strained fish stock in a large pan. To it add the 4 tablespoons wine, tomato paste, egg whites, and gelatine which has been dissolved in the cold water. Stir well to mix. Bring the liquid to a rolling boil and then remove from the heat. Leave to stand for 15 minutes, then strain. The liquid should now be completely clear.

Lightly grease a 3 pint (1.7 litre) mould with vegetable oil. (I like to use a large, shallow round one, about 12 in (30 cm) in diameter.) Pour in about ½ pint (300 ml) of the warm aspic* and set the pan in the refrigerator until the aspic has set.

On the jelled aspic arrange chopped carrot (from the fish stock), sliced pickle, olives, capers, lemon and pimiento in a decorative pattern. Carefully pour enough warm aspic over the vegetables to cover them. Put the pan in the refrigerator and chill until this layer has set.

Place the fish in a single layer on top of the aspic, then pour the remaining liquid over it. Chill for at least 4 hours, until completely firm.

* The amount of aspic poured into the bottom of the mould depends on its size and shape. There should be only a thin layer so that the pattern of vegetables will clearly show through once the aspic is inverted. If you are using a deep mould with a smaller diameter, pour in just enough aspic to cover the bottom in a thin layer. You may also want to add the fish in several layers alternating with aspic, instead of just one.

To turn out, run a knife around the edges of the mould to loosen, then dip the mould very briefly in hot water. Invert on to a plate. Serve the aspic with spicy Russian mustard, or with a Russian mayonnaise, if desired.

Serves 12 to 16 as *zakuska*.

Mayonnaise and sour cream sauce Sous provensal'

2 egg yolks	up to ½ pint (300 ml) olive oil
1 teaspoon prepared mustard	5 egg whites, stiffly beaten
2 tablespoons wine vinegar	¾ pint (450 ml) soured cream
1 teaspoon salt	

In a bowl mix together the egg yolks, mustard, vinegar and salt. Slowly, drop by drop, beat in the olive oil with a steady motion, until a good thick mayonnaise is formed, adding more oil if necessary.

Beat the egg whites until stiff but not dry. Fold them into the soured cream. Mix this soured cream mixture into the mayonnaise mixture. Chill.

Russian Liver Pâté Pashtet iz pechonki

Once, as I entered a Moscow restaurant, my attention was riveted by the *zakuski* displayed on a long table. There appeared to be tiny hedgehogs arranged in conversational clusters on a bed of chopped spring onions, as if at a garden party. However, closer inspection revealed them to be moulded out of liver pâté, with whole cloves for the eyes and piped butter for the quills. Although aware of the Russian penchant for small woodland creatures, I was still surprised at the strange shape that fancy took. Personally, I prefer the excellent Russian liver pâté served plain and unadorned, rather than in the shape of small animals. But that, of course, is a matter of taste. The *pashtet* may be prepared from either chicken or calf's liver.

1 lb (450 g) chicken livers (or calf's liver, cut into strips)	1 large egg
3 oz (85 g) butter	2 slices white bread, crusts removed
2 large onions, thinly sliced	¼ pint (150 ml) rich chicken stock
1 teaspoon salt	
⅛ teaspoon freshly ground black pepper	

Melt the butter in a large frying pan. Cook the onions in it until golden, then add the chicken livers and continue cooking for about 10 minutes, or until the livers are no longer pink.

In the bowl of a food processor or liquidiser combine the cooked onions, liver, salt, pepper, egg, bread and chicken stock. Chop very fine, until the texture is smooth.

Preheat the oven to 180°C/350°F/Gas 4. Grease a 9 in (22.5 cm) loaf tin, spoon the liver mixture into it, and bake for 45 minutes. Cool the pâté to room temperature, then chill it thoroughly before serving. Either turn the pâté out on to a plate or spoon it into a bowl.

Serves 8 as a first course; more as *zakuska*.

Roast Meat and Herring Soufflé Forshmak

This is a mixture of minced cooked meats and herring, blended with eggs to make a pudding not unlike a heavy soufflé. As so often happens in cross-lingual borrowings, the German *Vorschmack* (a 'foretaste' or 'foreboding') has come to mean 'appetiser' in this Russian dish. *Forshmak* is substantial enough to serve for a luncheon, but I prefer it as a *zakuska*, baked in a hollowed-out French loaf as in the variation below. The herring needs soaking overnight.

½ salt herring (about 6 oz/170 g)	¼ pint (150 ml) soured cream
1 lb (450 g) roast meat (beef, veal or lamb in any combination)	3 eggs, separated
	salt, freshly ground black pepper to taste
1 large onion, chopped	½ oz (15 g) grated Parmesan cheese
2 oz (60 g) butter	¼ oz (10 g) fine dry breadcrumbs
3 potatoes, boiled and peeled	

Soak the salt herring in milk or water to cover overnight. Next day, pat it dry and chop it coarsely, removing all fins and bones. It does not have to be skinned.

Fry the onion in half of the butter until golden. Then, in a mincer or food processor, finely mince together the roast meat, sautéed onion, chopped herring and boiled potatoes. Stir in the soured cream and the egg yolks. Season to taste, but be careful with the salt, as the herring is still rather salty.

Preheat the oven to 200°C/400°F/Gas 6, and grease a 3 pint (1.7 litre) ovenproof dish.

Beat the egg whites until stiff but not dry. Fold them into the meat mixture and turn the mixture into the greased dish. Sprinkle with the grated cheese and breadcrumbs. Dot with the remaining butter. Bake for 35 to 40 minutes until puffed and brown.

Serves about 10 as *zakuska*.

Variation: To make *Forshmak v kalache* (*forshmak* baked in a loaf), scoop the soft insides out of a loaf of French bread, a ring-shaped one if possible. Fill the hollow with the prepared *forshmak* mixture. Bake as directed above.

Chicken and Mushrooms en cocotte Zhul'yen kurinyi v kokotnitsakh

A French dish, adapted for the Russian table.

½ lb (225 g) cooked chicken	salt, freshly ground white
1 large onion	pepper to taste
¼ lb (120 g) mushrooms,	3 tablespoons soured cream
trimmed	freshly grated nutmeg
2½ oz (75 g) butter	2 oz (60 g) grated Gruyère cheese

Mince the chicken and set it aside. Mince the onion and the mushrooms, separately.

In a frying pan melt 2 oz (60 g) of the butter. Cook the minced onion for about 5 minutes, until it begins to soften, then stir in the mushrooms and the chicken. Continue to cook for about 5 minutes more, adding salt and white pepper to taste.

Remove the pan from the heat and stir in the soured cream. Add nutmeg to taste.

Preheat the oven to 200°C/400°F/Gas 6. Divide the chicken mixture between four greased ramekins. Top each ramekin with some of the grated cheese and a dab of the remaining butter. Bake for 10 minutes, or until bubbly. Serve hot.

Serves 4.

Veal or Pork Brawn Studen' *or* Kholodets

This classic Russian appetiser is none other than meat (or sometimes poultry) moulded in aspic. The names *studen'* and *kholodets* both derive from Slavic roots meaning 'chill' and 'cold', and indeed the aspic must be thoroughly chilled before unmoulding. Served on a decorative platter with hot Russian-style mustard, *studen'* is a notable addition to the *zakuska* table.

7 pints (4 litres) cold water	1 tablespoon salt
2½ lb (1 kg) calf's feet (or pig's trotters)	2 bay leaves
1 lb (450 g) lean beef chuck, plus bone (or pork loin)	1 whole head garlic
1 lb (450 g) chicken necks, skin removed	2 teaspoons salt
	½ teaspoon freshly ground
1 medium onion	black pepper (or to taste)
1 medium carrot	
8 black peppercorns	3 hard-boiled eggs

In a large stockpot heat the water until warm. Then add the calf's feet, beef, and chicken necks. Bring to the boil, then immediately reduce the heat to a simmer. Skim off the foam as it rises to the surface.

When the foam has stopped rising, add the onion, carrot, pepper-corns and 1 tablespoon salt. Partially cover the pot and cook the broth over very low heat, at a gentle simmer, for 6 hours, until the broth is rich. It should be reduced by about half.

One hour before the broth is ready, add the bay leaves. After 6 hours, strain the liquid through several layers of cheesecloth into a clean pot. There should be about 3½ pints (2 litres).

Discard the carrot and onion. Remove the meat from the chicken necks and shred it along with the beef. Peel the whole head of garlic and press the cloves through a garlic press. Stir in 2 teaspoons salt and the black pepper. Mix well with the shredded meat.

Prepare two 2 pint (1 litre) moulds by brushing them very lightly with vegetable oil. Pour in enough broth to cover the bottom of the mould generously, then refrigerate until the broth has jelled. Top the jelled layer with sliced hard-boiled eggs and other garnish, if desired. Place a layer of meat on top of the eggs and pour on the remaining broth to cover.

Place in the refrigerator and allow to chill for 8 hours or overnight. Scrape off any fat that has formed on the surface.

To turn out, run a knife carefully around the edges of the jelly to loosen it. Wrap the mould for just a moment in a hot tea towel, then place a serving platter over it and invert the *studen'* on to the plate. Serve it well chilled with a pot of spicy mustard on the side.

Serves 12 to 16.

Cocktail Sausages in Tomato Sauce   Sosiski sous-tomat

Always a favourite on the *zakuska* table.

½ lb (225 g) cocktail sausages	freshly ground black pepper to
1 small onion, chopped	taste
1 oz (30 g) butter	dash of cayenne
¼ pint (150 ml) tomato purée	2 tablespoons vodka
4 tablespoons beef stock	1 tablespoon chopped parsley
¼ teaspoon salt	

Fry the chopped onion in butter until soft but not brown. Add the sausages to the pan and fry them until browned on all sides. Then transfer the sausages to a chafing dish to keep warm, leaving the onions and butter in the pan.

Stir the tomato purée into the onions and butter, then add the beef stock, salt, pepper and cayenne. Stir in the vodka. Return the sausages to the pan, and heat them gently for about 15 minutes. Serve from a chafing dish, garnished with parsley.

Serves 4.

Kidneys in Madeira Pochki v madere

The railway buffet at Tsarskoye Selo, the royal retreat, was famed for its version of these succulent kidneys. Ironically, in Andrei Bely's novel *Petersburg*, they were also the dish chosen by Nikolai Apollonovich at a moment of high suspense, when he might be revealed as a political terrorist. But politics aside, Kidneys in Madeira is a lovely *zakuska*, befitting the tables of both anarchists and tsars.

3 veal kidneys (or 6 lamb)	½ pint (300 ml) Madeira
salt, freshly ground black pepper to taste	¼ pint (150 ml) beef or chicken stock
flour	6 tiny new potatoes, boiled and peeled
¼ lb (120 g) butter	finely chopped parsley
¼ lb (120 g) mushrooms, trimmed and sliced	

Remove the membrane from the kidneys and then soak them in cold water for 30 minutes. Pat dry. Cut the kidneys crosswise into ¼ in (6 mm) thick slices. Season with salt and pepper and dredge with flour.

In a frying pan melt half the butter. Quickly fry the mushrooms for about 4 minutes only, then transfer them to a dish. Place the remaining butter in the pan. Add the kidney slices and fry them quickly over high heat to brown, about 5 minutes. Transfer to the dish with the mushrooms.

Add a little Madeira to the pan to deglaze it. Then stir in the stock and the remaining wine. Return the kidneys and mushrooms to the pan and simmer gently for 15 minutes.

Just before serving, stir in the potatoes. Garnish with parsley. Serve with kidneys in a chafing dish.

Serves 6 as *zakuska*.

Aubergine Caviar Baklazhannaya ikra

For those unable to afford the luxury of fish roe at their table, this finely-chopped aubergine dish presents a tasty alternative – hence its nickname of 'Poor Man's Caviar'. This spicy 'caviar' originated in the Caucasus and was adopted by the Russians into their own cuisine. It is best served on thick slices of black bread. Try to resist eating the caviar right away so the flavours can combine overnight in the refrigerator.

3 aubergines (about 2½ lb/1 kg)	of plum tomatoes, drained
¼ pint (150 ml) olive oil	and finely chopped
2 medium onions, finely	1 generous teaspoon honey
chopped	1 tablespoon salt
1 green pepper, finely chopped	freshly ground black pepper to
4 cloves garlic, crushed	taste
3 large tomatoes, peeled and	juice of 1 lemon
finely chopped, *or* 1 large tin	

Place the aubergines in a baking dish and bake in a preheated 190°C/375°F/Gas 5 oven until tender, about 25 minutes. Set aside to cool.

Meanwhile, sauté the onions in the olive oil in a large, lidded frying pan until soft but not brown. Then add the chopped green pepper and the garlic and cook until the green pepper begins to soften.

Peel the baked aubergines and chop the pulp finely. Add to the pan along with the chopped tomatoes, honey, salt and pepper. Bring the mixture to the boil, cover, and then reduce the heat to low. Simmer for about 1 hour.

Remove the cover from the pan and continue to simmer the mixture until all excess liquid has evaporated and the mixture is thick, but not dry. Stir occasionally. This final simmering will take from 20 to 45 minutes, depending on the consistency of the vegetables. When the mixture is ready, stir in the lemon juice and taste for seasoning. I usually add black pepper liberally at this point.

Transfer the caviar to a bowl and chill, covered, in the refrigerator for several hours or overnight.

Serves 8 generously as a first course; more as *zakuska*.

Variation: **Marrow Caviar** Ikra iz kabachkov

Marrow is a favourite vegetable in southern Russia. The Russian word for marrow, *kabachok*, also means 'little tavern'. The mass of tiny seeds clustered in the flesh of the vegetable is said to be reminiscent of people clustered in a tavern.

This is a good way to use up an over-abundance of marrow from a summer garden. Simply follow the directions above for Aubergine Caviar, substituting 2½ lb (1 kg) marrow or courgettes for the aubergines. Do not peel them. Bake them for only 15 to 20 minutes in the oven, and then proceed as directed above.

Note: Olive oil *must* be used in these recipes for 'caviar'.

Mushroom Caviar   Gribnaya ikra

This version of 'caviar', made with finely chopped mushrooms and soured cream, is hardly inferior to the real thing. Thrifty cooks used to use leftover mushroom trimmings to make this dish, but it tastes even better with fresh caps and stems.

3 large spring onions
  (including green tops), finely
  chopped
1½ oz (45 g) butter
¾ lb (340 g) mushrooms,
  trimmed and finely chopped
juice of half a large lemon
salt, freshly ground pepper to
  taste

cayenne pepper to taste
¼ pint (150 ml) soured cream
3 tablespoons snipped fresh
  dill, *or* 1 tablespoon dried dill

parsley
tomato slices

Briefly sauté the chopped spring onions in the butter. Add the chopped mushrooms and the lemon juice. Season to taste. Cook over medium heat, stirring occasionally, for 5 minutes. Remove from the heat. Stir in the soured cream and the dill. Check for seasoning. Set aside to cool. Serve at room temperature, garnished with parsley and tomato slices.

Serves 6 to 8.

Note: Make sure not to chop the mushrooms and spring onions too finely, or you will end up with a sauce instead of 'caviar'.

Marinated Mushrooms   Griby, marinovannye v tomatnom souse

Every *zakuska* table should offer at least one mushroom dish. This recipe is well suited for the cultivated mushrooms one buys regularly, since the marinade lends great flavour to mild mushrooms. Although they may be eaten after only 12 hours in the refrigerator, these mushrooms taste best when allowed to soak for a full week. Any leftover marinade may be used as a rich dipping sauce for thick chunks of black bread.

4½ lb (2 kg) button
  mushrooms, wiped and
  trimmed*
¼ pint (150 ml) olive oil
6 tablespoons freshly squeezed
  lemon juice

6 tablespoons olive oil
3 large onions, sliced
5 cloves garlic, crushed
¾ teaspoon thyme
¾ teaspoon marjoram
1 teaspoon freshly ground
  black pepper

4 bay leaves
3½ lb (1.6 kg) canned plum
  tomatoes, drained (reserve
  the juice) and chopped
¼ pint (150 ml) of the reserved
  juice from the tomatoes
½ pint (300 ml) red
  wine vinegar
1½ teaspoons sugar
¼ teaspoon hot pepper sauce
  or cayenne
salt to taste

Heat the ¼ pint (300 ml) olive oil in a large frying pan. Add the mushrooms (in batches, if necessary) and sauté them until just tender, before they begin to shrink. Transfer them to a large bowl and toss with the lemon juice.

Add the 6 tablespoons olive oil to the frying pan. Sauté the sliced onions and garlic until soft, but not browned. Add the herbs and pepper; sauté a minute more. Stir in the tomatoes, then add the juice, vinegar, sugar and hot pepper sauce or cayenne. Simmer, covered, for 25 minutes.

Pour the sauce over the mushrooms and season with salt to taste. Add more black pepper, if desired. Let the mushrooms cool to room temperature and then chill them, covered, for at least 12 hours, or up to 10 days in the refrigerator. Bring to room temperature before serving.

Serves 12 to 15 as *zakuska*.

Russian Salad Stolichnyi salat *or* Salat Oliv'ye

This famous Russian salad is actually the brainchild of a French chef, Olivier, who caused a sensation in Moscow in the 1860s when he concocted a salad of cooked chicken and potatoes masked with mayonnaise. For many years the matrons of Moscow society vied with one another in hiring Olivier as chef for their elaborate banquets, and his restaurant, 'Olivier's Hermitage', remained in vogue well into the 1890s.

Since Olivier's initial inspiration, Russian Salad has evolved into the complex combination of meat and vegetables that is served today. Its close cousin is *Salade Bagration*, named after Prince Pyotr Bagration who led his Russian troops to victory over Napoleon at Eylau, and which is made with boiled macaroni instead of potatoes.

* Larger mushrooms may be used if they are sliced, but they are not as nice for the *zakuska* table.

½ lb (225 g) cooked chicken, in bite-sized pieces
2 lb (900 g) boiling potatoes
1 large carrot, scraped
2 tart apples, cored and chopped, but not peeled*
1 orange, peeled and cut into chunks
2 whole spring onions, chopped
4 oz (120 g) freshly shelled peas

3 hard-boiled egg yolks
2 tablespoons olive oil

2 tablespoons white wine vinegar
8 tablespoons mayonnaise
8 tablespoons soured cream
salt, freshly ground white pepper to taste

4 tablespoons mayonnaise
4 tablespoons soured cream
1 tablespoon olive oil
1 tablespoon white wine vinegar

fresh parsley or dill

Boil the potatoes in salted water until just tender; drain and peel. While still warm, cut them into chunks. In a separate pot boil the carrot until just tender; drain and cut it into rounds, setting a few rounds aside for the garnish. Boil the peas in salted water for 5 minutes; drain.

Peel the orange and remove all of the white membrane. Cut the orange into 1 in (2.5 cm) chunks. Chop the apples and spring onions.

Mix all the vegetables and fruits with the cooked chicken in a large bowl.

Prepare the dressing. Press the hard-boiled egg yolks through a fine sieve. Mix in 2 tablespoons olive oil until a smooth, creamy paste is formed. Stir in 2 tablespoons vinegar, and 8 tablespoons each of mayonnaise and soured cream. Season to taste. Pour over the warm vegetables and chicken in the bowl, and toss to mix thoroughly. Turn the salad into a clean bowl and chill, covered, overnight.

To serve, form the salad into a high mound on a decorative platter. Mix together the remaining mayonnaise, soured cream, olive oil and vinegar. Pour this dressing over the top of the mound so that it cascades down the sides. Garnish the salad with the leftover carrot rounds and with fresh parsley or dill.

Serves 8 to 10 as *zakuska*.

Note: The ingredients for this salad may be varied. Try substituting fresh peaches for the oranges, or crab meat for the chicken.

---

* Either red or green apples may be used, but the red will add more colour to the salad.

Salade Bagration

8 oz (225 g) uncooked elbow
macaroni or pasta shells

8 oz (225 g) cooked chicken or
turkey, cut into bite-sized
pieces

4 oz (120 g) cooked ham, cut
into bite-sized pieces

2 tart apples, cored and
chopped, but not peeled

2 whole spring onions,
chopped

4 oz (120 g) freshly shelled peas

2 oz (60 g) chopped black olives

3 hard-boiled egg yolks
3 tablespoons olive oil
3 tablespoons white
wine vinegar
¼ pint (150 ml) mayonnaise
¼ pint (150 ml) soured cream
salt, freshly ground white
pepper to taste
6 tablespoons chili sauce

Basically, this salad is prepared in the same way as Russian Salad. Boil the macaroni in salted water until just tender. Drain. While the macaroni is still warm, toss it with the prepared meats and vegetables, and pour over it the dressing which has been made by beating together the egg yolks, oil, vinegar, mayonnaise, soured cream and chili sauce. Season to taste, then chill overnight before serving.

Serves about 10 as *zakuska*.

Pink Potato Salad Vinegret iz kartofelya i svyokly

There are many variations of Russian potato salad. Some include meat or fish; others use only mayonnaise instead of soured cream; still others have an oil base. The salad offered here is a basic one made festive by the addition of beetroot, which turns the potatoes a lovely deep rose colour. It is sure to attract attention.

2 lb (900 g) potatoes
1 large beetroot
3 hard-boiled eggs, chopped
1 large cucumber, diced
3 oz (85 g) dill pickle, diced
3 spring onions, including the
green tops, chopped
1 heaped tablespoon capers
2 tablespoons olive oil

3 tablespoons white
wine vinegar
1 teaspoon salt
freshly ground black pepper to
taste
2 teaspoons fresh dill *or* ½
teaspoon dried dill
¼ pint (150 ml) soured cream

In separate pots, boil the potatoes and the beetroot until just tender. Drain them and remove the skins. Chop the potatoes into coarse chunks; dice the beetroot. Put both into a large bowl.

Add the chopped hard-boiled eggs, the cucumber, pickle, spring onions and capers, and mix well. Mix in the olive oil, vinegar, salt, pepper and dill. Finally, stir in the soured cream, mixing well to make sure each piece of the salad is coated. Chill, covered, overnight in the refrigerator before serving.

Serves 8 to 10 as *zakuska*.

Russian Egg Salad Salat iz yaits

This strongly-flavoured salad is a 'must' for the *zakuska* table. The egg slices are traditionally spread out in a long oval or rectangular cut-crystal dish, then masked with mayonnaise, rather than being mixed together with it.

6 hard-boiled eggs	¼ teaspoon salt
¼ pint (150 ml) mayonnaise (preferably home-made)	2 tablespoons finely chopped spring onion tops or chives
5 tablespoons soured cream	
1 small clove garlic, crushed	carrot or pimiento
¼ teaspoon hot mustard	

Slice the eggs thinly. Mix together the mayonnaise, soured cream, garlic, mustard and salt. Mask the eggs with this mixture. Sprinkle the chopped spring onion on top. Garnish with a little carrot or pimiento for colour.

Serves 4.

Mushroom-Stuffed Eggs Yaitsa, farshirovannye gribami

Stuffed eggs complement any *zakuska* table. They may be filled with whatever is on hand, from leftover *Stolichnyi salat*, to smoked fish and mayonnaise, to glistening grains of caviar. Here, the eggs are stuffed with a savoury mixture of minced mushrooms and egg. Mound the filling high in the cradles of egg.

4 hard-boiled eggs	freshly ground pepper to taste
2 oz (60 g) butter	a few drops of hot pepper sauce
1 small onion, minced	4 teaspoons mayonnaise
½ lb (225 g) mushrooms, trimmed and minced	2 teaspoons sour cream
2 tablespoons parsley	pinch of salt
2 teaspoons fresh dill, *or* ½ teaspoon dried dill	pimiento (optional)
½ teaspoon salt	

Sauté the onion in half the butter until golden. Add the remaining butter and the mushrooms and cook for 5 to 8 minutes more. Remove from the heat.

Peel the hard-boiled eggs and cut them in half lengthwise. Scoop out the yolks and chop them finely. Add them to the mushroom mixture along with the parsley, dill, salt, pepper and hot pepper sauce. Mix together the mayonnaise, sour cream and pinch of salt.

Fill the eggs with the mushroom mixture, mounding it high to form tall peaks. Dribble the mayonnaise mixture over the top so that it runs slightly down the sides. Garnish with a little pimiento, if desired.

Serves 4.

Sweet and Sour Beetroot Svyokla v tomatnom souse

Even inveterate beetroot haters will eat this salad with surprise and pleasure. The deep red of the beetroot merges with the orange carrots to yield a beautiful ruby colour. The salad tastes slightly more sweet than sour. If any is left over, it will keep well in the refrigerator for up to a week.

1 lb (450 g) fresh beetroot, tops removed	1 tablespoon red wine vinegar
1 lb (450 g) carrots	2 teaspoons sugar
1 large onion	¾ pint (450 ml) Basic Tomato Sauce (see below)
6 tablespoons olive oil	

Peel the beetroot and the carrots. Grate them together with the onion. (This is most easily done with the shredding disc of a food processor.)

In a large frying pan heat the olive oil. Add the shredded vegetables, mixing well. Sauté the vegetables over medium high heat for 10 to 12 minutes, until just barely tender. Stir in the vinegar, sugar, and the tomato sauce. Continue to cook over medium heat, stirring occasionally, until all the moisture evaporates, about 20 to 25 minutes. Transfer to a dish and chill before serving.

Serves 8 to 10 as *zakuska*.

Basic Tomato Sauce Tomatnyi Sous

2 tablespoons olive oil	freshly ground black pepper to taste
1 large onion, coarsely chopped	½ teaspoon dried basil
1 large clove garlic, crushed	a few drops of hot pepper sauce
1½ lb (700 g) ripe tomatoes, quartered	½ oz (15 g) butter
1 small green pepper, deseeded and chopped	1 tablespoon flour
1 teaspoon salt	1 tablespoon tomato paste
	½ teaspoon sugar

Sauté the onion and garlic in the olive oil until soft but not brown. Stir in the tomatoes, green pepper, salt, pepper, basil and hot pepper sauce. Cover the pan and simmer for 30 minutes. Then put the mixture through a vegetable mill.

In a saucepan melt the butter. Stir in the flour, then cook for a few minutes. Stir in the puréed tomato mixture, then add the tomato paste and sugar. Simmer for 10 minutes.

Makes ¾ pint (450 ml).

Beetroot Vinaigrette Vinegret iz svyokly

Lest you wince at the sight of another recipe for beetroot, it's best to keep in mind the old adage, 'Beets make the blood rich'. And if that isn't justification enough, this savoury beetroot salad should speak for itself.

1 lb (450 g) beetroot	salt, freshly ground black
4 tablespoons olive oil	pepper to taste
4 tablespoons red wine vinegar	
1 teaspoon hot mustard	finely chopped parsley

Preheat the oven to 190°C/375°F/Gas 5. Bake the unpeeled beetroot for 1 to 1½ hours, until tender. (If in a hurry, the beetroot may be boiled, but the flavour will not be as good.)

Meanwhile, mix together the remaining ingredients. When the beetroot is tender and cool enough to handle (but still warm), slip off the skins and slice. Cover the beetroot slices with the vinegar and oil mixture. Chill before serving. Garnish with finely chopped parsley.

Serves 4 to 6.

Cauliflower with Mayonnaise Tsvetnaya kapusta pod mayonezom

Here are two ways of preparing cauliflower to brighten the *zakuska* table. In both recipes the cauliflower is left whole and then crowned with a colourful dressing: a golden mustard-and-horseradish mayonnaise or a brilliantly tinted beetroot mayonnaise. Both preparations look very festive and, of course, taste delicious.

Cauliflower with Mustard and Horseradish Mayonnaise Tsvetnaya kapusta pod mayonezom iz gorchitsy i khrena

1 head cauliflower	⅛ teaspoon salt
5 tablespoons mayonnaise	white pepper to taste
(preferably home-made)	½ teaspoon prepared
5 tablespoons soured cream	horseradish (see p. 170)
2 tablespoons hot mustard	1½ tablespoons finely chopped
1 teaspoon fresh lemon juice	parsley

Steam the whole head of cauliflower over boiling water for 10 minutes. Drain and chill thoroughly in the refrigerator.

Just before serving, mix together the mayonnaise, soured cream, mustard, lemon juice, salt, pepper and horseradish, blending well. Spread this mixture over the top and sides of the chilled cauliflower, masking it completely. Sprinkle the chopped parsley over the top. To serve, cut the cauliflower in wedges with a sharp knife.

Serves 6.

Cauliflower with Beetroot Mayonnaise Tsvetnaya kapusta pod mayonezom iz svyokly

1 head cauliflower	½ teaspoon fresh lemon juice
1 tiny beetroot (about 1 oz/30 g)	salt to taste
¼ pint (150 ml) mayonnaise (preferably home-made)	snipped dill
2 teaspoons prepared horseradish (see p. 170)	

Steam the whole head of cauliflower over boiling water for 10 minutes. Drain and chill thoroughly in the refrigerator.

Meanwhile, boil the beetroot until tender. Peel it and put it through a fine strainer. Mix together the sieved beetroot, the mayonnaise, horseradish, lemon juice and salt.

Just before serving, mask the chilled cauliflower with the beetroot mayonnaise, covering the top and sides. Garnish with freshly snipped dill, and cut into wedges to serve.

Serves 6.

Note: Be sure not to overcook the cauliflower. It must remain firm.

Onions with Dill Luk marinovannyi

The perfect complement to a glass of vodka!

1 lb (450 g) jar pearl onions, drained	1 teaspoon caraway seed
½ pint (300 ml) cider vinegar	1 teaspoon crushed hot dried pepper
5 oz (150 g) sugar	12 black peppercorns
1 teaspoon salt	
2 tablespoons fresh snipped dill, *or* 1 teaspoon dried dill	

Place the drained onions in a 1½ pint (900 ml) jar. Combine the vinegar, sugar, salt, dill and spices in a medium saucepan. Bring to boil and then pour the mixture over the onions. Close the jar tightly and cool to room temperature. Refrigerate the onions for two weeks before serving.

Open-Faced Radish Sandwiches Buterbrody s rediskoi

Russians love radishes, from the mild red garden variety to the thick-skinned black balls of large dimension, and the versatile vegetable is firmly rooted in the Russian cuisine. One old adage even testifies to its ubiquity: 'We've had seven meals, and it's radishes still: radishes in thirds and slices; radishes with butter and kvass; radishes in bits and pieces; and radishes just as they are.'

Here, red radishes are finely chopped and mixed with cream cheese for a canapé spread which is as lovely to look at as it is to eat.

6 pieces thinly sliced black bread, cut into quarters	1 teaspoon lemon juice
16 red radishes	½ teaspoon coarse salt
4 oz (120 g) cream cheese	1 tablespoon chopped parsley
1 teaspoon fresh *or* ¼ teaspoon dried dill	

In a small bowl cream the cream cheese. Chop 8 of the radishes very finely, and slice the remaining 8 thinly. Add the chopped radishes to the cream cheese. Stir in the dill, lemon juice, salt and parsley. Spread the mixture on the slices of bread. On top of each canapé place overlapping slices of radish from the remaining 8 radishes.

Makes 2 dozen canapés.

Garlic-Cheese Spread Syr i chesnok pod mayonezom

The garlic available in the Soviet Union is very pungent, so it's no wonder Russia is a nation of garlic lovers. After tasting this excellent garlic-cheese spread, no one can remain impartial to it for long. This spread can also be used as the base for delicious *buterbrody*: try it over a slice of ham on black bread, or generously topped with watercress.

8 oz (225 g) Munster cheese, grated	1 tablespoon fresh snipped chives
3 large cloves garlic, crushed	sprinkling of salt
5 tablespoons mayonnaise	

Grate the cheese into a medium bowl, and add the garlic. Stir in the mayonnaise, mixing thoroughly with a wooden spoon until a creamy mass is achieved. (A few lumps are all right.) Stir in the chives, sprinkle with salt, and blend well.

Refrigerate the cheese spread, but bring it to room temperature before serving. Serve with thin slices of black bread or lightly toasted rounds of French bread.

Makes about ¾ pint (450 ml).

Note: The spread must be served at room temperature for the best flavour.

In the Days of the Tsar
Classic Recipes

Russian cookery had its heyday in the late-nineteenth-century Court of the Tsar and the homes of the gentry and nobility, when fantastic dishes were created to please discerning masters – Salad Demidoff, Pheasant Souvaroff, Veal Orloff, Beef Stroganoff, Nesselrode Pie. The fanciest chefs were all French, and the fanciest dishes resulted from a mixture of traditional French cookery and native Russian methods, as the original Russian foods received a flair they had previously lacked.

Still, Russian cookery did not blossom overnight. It took many years before gastronomy in Russia reached that state of refinement we consider its *haute cuisine* today. This evolution seems striking when one considers that the early Slavic tribes subsisted mainly on coarse gruels and primitive brews. The first written account of food occurs in the Russian *Primary Chronicle*, a history set down by a clerical scribe in Church Slavonic, a language now dead for many centuries. The entry is dated 997 AD; the scene is the ancient town of Belgorod.

Heathen Pecheneg tribes laid siege to the town, and Belgorod was beset by famine. When the inhabitants learned that Great Prince Vladimir was unable to come to their aid, they began to despair. They were on the verge of surrender when a sage old man formulated a plan to trick the Pechenegs. He bid the townspeople to gather all the oats, wheat and bran to be found and brew them into a porridge (*kasha*), then to gather as much honey as possible and dilute it to make mead. The grains were mixed with water and poured into a tub, as was the honey. Then the tubs were set into large pits in the ground, and a messenger invited the Pechenegs to send envoys to the town and observe the state of affairs. The Pechenegs, expecting the townsfolk's surrender, were astonished to find them eating copious amounts of boiled *kasha* and mead. Between mouthfuls, the people informed their enemies that they received their sustenance from the earth itself, and even if the

Pechenegs were to besiege them for ten years, they would not starve. Thus the siege was raised, thanks to simple food and drink and the cunning of a wise old man: an apocryphal tale to be sure.

As the years passed, the status of *kasha* rose from plebeian to plush. By the twelfth century we find the great princes of Russia dining on buckwheat porridge at their feasts, using the spoon as their utensil. (Even when the fork was introduced several centuries later, people balked, saying, 'A fork's like a fishing rod, but a spoon's a net!' Apparently, the idea was to load as much food as possible into a single mouthful.) Buckwheat continued to be food for the wealthy until the sixteenth century, when the nobles discovered diversity and the coarse groats finally became accessible to the common man. Since that time it has been firmly rooted in the peasant tradition, the upper classes turning instead to such delicacies as sturgeon roe and breast of chicken – never entirely scorning their buckwheat, though.

The elaborate feasts of the boyars in the sixteenth-century court of Ivan the Terrible, vividly described by Count Alexis Tolstoy in his historical novel, *Prince Serebryanyi*, bear witness to the new diversity in food among the well-to-do. These feasts stretched on for six to eight hours at a time. The guests were regaled with ten different courses, each consisting of up to twenty distinct dishes of a given type: there might be ten roasts of wild fowl and five varieties of fish. Each course was presented separately at table, until an array of sculpted masterpieces for dessert signalled the ending of the meal. Considering the massive amounts of food people consumed in those days, it is hardly surprising that their life expectancy was short.

By the late eighteenth century, the standard feast menu had been sensibly toned down, offering only eight different courses with just one dish for each course. The order was as follows: hot soup, cold soup, roast meat or fowl, poached or baked fish, Russian pie (*pirog* or *kulebyaka*), *kasha*, sweet pastry, and sweetmeats. Such a progression of courses did not seem extreme at the time; if anything, to the nobility it seemed restrained. Even so, the gifted eighteenth-century poet Derzhavin felt inspired to write a cautionary ode entitled *Invitation to Dinner*, which opens with a description of the delights of the dinner table awaiting the guests, but ends with the grave admonition that bliss is not to be found in sensual delights, for 'Moderation is the best of feasts'. The Russians were finally learning from the Greeks.

Perhaps Derzhavin's words were taken to heart. Eating habits were gradually becoming more temperate. By the time of Tolstoy, a wide choice of menu was available to the connoisseur, depending on how fancy a meal was desired. Dinners could range from two courses (soup and roast) to twelve (several different soups, roasts, fish, *entremets*, vegetables and desserts), the most common consisting of six: a hot soup, a cold one, fish, roast meat or fowl, vegetable or salad – always served as a separate course – and dessert. A strict progression of wines from soup to dessert was observed throughout the meal. The cookery books of the time show that for those who had money, a great diversity of products both wild and cultivated was available in the larger cities of Moscow, St Petersburg and Kiev. English lamb imported from London was considered the finest, while the native Ukrainian pork was said to be surpassed by no other. Circassian beef from the Caucasus was believed to be the best. In Turgenev's *Fathers and Sons*, it is not unrealistic that when a special meal is prepared, a servant is sent off at dawn for Circassian beef, while the bailiff of the estate is sent to fetch fresh fish and crayfish from the local waters.

Each area of Russia enjoyed the fish from its own rivers and lakes, and these local delicacies often could not be had outside a small radius. The people of St Petersburg ate fish from the River Neva and the Gulf of Finland, which harboured trout, salmon, whitefish, turbot, bream, ruff, perch, eel, pike, smelt, crayfish and other delights too numerous to name. High-living members of society paid exorbitant prices to import the prized Volga sterlet to St Petersburg in special tanks kept at carefully controlled temperatures. Most families enjoyed wild fowl such as capercailzie, blackcock, pheasant, hazel hen, woodcock, snipe and quail. Those lucky enough to know a hunter feasted on bear cub and wild boar, both great delicacies of the time. More easily obtainable were elk, wild goat, deer and hare, of which the russet variety was reputed tastier than the white. Domestic geese and turkeys, often bought live and fattened at home, complemented the heavier wild fowl.

The nineteenth-century table took excellent advantage of the abundance in Russia's forests and waterways. And as the influence of French taste on Russian life grew, so did the interest in food and its fine preparation. Yet even as many dishes gained new refinements (and some, fancy new French names), their bases remained typically Russian. Those who carried the French mode of the day too far were often ridiculed, as in Tolstoy's *Anna Karenina*, when Princess Myakhkaya tells in a loud voice of a dinner she and her husband attended where a fancy sauce ostensibly costing 1,000 roubles was served. 'It was a green mess!' the Princess declares. Nevertheless, according to etiquette, the dinner invitation had to be reciprocated. The Princess retaliated (and claims to have triumphed) by making a Russian sauce for only 85 kopecks, which tasted far better. Tolstoy himself detested pretensions to the French, preferring instead the native Russian fare as served by his hero Levin at his country estate: fresh bread and dairy butter, smoked goose, and salted mushrooms for an appetiser, followed by a soup of wild nettles with *pirozhki*, then roast chicken with white sauce, served with a white Crimean wine, and ending with a draught of home-made herb vodka. In spite of the influx of French wines, vodka still remained a preferred beverage, even among cosmopolitans. Shunning the more common wine cellar, Tsar Alexander II was said to have had a vodka cellar of 750,000 bottles.

One of the landmarks of traditional Russian dining in the mid-nineteenth century was Moscow's famed Merchants' Club. In the 1840s the club took over an old noble establishment, transforming its modish French menu into a splendid Russian table. Suckling pigs were ordered from the restaurateur Testov, well known in his own right for hand-feeding his piglets and keeping them in pens so small they could barely move their feet. Capons and *poulardes* were brought in from Rostov Yaroslavsky, milk-fed veal from the Trinity Monastery. The popular late-night dinners at the Merchants' Club are described by V. A. Gilyarovsky in his entertaining book, *Moscow and Muscovites*. These 'second' dinners often included fish soup (*ukha*) with sterlet, sturgeons two *arshins* (almost five feet) in length, Beluga sturgeon in brine, 'banquet' veal, walnut-fed turkeys 'as white as cream', fish pies (*rasstegai*) with burbot liver and sturgeon, suckling pig with horseradish and suckling pig with *kasha*. After the last toast ('To excess!'), the diners retired to the parlour where they sipped coffee and post-prandial liqueurs. If they were lucky, Nikolai Agafonych might appear and take orders for their favourite drinks. Nikolai Agafonych was the Merchants' Club's master brewer of kvasses and fruit drinks, for which the club was renowned. The diners, languorously reclining in easy chairs after the night's immoderations, would perk up the moment Nikolai Agafonych appeared. Then they'd begin calling out their orders for drinks infused with black-currant buds, so aromatic that the scent of early spring lingered long in one's nostrils, for nectars of ruby-red cherries or delicate raspberries, for kvass brewed from white bread instead of the usual black. Some hearty souls swore by Nikolai Agafonych's sour *shchi*, a fermented brew so gaseous that it had to be kept in tightly-stoppered bottles to avoid explosions. The Merchants' Club's notorious cook, the 360 pound Lyonechka, drank the *shchi* alongside frozen champagne, claiming that 'sour *shchi* might sock you in the nose, but it socks out drunkenness too!'

This same Lyonechka was the inventor of a fabulous twelve-layered *kulebyaka* which could be had only at the Merchants' Club or Testov's Tavern. Enclosed in his rich pastry crust were generous layers of meat, fish, mushrooms, chicken, and all sorts of game. Lyonechka's creation was so elaborate that it had to be ordered a good twenty-four hours in advance.

Entertainment at these meals was usually provided by Russian, Hungarian or gypsy singers and dancers. A touch of the exotic was much sought after by Muscovites of the time. One legendary merchant, Misha Khludov, regularly held lavish banquets at which he always appeared in different wild garb, accompanied by his pet tiger. By contemporary account, the ladies of Moscow were thrilled to see him as a Roman gladiator, clad only in a tiger skin which revealed the tautness of his physique; but they were probably less thrilled by the inevitable tiger stalking among them, sniffing at their plates.

In spite of all the hoopla of many nineteenth-century dinners, there was also a very serious side to Russian dining, one impelled by the deep religious feelings of the people. What determined the character of the Russian table more than anything else was the strict progression of feast and fast days in the Orthodox religious year, which most Russians observed. Because there were so many fast (*postnyi*) days when all meat, egg and milk products were proscribed (from 192 to 216 days of the year!), the feast (*skoromnyi*) days turned into extravaganzas – hence the liberal use of butter-rich foods in Russian cookery. Cooks had to be inventive to come up with tasty dishes for the many lean days of the year, and this fact accounts for Russia's wonderful fish and mushroom preparations. In addition, many ordinary foods could still be enjoyed on fast days if the ingredients were changed slightly, and such experimentation ultimately enriched the cuisine. Hemp, mustard, or nut oils were found to be substitutes for butter in cooking; pastries and breads were baked with almond milk or rose water instead of milk from cows.

To help guide cooks and home-makers through the maze of religious rules and direct them in the use of the abundant ingredients, popular cookery books began appearing in the mid-1800s. But the concept of a popular cookery book was hardly new in Russia. As early as the sixteenth century, a book appeared offering advice on food preparation and preserving. This was the *Domostroi*, or book of 'Household Order', attributed to the monk Sylvester from Novgorod, a city with a large and prosperous middle class. In an attempt to reach beyond the ecclesiastical community, the *Domostroi* was written in conversational style. It contains chapters on brewing beer and *sbiten'* (a hot, spiced honey drink), chapters on putting up preserves and storing vegetables ('when others must go to the market, you need only go as far as your cellar'), instructions for making *shchi*, and tips on preparing other such ultra-Russian foods as *kisel'* (fruit pudding), *blini*, *pirogi* and *grechnevaya kasha*. Sylvester also offers helpful hints for keeping the kitchen orderly and for receiving and feeding guests – the essential concept of hospitality is never overlooked. Naturally, the *Domostroi* dwells rather tediously on the importance of keeping the fast and feast days, but it also gives sound advice on how most pleasantly to observe them. Even today it is a delightful document affording insight into sixteenth-century life.

Much later, in 1816, the first recipe book appeared in Moscow: *The Russian Kitchen*, written by a chef named Levshin. But the most popular cookery book of all did not appear until 1861; this was Elena Molokhovets's *A Gift to Young Housewives; or a means of Reducing Household Expenses*. What began as a personal collection of favourite recipes turned into a best-seller, going through twenty-eight editions between 1861 and 1914. For the first time in a Russian cookery book, Molokhovets carefully detailed the ingredients and procedures necessary for the success of a myriad of dishes. Besides providing over 4,000 diverse recipes, she included menu suggestions and tips on household economy. Molokhovets has all too often been called the Mrs Beeton of Russia, and the similarities between the two are undeniable. Her book is still considered a classic in the Soviet Union today, where the contemporary housewife can read with longing of larders stocked with foods she has never even seen, let alone tasted. Because of the expectations such reading material might engender, *A Gift to Young Housewives* has never been reprinted in the Soviet Union and has long since disappeared from the shelves of antiquarian booksellers, as each treasured volume is passed down through family generations.

Molokhovets's cookery book was a tribute to the abundance and fine preparation of Russian food. Ironically, within ten years of its final edition, people throughout the newly-formed Soviet Union were brewing 'tea' from carrots and making bread out of coarse grains and sawdust. Of course, the food situation gradually stabilised, but the era of surfeit had finally come to an end, to be replaced by what Nabokov has termed 'the sadness of balanced meals'. It is true that the standard Russian meal of today is more balanced, more 'sensible' than its counterpart one hundred years ago, but much of its *éclat* has been lost. This chapter, then, is intended to resurrect the glories of the Russian cuisine as it was once prepared for banquets and feasts, when cooking and dining were both highly prized arts, and when calories did not count.

Sturgeon Soup with Champagne Sup iz osetriny s shampanskim

This soup, a favourite of the Empress Catherine the Great, is very elegant – and very expensive. Legend has it that Catherine planned a visit to her consort, Count Potemkin, at a time when no sturgeon was to be had in all of Moscow. Potemkin, never one to give up easily, sought out a cunning fishmonger who supplied him with enough fish for the soup. But it cost him dearly. In exchange for the sturgeon Potemkin relinquished a painting he had recently purchased for 10,000 roubles. But when Catherine the Great is coming for dinner, what else can one do?

   In old Russia a whole fillet of sturgeon was placed in each soup bowl and the broth poured over. The diners sipped the broth and then attacked the fish with knife and fork. The method presented here is more streamlined – and more economical.

1¼ pints (750 ml) fish stock
  (see p. 160)
1 lb (450 g) fresh sturgeon,
  trimmed and cut into cubes

½ pint (300 ml) dry champagne

lemon slices
chopped spring onion

Place the fish stock and the cubed sturgeon in a stockpot and bring to the boil. Simmer gently for about 10 minutes until the fish is cooked through.

Pour the champagne into the fish soup and just barely heat through. Ladle the soup into individual bowls and garnish each with some thinly sliced lemon and chopped spring onion.

Serves 4.

Clear Fish Soup Ukha

Ukha is the Russian fisherman's soup, traditionally prepared by simmering the catch of the day over a wood fire on the sandy shore. No doubt it is these bucolic associations which cause Russians to sigh when *ukha* is mentioned, for they rarely make the soup at home. Basically, *ukha* is a clear fish broth to which potatoes are sometimes added to fill it out. Almost any fish may be used, provided it is very fresh, since old fish turns the soup cloudy. The Russians claim that 'Bony fish make *ukha* sweet'. They themselves favour the *omul'*, a fish of the salmon family that emits a weird cry when caught.

4 pints (2 litres) cold water
2 lb (900 g) fish (including some
  trimmings)
1 onion, quartered
3 sprigs parsley
2 bay leaves

5 white peppercorns plus
  ground white pepper to taste
1½ tablespoons salt
2 potatoes, peeled and cubed
  (optional)

In a large pan put the water and the fish which has been cut into serving-sized pieces. (Perch, flounder, sea bass, etc. are all good in this soup, and a mixture of fish is to be preferred, but avoid using cod.) Bring the fish and water to the boil, skimming the foam from the surface. Then add the remaining ingredients. Cover and simmer for 1 hour.

To serve, place a piece of fish in each bowl and pour broth over.

Serves 6 to 8.

Note: Although purists insist that *ukha* must be made with a variety of fish and without any potatoes, my friend Klara makes an excellent version using 2 lb (900 g) salmon (including some salmon collars) and 2 potatoes. Proceed as directed above.

Russian Lemon Soup Limonnyi sup

An unusual and delightful soup.

2 oz (60 g) uncooked rice	juice and rind of 1 large lemon
1 oz (30 g) butter	
2 pints (1 litre) clear chicken broth	finely chopped parsley
	lemon slices
¼ pint (150 ml) double cream	

In a medium-sized saucepan cook the rice and the butter in ½ pint (300 ml) chicken broth until tender, about 20 minutes. Stirring the rice with a fork, gradually add the remaining chicken broth. Stir in the double cream and then the finely grated rind and juice of the lemon. (If an even tarter taste is preferred, more lemon juice may be added.)

When the ingredients are well blended, ladle the soup into individual bowls, making sure that some rice is placed in the bottom of each bowl. Garnish with thin slices of lemon and chopped parsley.

Serves 4.

Variation: To serve the soup cold, cook the rice as directed above and then stir in the remaining broth. Chill. Skim off any fat that has hardened on the surface, and then add the cream and lemon juice and rind. Chill well before serving.

Kidney and Dill Pickle Soup Rassol'nik

The classic Russian sour soup, provocative both in its flavour and in its scent.

1 veal kidney (or 2 lamb) flour	2 tablespoons brine from the pickle jar
1 large carrot, scraped	2 oz (60 g) uncooked pearl barley
1 medium leek, peeled	¾ teaspoon salt
1 medium potato, peeled	freshly ground black pepper to taste
2 oz (60 g) butter	soured cream
4¾ pints (2½ litres) beef stock	
3 dill pickles, insides scraped out, cut into julienne strips	

Remove all membrane from the kidney and soak it in cold water for 30 minutes. Then pat it dry and cut into slices. Dredge with flour.

Meanwhile, prepare the vegetables. Cut the carrot, leek and potato into julienne strips. Melt 1 oz (30 g) butter in a large stockpot and sauté the vegetables in it for 10 minutes.

In a small frying pan melt the remaining butter and fry the kidneys in it over high heat to brown, for about 5 minutes.

Add the fried kidneys and the beef stock to the vegetables in the stockpot. Then add the pickles in julienne strips, the barley, the salt, and freshly ground pepper to taste. Bring to the boil, skimming the foam that rises to the surface. When the foam has subsided, cover the pot and simmer the soup for 45 minutes.

Stir in the pickle brine. Test for seasoning. At this point soured cream may be stirred into the soup for serving, or it may be passed at the table and the soup served clear.

Serves 10 to 12.

Cold Raspberry Soup Malinnik

A lush and elegant soup.

1 lb (450 g) fresh raspberries	¾ pint (450 ml) claret
4 oz (120 g) sugar (or more, to taste, depending on the sweetness of the berries)	2 tablespoons sparkling water

Put 12 oz (340 g) of the berries through a vegetable mill, reserving the rest for garnish. Stir in the sugar and then add the claret. Chill well.

Just before serving, stir in the sparkling water and the reserved berries. This soup looks lovely when presented in a glass bowl. A dollop of whipped sweet or soured cream may be placed in each portion, if desired. Serve with plain biscuits.

Serves 4 to 6.

Note: If fresh raspberries are not available, two 10 oz (280 g) packets of frozen raspberries in syrup may be substituted. In this case, eliminate the sugar entirely.

Russian Pies Pirozhki

There's a folktale in which a child asks a large Russian stove, 'Where have all the magic birds flown?' And Mother-stove replies, while coaxing the child with a hot ryemeal pie, 'Eat! Eat! And then I will tell you.' The Russian pie (*pirog* or *pirozhok*) is as ubiquitous in Russian life as it is in literature. Street corners are dotted with hawkers selling their pies hot from portable ovens; cafés offer meat pies along with bowls of steaming soup. The importance of the *pirog* cannot be underestimated: in one of Gogol's *Dikanka* tales the narrator is alarmed to find that his wife has made off with half the pages of his book to use as baking paper for her pies, which, he confesses, are indeed the tastiest around.

The practice of enclosing all sorts of fillings, both savoury and sweet, in an envelope of dough is an old one, and very characteristic of the Russian cuisine. The pies range from the complex and extravagant (the many-layered salmon *kulebyaka*, for instance) to the simple and plain (deep-fried half-moons of dough stuffed with leftovers). The large pies are called *pirogi*. They are usually square or rectangular in shape. Their diminutive cousins, the *pirozhki*, are pocket-sized and oval. All can be made from a variety of doughs – yeast, short or flaky pastry – depending on which suits the filling best.

The word *pirog* comes from *pir* or 'feast': *pirogi* were, and still are, integral to Russian entertaining. The recipes below are for some of the more popular pie fillings, but improvisation is encouraged, as the possibilities are endless.

Basic Raised Pirozhki Dough Drozhzhevoye testo

1 tablespoon dried yeast	1 teaspoon salt
4 tablespoons warm water	2 teaspoons sugar
8 fluid oz (225 ml) milk	2 whole eggs
4 oz (120 g) butter, cut into	2 egg yolks
small pieces	1–1¼ lb (450–550 g) plain flour

Dissolve the dried yeast in the warm water. Heat the milk to lukewarm and add the butter. Stir the milk and butter mixture into the yeast. Add the salt, sugar, one of the eggs, and the egg yolks, mixing well. Gradually stir in enough flour to make a soft dough.

Turn the dough out on to a floured board and knead it lightly until smooth and elastic. Place it in a greased bowl, turning to grease the top, and cover it with a clean towel. Let rise in a warm place until doubled in bulk, about 1½ hours.

Knock back the dough and divide it into 48 balls of equal size. On a floured board roll each ball out to a circle 3½ in (9 cm) in diameter. Place a heaped tablespoon of filling on each circle, then press the edges of the dough together firmly to seal. Gently shape the pies into elongated ovals.

Place the pies seam-side down on a greased baking tray. Cover and let rise until they are just doubled in bulk, about 40 minutes. Preheat the oven to 180°C/350°F/Gas 4.

Beat the remaining whole egg and brush each pie with it. Bake for 20 minutes or until golden.

Makes 4 dozen *pirozhki*.

Variations:
1. To make a sweet raised dough for dessert *pirozhki*, increase the amount of sugar to 2 tablespoons. Proceed as directed above.
2. *Pirozhki* may be deep-fried instead of baked, and then they are usually shaped into round balls instead of ovals. After the *pirozhki* have risen on the baking tray, drop them, a few at a time, into deep hot fat (185°C/365°F) and fry them until golden, about 5 minutes, turning them once. Drain on kitchen paper and serve immediately.
3. To make 2 large *pirogi*, divide the risen dough into 4 pieces. Roll out each piece of dough into a 10 in (25 cm) square. Spread 2 of the

pieces with the desired filling, and then top each filling with the remaining squares of dough. Turn the bottom edge of the dough up over the top piece to seal. Shape any leftover scraps of dough into fancy shapes and affix them in a decorative pattern to the top of the *pirogi* with beaten egg. Let the *pirogi* rise in a warm place, covered, until doubled in bulk. Brush them with beaten egg and bake them in a preheated 180°C/350°F/Gas 4 oven for about 45 minutes, or until golden.

4. A four-cornered *pirog* is made for special occasions (such as a Name Day). Roll out the dough as for the 2 large *pirogi* above, but instead of using only 1 filling, spread the bottom squares of dough with 4 different fillings, using 1 filling to cover each corner of the squares of dough. Top with the remaining dough and proceed as directed above.

Soured Cream Pastry for Pirozhki Bezdrozhzhevoye testo

12 oz (340 g) plain flour	9 oz (250 g) butter
¾ teaspoon salt	¼ pint (150 ml) soured cream
1 oz (30 g) sugar	

In a medium bowl mix together the flour, salt and sugar. Cut in the butter until the dough is the consistency of cornmeal. Add the soured cream, mixing well. Wrap the dough in waxed paper and chill in the refrigerator for 2 hours.

Roll the dough out ⅛–¼ in (3–6 mm) thick. With a round biscuit cutter, cut out circles 4 in (10 cm) in diameter. Place a generous tablespoon of filling on one half of each circle; fold the other half over to form half-moons. Crimp the edges together with a fork to seal.

Preheat the oven to 190°C/375°F/Gas 5. Place the *pirozhki* on a very lightly greased baking tray and bake them for 20 minutes, or until golden.

Makes 2 dozen *pirozhki*.

Variation: For sweet *pirozhki*, increase the amount of sugar to 6 tablespoons and proceed as directed above.

Biscuit Dough for Sweet Pirozhki Sladkoye bezdrozhzhevoye testo

Sweet *pirozhki* made from this dough are irresistible, as the servant Natasha in Fyodor Sologub's novel *The Petty Demon* knows. She wants to steal a *pirozhok* and eat it on the sly, but because the pastries are so rich they leave a trace on the baking tray, and Natasha's suspicious mistress always examines the tray to see if the number of buttery patterns left on it matches the number of *pirozhki* brought to table. Natasha is afraid of being caught, so she doesn't yield to temptation – at least not this time.

12 oz (340 g) plain flour
½ teaspoon salt
6 oz (170 g) sugar
½ teaspoon bicarbonate of
  soda

4 oz (120 g) butter
8 tablespoons soured cream
3 eggs, 1 of them beaten for
  brushing before baking

Follow exactly the same procedure as for the Soured Cream Dough above, but brush these *pirozhki* with the beaten egg before baking.

Makes 2 dozen *pirozhki*.

Variation: This dough may also be used to make small biscuits called 'pigtails' (*kosichki*): Roll the dough out ⅛ in (3 mm) thick. Cut it into strips ½ in (12 mm) wide and 5 in (12.5 cm) long. Take 3 strips and braid them together, repeating until all the dough has been braided. Place the 'pigtails' on a lightly greased baking sheet, brush them with beaten egg, and sprinkle them with poppy seed. Bake in a preheated 190°C/375°F/Gas 5 oven for 15 minutes. These make a good plain biscuit for tea. Makes 2 dozen biscuits.

Savoury Fillings for Pirozhki

Beef Filling Nachinka iz rublyonogo myasa

1 oz (30 g) butter
1 tablespoon olive oil
2 large onions, minced
1 lb (450 g) lean minced beef
2½ teaspoons salt
freshly ground black pepper to
  taste

2 tablespoons snipped fresh
  dill *or* 2 teaspoons dried dill
2 hard-boiled eggs, minced
2 tablespoons soured cream

Sauté the onion in the butter and oil until transparent. Stir in the beef and cook it until no trace of pink remains. Then stir in the remaining ingredients, mixing well. Set aside to cool before using as filling.

Makes filling for 4 dozen *pirozhki* or 2 *pirogi*.

Cabbage Filling Nachinka iz kapusty

1 lb (450 g) white cabbage,
  finely shredded
2 oz (60 g) butter
2 tablespoons olive oil
2 large onions, minced
4 teaspoons snipped fresh dill
  or 1¼ teaspoons dried dill

1 tablespoon salt
freshly ground black pepper to
  taste
2 hard-boiled eggs, minced

Sauté the onion in the butter and oil until transparent, then add the shredded cabbage and continue cooking for 15 to 20 minutes more, until the cabbage is tender but not browned. Stir in the remaining ingredients, mixing well. Let cool slightly before using.

Makes filling for 4 dozen *pirozhki* or 2 *pirogi*.

Mushroom Filling Gribnaya nachinka

4 oz (120 g) butter
2 medium onions, minced
1 lb (450 g) mushrooms, minced
2 hard-boiled eggs, minced
2 oz (60 g) uncooked rice, cooked according to directions on packet

6 tablespoons minced fresh parsley
1 teaspoon salt
freshly ground black pepper to taste
2 tablespoons fresh dill *or* 2 teaspoons dried dill

Cook the onion until soft but not brown in the butter. Stir in the mushrooms and sauté for 5 minutes more. Off the heat, stir in the remaining ingredients, mixing well. Let cool slightly before using.

Makes enough to fill 4 dozen *pirozhki* or 2 *pirogi*.

Spring Onion Filling Nachinka iz zelonogo luka

6 to 8 large spring onions, finely chopped
6 oz (170 g) butter
8 tablespoons minced fresh parsley
4 hard-boiled eggs, finely chopped

3 tablespoons fresh snipped dill *or* 1 tablespoon dried dill
2 teaspoons salt
freshly ground black pepper to taste
4 tablespoons soured cream

Sauté the spring onion in the butter for 5 minutes. Off the heat, stir in the remaining ingredients, mixing well. Leave to cool slightly before using.

Makes enough to fill 4 dozen *pirozhki* or 2 *pirogi*.

Carrot Filling Nachinka iz morkovi

6 medium carrots, scraped
4 oz (120 g) butter
1 spring onion, finely chopped
3 slices day-old white bread, crusts removed, crumbled
2 tablespoons snipped chives

1½ teaspoons salt
freshly ground black pepper to taste
3 tablespoons soured cream
6 tablespoons minced fresh parsley

Boil the carrots in salted water until tender, then chop them finely. Sauté them for 5 minutes in the butter, along with the chopped spring onion and the breadcrumbs. Off the heat, stir in the remaining ingredients, mixing well.

Leave to cool slightly before using.

Makes enough to fill 4 dozen *pirozhki* or 2 *pirogi*.

Sweet Fillings for Pirozhki

Apricot Filling Abrikosovaya nachinka

1 lb (450 g) dried apricots, cut into fairly small pieces	1 lb (450 g) sugar

Place the apricot pieces in a large pan, and pour in enough water just to cover them. Leave them to soak overnight.

The next day, stir the sugar into the apricots and water. Bring the mixture to the boil over medium heat. Then cook slowly, stirring, until the apricots are soft, about 30 minutes. Cool before using.

Makes enough to fill 2 dozen *pirozhki* or 1 *pirog*.

Apple Filling Yablochnaya nachinka

1½ lb (700 g) tart cooking apples, peeled, cored, and coarsely grated	scant ½ teaspoon cardamom (or less, to taste)
juice of 1 lemon	1 tablespoon flour
6 oz (170 g) sugar	1½ oz (45 g) butter
¾ teaspoon cinnamon	sugar

Grate the apples and immediately mix them with the lemon juice in a large bowl. Stir in the sugar, cinnamon, cardamom, and flour. Place a heaped tablespoon of the filling on each round of dough. Top the filling with a dot of butter.

After the dough has been brushed with beaten egg, sprinkle each pie lightly with granulated sugar before baking.

Makes enough to fill 2 dozen *pirozhki* or 1 *pirog*.

Poppy Seed Filling Makovaya nachinka

4 oz (120 g) poppy seed, ground in a blender or food processor	2 oz (60 g) unsalted butter
	3 oz (85 g) honey
3 oz (85 g) almonds, toasted, then very finely chopped	white of 1 large egg

Toast the almonds for 10 minutes at 150°C/300°F/Gas 2 until lightly browned. Grind the poppy seed. Cream together the butter and the honey, then stir in the chopped almonds and the poppy seed. Whip the egg white until stiff and fold into the poppy seed mixture.

Makes enough to fill 2 dozen *pirozhki* or 1 *pirog*.

Walnut-Honey Filling Orekhovaya nachinka

An especially good filling for the biscuit dough.

8 oz (225 g) walnut halves, finely chopped	2 oz (60 g) sugar
3 oz (85 g) honey	¼ teaspoon cinnamon
	grated rind of 1 lemon

Mix together the sugar and honey, then stir in the cinnamon. Add the chopped walnuts and the lemon rind, mixing well. Place a heaped tablespoon of the filling on each round of dough.

Makes enough to fill 2 dozen *pirozhki* or 1 *pirog*.

Small Fish Pies Rasstegai

These charming pies are the traditional accompaniment to fish broth, *ukha*. Their name comes from the Russian *rasstegnut'*, 'to come undone', because the pies' fanciful shape (with their filling exposed) makes one suspect they've popped open in the baking.

In the past, when appetites were larger, *rasstegai* were often made the size of a salad plate. One noted Moscow tavern, Yegorov's, claimed to serve the best *rasstegai* in town. When these fish pies were ordered, the *ukha* came free. It was Yegorov's showy waiter, Pyotr Kirilych, who perfected the serving of *rasstegai* at the table. With a bold flourish of knife and fork, he frenetically attacked the warm pastry, then stood back to admire his workmanship: ten thin slices artistically stretching out from the centre of the pie to its well-browned edges. This method of slicing soon became the rage in Moscow, but no one could do it quite as stylishly as Pyotr Kirilych.

Yegorov's *rasstegai* were filled with a mixture of cooked fish and *vesiga*, the dried backbone of sturgeon. A slice of sturgeon topped with burbot liver peeked through the central opening. In the recipe below, both the fish liver and the sturgeon backbone have been omitted. Nor does one have to worry about carving these pies artistically, for they are conveniently made in individual portions.

1½ teaspoons active dry yeast	1 oz (30 g) butter
2 tablespoons warm water	¼ lb (120 g) mushrooms,
pinch of sugar	minced
1 oz (30 g) butter, melted	¼ lb (120 g) smoked salmon
2 egg yolks	2 tablespoons minced parsley
6 tablespoons milk	2 tablespoons soured cream
¼ teaspoon salt	freshly ground white pepper to
8 oz (225 g) plain flour	taste
½ lb (225 g) fish fillets (trout is especially good)	1 egg yolk
	1 tablespoon cold water

Dissolve the yeast in the warm water along with the sugar. Then stir in the melted butter, egg yolks, salt, and milk which has been heated to lukewarm. Mix in the flour to make a soft dough. Turn out on to a floured board and knead until smooth and elastic. Place the dough in a greased bowl, turning once to grease the top of the dough. Cover and leave to rise in a warm place until doubled in bulk, about 2 hours.

Meanwhile, prepare the filling. Sauté the fillets in half the butter until they are done. Sauté the minced mushrooms in butter for just a few minutes. Flake the fish into a bowl and stir in the mushrooms, the smoked salmon which has been finely chopped, the parsley and the soured cream. Add pepper to taste.

When the dough has risen, knock it back and then turn it out on to a floured board. Roll it out very thinly and with a 3 in (5 cm) biscuit cutter, cut out 2 dozen rounds. On each round of dough place a heaped tablespoon of the filling down the centre.

Now shape the *rasstegai*. Starting just to the left of centre of one of the rounds, bring two edges together to meet. Overlap one edge over the other to seal, and seal the left side of the pie. Now bring the two edges of dough together just to the right of the centre of the pie, overlapping one edge over the other and sealing the whole side. The result is an enclosed pie with a hole 1½ in (3 cm) in diameter in the top centre. Flare the edges of dough around the hole slightly to make it look rounder. Continue in this manner until all the pies have been shaped.

Place the pies on a greased baking tray. Cover and leave to rise until almost doubled in bulk, 45 minutes to 1 hour. Brush the pies with a mixture of egg yolk and cold water.

Preheat the oven to 180°C/350°F/Gas 4. Bake the pies for 15 minutes, until golden. Serve warm or at room temperature.

Makes 2 dozen pies.

Coulibiac of Salmon Kulebyaka

Of all Russian pies, *kulebyaka* is the most glorious, the *pirog par excellence* of the Russian cuisine. When made in the classical manner, it is elaborate and time-consuming, but the results are well worth the effort. *Kulebyaka* differs from the more common *pirog* in that the filling is assembled in layers, rather than being mixed all together, and its finished shape is narrow and high instead of wide and flat. According to the court stenographer in Chekhov's *The Siren*, 'The *kulebyaka* should be appetising, shameless in its nakedness, a temptation to sin . . .'

Start preparing the puff pastry for the *kulebyaka* a day ahead of time.

Puff Pastry

½ lb (225 g) plain flour	½ lb (225g) unsalted butter
¾ teaspoon salt	1 egg, lightly beaten
4 fluid oz (125 ml) water	

In a medium-sized bowl, mix together the flour and salt. Add enough water to make a fairly soft dough. Knead it lightly.

Place the butter in a large bowl of iced water. Working quickly, knead it with your fingers and shape it into a 4 in (9 cm) square. Do not let the butter get too soft.

Roll the dough out to a 12 in (30 cm) square. Place the butter in the centre of the dough, then fold the sides of the dough up around the butter. Wrap in waxed paper and refrigerate for 30 minutes.

Roll the dough out into a long rectangle. Fold it into thirds. Turn the dough so that the raw edges are facing you and roll it out once more into a long strip. Fold in thirds once more. You have just completed two 'turns' of the dough. Wrap the dough in waxed paper and refrigerate for 30 minutes.

Roll the dough out for a third time into a long strip; fold it into thirds. This is the third 'turn'. Refrigerate for 30 minutes.

Roll out the dough a fourth time, fold it in thirds and refrigerate. At this point the dough may be held overnight in the refrigerator – in fact, it is a good idea.

The next day, roll out the dough into a long strip and then fold it into thirds. This is the fifth 'turn'. Refrigerate for 30 minutes.

Roll out the dough into a long strip, fold in thirds, and wrap in waxed paper again. You have just completed the sixth and final 'turn'. The dough is now ready to be used. Keep it wrapped in the refrigerator until you are about to assemble the *kulebyaka*.

The next step in preparing *kulebyaka* is to make thin pancakes or *blinchiki*. These also may be prepared a day ahead and held at room temperature overnight.

Blinchiki

1 egg, separated	pinch of salt
½ pint (300 ml) milk	pinch of sugar
2 oz (60 g) butter, melted	
4 oz (120 g) plain flour	butter for frying

Beat the egg yolk with the milk. Add the melted butter. Stir in the flour, sugar and salt. Beat the egg white until stiff but not dry, then fold it into the batter.

Heat a crêpe pan or frying pan and brush it with butter. Fry the *blinchiki* one at a time until all the batter has been used up. Use only about 1 tablespoon of batter for each pancake, as they should be as thin as crêpes.

If you are preparing them ahead of time, brush each pancake with melted butter and stack them one on top of the next. Cover with plastic wrap or foil.

When ready to use the *blinchiki*, trim them into rectangles.

Next, prepare the remaining ingredients for the filling.

Filling

4 eggs, hard-boiled	1½ lb (700 g) salmon fillets
	3 oz (85 g) uncooked rice
½ lb (225 g) mushrooms, trimmed and sliced	1 tablespoon snipped fresh dill
1 tablespoon freshly squeezed lemon juice	1 onion, chopped
	1 oz (30 g) *vesiga* or Chinese
3 oz (85 g) butter	vermicelli*
salt, freshly ground white pepper to taste	melted butter
8 tablespoons dry white wine	

Cut the hard-boiled eggs into thin slices. Set aside.

Toss the sliced mushrooms with the lemon juice. In a large pan melt 1 oz (30 g) butter and stir in the mushrooms. Add salt and pepper to taste. Pour in the wine. Cover and steam the mushrooms for 5 minutes. Then place the salmon fillets on top of the mushrooms and poach them, covered, until done, about 10 minutes. Do not overcook them.

With a slotted spoon remove the salmon and mushrooms from the pan and set them aside. Measure the liquid remaining in the pot. There should be 6 fluid oz (175 ml). (If there is not, add enough more wine to make up the amount.) Cook the rice in this liquid until it is done. Stir in the freshly snipped dill.

Sauté the onion in the remaining butter until golden.

Boil the Chinese vermicelli in salted water until soft and transparent, about 20 minutes. Drain. Mince the vermicelli and add to the sautéed onion.

Now you are ready to assemble the *kulebyaka*. On a floured cloth, roll the dough out to a 12 in (30 cm) × 18 in (45 cm) rectangle. (Throughout this whole process, try to work as quickly as possible so that the dough does not soften too much.)

Spread half of the *blinchiki* (which have been cut into rectangles) in a strip 5 in (12 cm) wide down the centre of the dough, leaving a good inch (2 cm) of dough at either end. On top of the *blinchiki* place half of the rice mixture. On top of the rice place half of the onion-vermicelli mixture, then half of the sliced hard-boiled eggs, then half of the mushrooms. On top of the mushrooms place all of the poached salmon fillets, pressing down gently with the palm of your hand.

Now reverse the order: top the salmon with the rest of the mushrooms, then the egg slices, the onion-bean thread mixture, and the rice. Top the rice with the remaining trimmed *blinchiki*. Press down gently on the filling to mould it together.

* *Vesiga* is the gelatinous dried backbone of the sturgeon. If available, it gives a unique flavour to the *kulebyaka*. To prepare *vesiga*, soak it for several hours in cold water. Then rinse. Put it in a pot with clean water, bring to the boil, and simmer until tender, about 2½ hours. Drain and mince. I find that the Chinese vermicelli are a good substitute, as do the Russians living in San Francisco, who shop at the Chinese supermarkets.

Bring the two short ends of the dough up over the filling to enclose it, then carefully bring the two long sides of the dough up over the filling to meet in the centre. Seal the edges securely, using a little cold water if necessary to help them adhere. Very carefully invert the *kulebyaka* on to a large baking tray which has been brushed with cold water.

Cut three small holes in the top of the dough. Decorate the *kulebyaka* with leftover bits of dough, using some of the beaten egg to help them adhere. Brush the dough all over with the beaten egg. Place the *kulebyaka* in the refrigerator and chill for 30 minutes.

Preheat the oven to 200°C/400°F/Gas 6. Bake the *kulebyaka* for 10 minutes, then reduce the heat to 180°C/350°F/Gas 4 and continue baking for 20 to 25 minutes, until puffed and brown.

Serve with plenty of melted butter. (If desired, some melted butter may be poured into the holes in the *kulebyaka* when it is removed from the oven, but be careful not to add too much, lest the dough become soggy.)

Makes 8 to 10 servings.

Variations: Cream cheese pastry (below) may be substituted for the puff pastry.

Substitute thickly sliced smoked salmon for the fresh salmon.

Russian Chicken Pie Kurnik

Kurnik, whose name derives from the Russian word for hen, is yet another sort of pie enclosed in rich pastry top and bottom. It is good party fare, since it may be made early in the day and reheated at the last minute.

Pastry

12 oz (340 g) butter, at room temperature	12 oz (340 g) plain flour
	½ teaspoon salt
12 oz (340 g) cream cheese, at room temperature	2 teaspoons baking powder
2 egg yolks	

Cream the butter and cream cheese. Mix in the egg yolks. Stir in the flour, salt and baking powder until smooth. Divide the dough into two balls, one larger than the other. Wrap each ball in greaseproof paper and chill in the refrigerator for at least 30 minutes before using.

Chicken

4 lb (1.8 kg) boiling fowl	1 bay leaf
1½ pints (900 ml) cold water	8 black peppercorns
1 sprig parsley	1 teaspoon salt
1 large carrot, scraped	1 teaspoon tarragon
1 onion, quartered	

In a large stockpot bring all the above ingredients to the boil. Simmer, covered, for 1½ hours, or until the chicken is tender. Then strain, reserving the chicken stock.

Remove the skin from the chicken and discard it. Separate the meat from the bones and cut the meat into small pieces. Chop the giblets.

Reserve the carrot and cut it into ¼ in (6 mm) thick slices.

Filling

scant 1¼ pints (750 ml) reserved chicken stock	1 lb (450 g) mushrooms, trimmed and sliced
4 tablespoons soured cream	4 tablespoons chopped parsley
1 tablespoon snipped fresh dill or 1½ teaspoons dried dill	4 hard-boiled eggs, coarsely chopped
¾ teaspoon salt	
8 oz (225 g) uncooked rice	1 egg yolk
3 oz (85 g) butter	2 teaspoons cold water
2 onions, sliced	

First, heat 8 fluid oz (225 ml) of the reserved chicken stock. Stir in the soured cream and the dill, mixing well. Stir in ¼ teaspoon salt. Pour the mixture over the chopped chicken pieces, stirring to coat them well. Set aside.

Cook the rice in ¾ pint (450 ml) of the reserved chicken stock along with the remaining ½ teaspoon salt, just until the liquid is absorbed. Do not overcook. Set aside.

Sauté the sliced onions in 2 oz (60 g) butter until soft and golden; then stir in the remaining butter and the mushrooms. Sauté for about 3 minutes until the mushrooms are just barely cooked. Stir in the parsley and the reserved sliced carrot. Drain off excess liquid and set aside.

Remove the larger ball of dough from the refrigerator. Roll it out on a floured board to a circle about 12 in (30 cm) in diameter. Line a 9 in (22.5 cm) springform tin with the dough. Preheat the oven to 200°C/400°F/Gas 6.

Taking one-third of the rice, place a layer of it on the bottom of the pastry. Top the rice with half of the chicken, then half of the chopped hard-boiled eggs, then half of the vegetable mixture. Top the vegetables with half of the remaining rice in an even layer, and then repeat the layering with the remaining ingredients, ending with a layer of rice on the top. (There will be 3 layers of rice and 2 of the other ingredients.)

Roll out the second ball of dough and cover the pie with it, sealing the edges well. Cut a round hole 1½ in (3 cm) in diameter in the centre of the top crust to allow steam to escape. Decorate the top crust with cut-out scraps of dough in a fanciful pattern.

Beat the egg yolk with 2 teaspoons cold water. Brush the mixture over the dough. Bake the *kurnik* at 200°C/400°F/Gas 6 for 20 minutes, then reduce the heat to 180°C/350°F/Gas 4 and continue baking it for

25 minutes longer, or until the crust is golden. Allow the *kurnik* to cool in the tin for 20 minutes, then remove the sides of the tin and serve the pie immediately.

Serves 8 to 10.

Variation: It is a little less complicated to bake the *kurnik* in an ordinary pie tin, although the result will not be as spectacular: Roll out half of the dough and fit it into a 10 in (25 cm) pie tin. Proceed as directed above, covering the filling with the remaining dough and crimping the edges well to seal. Cut a hole in the top crust to allow the steam to escape and bake as directed above. This version of *kurnik* is served directly from the tin.

Chicken Kiev Kievskie kotlety

These rich rolls of chicken encasing lightly herbed butter are a symbol of Russian *haute cuisine*. No one knows exactly when they were created, but their origin can be traced to the Ukrainian city of Kiev. Long before Moscow became the Russian capital, Kiev served as the major centre of trade and culture. It was the first seat of the medieval Russian empire, founded on three hills overlooking the Dnepr River. Stimulated by the fertile soils and abundant wild food of the region, the culinary art has been practised for many centuries in the Ukraine, producing such gastronomic *tours de force* as *borshch*, *pampushki*, *galushki*, and the rightly renowned Chicken Kiev.

When cutting into Chicken Kiev, beware! When properly prepared, the cutlets will release a spurt of hot, rich butter, sometimes greeting the diner unawares.

2 large whole chicken breasts, split	salt, freshly ground pepper to taste
4 oz (120 g) butter, slightly softened	Dijon mustard
freshly chopped parsley, chives and tarragon to taste	2 eggs, lightly beaten
1 teaspoon freshly squeezed lemon juice	flour
	fine, dry breadcrumbs
	vegetable oil for deep frying

Cream the butter with any combination of finely chopped herbs you desire. I use about 1 teaspoon each freshly snipped chives and tarragon and a bit more parsley. Blend in the lemon juice. Shape the butter into four rolls, long enough to be placed lengthwise on the chicken pieces without extending over the edge of the meat and leaving a 1 in (2.5 cm) border. Place the rolls of butter in the refrigerator to chill until firm.

Meanwhile, skin and bone the split chicken breasts. Then, between two sheets of waxed paper, pound each half-breast with a mallet until thin and flat, about ⅛ in (3 mm) thick, being careful not to tear the meat. Lightly salt and pepper the chicken, and set it aside.

When the butter is firm, remove it from the refrigerator. Spread each chicken fillet with a thin layer of Dijon mustard. Place a roll of butter lengthwise along each piece. Tuck in the ends of the fillets and roll them up, making sure that the butter is completely enclosed within the chicken packet. Dredge each fillet in flour, dip it in the beaten eggs, and then in the dry breadcrumbs, so that it is completely coated. Adjust the fillets into uniform ovals. Put them in the refrigerator and leave to chill for at least one hour (they can be held for 3 to 4 hours).

Preheat vegetable oil to 182°C/360°F in a deep-fat fryer. Remove the fillets from the refrigerator and immerse them, only one or two at a time (depending on the size of the fryer) in the hot oil. Do not crowd them. Fry the fillets for 5 to 8 minutes, or until golden. Serve immediately. (If they must be held until the remaining breasts are fried, place them in a warm oven for no more than 5 minutes.)

The *Kievskie kotlety* are traditionally served with fried potato baskets filled with tender green peas (see Straw Potatoes, p. 83).

Serves 4.

Notes: If no deep-fat fryer is available, the dish also works well when the fillets are simply fried in a frying pan over medium high heat in a mixture of 2 oz (60 g) butter and 1 tablespoon vegetable oil. Cook the fillets for about 5 minutes on each side.

A highly unorthodox but delicious variation of Chicken Kiev is made by replacing the herb butter with a flavoured cream cheese such as 'Boursin', which has been shaped into rolls. Proceed as directed above.

For traditional Chicken Kiev, the wing bone is left attached to the chicken breast. Bone the breast as described above, then cut off the tip of the wing so that only a short projection remains. At serving time this stump is usually outfitted with an aluminium or paper frill to look fancy; I myself prefer the sleeker look of the cutlets without the wing bone.

Chicken Cutlets Pozharskie kotlety

Like Chicken Kiev, these delicate cutlets are a classic of Russian cuisine, evoking the elegant meals of the days of the Tsar. Unlike Chicken Kiev, their origin can be traced back to the nineteenth century and the small merchant town of Torzhok. Before the advent of the Moscow–St Petersburg railway, well-heeled Russians travelled by coach between the two cities, stopping frequently at way stations to rest and refresh themselves. One such way station was at Torzhok, where the head chef was a culinary wizard named Pozharsky. These cutlets are his legacy to the Russian cuisine.

Pozharsky originally made his cutlets from wild game trapped in the surrounding woods, but today they are most often prepared from chicken or veal. And today the traveller, well-heeled or not, simply hops on the Red Arrow Express between Moscow and Leningrad, finding himself at his destination overnight and having feasted on nothing more substantial than a glass of hot tea and any sandwiches he had the foresight to bring along.

2 large, whole chicken breasts, skinned and boned	¾ teaspoon salt
	¼ teaspoon freshly ground
3 large slices day-old French bread (preferably sourdough), trimmed of crusts and torn into pieces	black pepper
	flour
	2 oz (60 g) butter
¼ pint (150 ml) single cream	1 tablespoon cooking oil
1 egg yolk	
3 oz (85 g) butter, softened at room temperature and creamed	sliced mushrooms, sautéed

In a food processor or mincer, mince the raw chicken finely.

Pour the cream over the crumbled bread in a large bowl. Mix with a spoon until the bread has absorbed all the liquid. Add the chicken to the bread mixture, along with the egg yolk, creamed butter, salt and pepper. Beat until smooth and well blended.

In a large, heavy frying pan heat the 2 oz (60 g) butter and the oil together.

Shape the chicken mixture into 8 patties, dredging each one well in flour so that it is not sticky. (It helps if your hands are also well floured.)

When the butter is hot, put the patties in the frying pan and cook them over medium high heat until they are golden brown, about 5 minutes on each side. Be careful not to overcook them, as they must remain moist. Serve immediately, garnished with sautéed sliced mushrooms.

Serves 4.

Variation: Substitute 1 lb (450 g) veal for the chicken; proceed as directed above. Or use a combination of half veal and half chicken.

Chicken Stuffed with Parsley and Lemon Kuritsa, farshirovannaya petrushkoi

A noteworthy combination.

5 lb (2.25 kg) roasting chicken
1 lemon, quartered
salt, pepper to taste

½ oz (15 g) butter
2 tablespoons olive oil
3 medium onions, finely
  chopped
2 cloves garlic, crushed
salt, freshly ground pepper to
  taste

½ teaspoon sweet paprika
⅛ teaspoon cayenne
1 teaspoon crushed savory
6 oz (170 g) parsley, stems
  removed, finely chopped
juice of 1 large lemon
4 oz (120 g) butter, cut into
  small pieces

4 oz (120 g) butter
¼ pint (150 ml) chicken broth

Wipe the chicken and rub it inside and out with the lemon quarters, squeezing out as much juice as possible on to the chicken. Sprinkle the chicken with salt and pepper. Set aside.

In a large heavy-bottomed frying pan melt the ½ oz (15 g) butter and the olive oil. Stir in the finely chopped onions and garlic and cook over medium heat until soft and translucent, but not brown. Season with the salt, pepper, paprika, cayenne and savory. Stir in the chopped parsley. Pour the lemon juice over all. Stir in 4 oz (120 g) butter and cook, stirring constantly, until the butter melts. Leave the mixture to cool slightly, then stuff the chicken with this mixture. Close the cavity opening well.

Melt the remaining 4 oz (120 g) butter in a casserole large enough to hold the chicken. Brown the chicken in the butter, turning it to cook evenly on all sides. Be careful not to tear the skin. When the chicken is brown, add about ¼ pint (150 ml) chicken broth. Cover the pot tightly. Simmer until the chicken is tender, about 1½ hours. Check periodically to make sure there is enough liquid in the pot; add more if necessary. Transfer to a platter and serve.

Serves 4 to 6.

Note: This dish will be only as good and as tender as the chicken you use. Go to a reliable butcher, otherwise the result may be less than delectable.

Spring Chicken with Gooseberry Sauce Tsyplyonok pod scusom iz krizhovnika

In old Russia, so many spring chickens were sacrificed in the name of genteel dining that they were commonly called the 'great martyrs', *velikomuchenitsy*. Here, the young fowl is accompanied by gooseberry sauce in this subtle and delicate dish.

2 spring chickens (2 lb/900 g each)	1 tablespoon flour
½ onion	¼ pint (150 ml) chicken stock
2 sprigs parsley	¼ teaspoon salt
1 tablespoon dried tarragon	freshly ground white pepper
1 oz (30 g) butter	2 egg yolks
	1½ tablespoons freshly squeezed lemon juice
8 oz (225 g) fresh gooseberries*	1 tablespoon soured cream
½ oz (15 g) butter	freshly ground nutmeg to taste

Preheat the oven to 230°C/450°F/Gas 8. Salt the chickens inside and out. Place quarter of a onion, 1 sprig parsley and 1½ teaspoons tarragon in the cavity of each chicken. Place the chickens in a roasting dish and dot them with 1 oz (30 g) butter. (If desired, new potatoes and onions may be roasted along with the chickens.) Place the chickens in the oven and immediately reduce the heat to 180°C/350°F/Gas 4. Roast until tender, about 20 minutes to the pound, basting occasionally.

Meanwhile, prepare the sauce. Cook the gooseberries in the chicken stock until tender, about 15 minutes. Drain them, reserving the stock. Press the berries through a fine sieve to make a purée; set aside.

Measure the reserved chicken stock, adding more if necessary to make ¼ pint (150 ml). In a saucepan melt the ½ oz (15 g) butter; stir in the flour and cook for a minute. Gradually whisk in the reserved chicken stock, then add the gooseberry purée.

Carefully add a little of the hot sauce to the egg yolks which have been lightly beaten, then whisk the yolks into the sauce. Stir in the lemon juice, soured cream, salt and pepper to taste. If the berries are especially tart, add a little sugar to taste. Just before serving, grind some nutmeg into the sauce. Serve in a sauceboat with the roast chicken.

Serves 4.

---

* If fresh gooseberries are not available, substitute a 16 oz (450 g) can of gooseberries, drained. Press the berries through a sieve to make a purée, and then proceed as directed above.

Turkey Breast with Apples File indeiki s yablokami

A novel way to prepare turkey – and an excellent one.

2 lb (900 g) boned and rolled
  breast of turkey
¾ pint (450 ml) rich chicken
  stock
6 black peppercorns
1 sprig parsley
1 onion, quartered
1 carrot, scraped and cut in half
3 oz (85 g) butter
3 medium-sized tart apples,
  peeled, cored and sliced

1 tablespoon flour
3 tablespoons soured cream
salt, freshly ground pepper to
  taste
¼ teaspoon crushed thyme
2 oz (60 g) grated sharp
  Gruyère cheese

parsley

In a casserole, braise the turkey breast in the stock along with the peppercorns, parsley, onion and carrot for 45 minutes to 1 hour, or until tender. Cool slightly; remove the string from the turkey roll and cut the meat into 8 slices, each about 1 in (2.5 cm) thick. Strain and reserve the stock.

Melt 2 oz (60 g) butter in a large frying pan. Add the sliced apples and cook them over medium heat until just tender, about 5 minutes. Remove the apples with a slotted spoon and set aside. Put the turkey slices in the frying pan and cook them over medium heat, turning once, until they are lightly browned.

Grease an ovenproof casserole large enough to hold the turkey slices in a single layer. Place the slices in the casserole and top them with the apples.

Make a sauce: in a saucepan melt the remaining 1 oz (30 g) butter, then stir in the flour and cook for just a minute. Gradually whisk in 6 fluid oz (170 ml) of the stock the turkey was cooked in, stirring constantly until thickened. Then stir in the soured cream, salt, pepper and thyme.

Pour the sauce over the turkey and apples, and then sprinkle the cheese over all. Place the casserole under the grill and grill until browned and bubbly. Garnish with parsley and serve at once.

Serves 4 to 6.

Braised Rabbit in Soured Cream Krolik, tushonyi v smetane

1 rabbit (3 lb/1.5 kg), cut into serving pieces	8 fluid oz (225 ml) rich chicken stock
3½ tablespoons flour	3 tablespoons red wine vinegar
salt, pepper	8 fluid oz (225 ml) soured cream
2 oz (60 g) butter	salt, freshly ground pepper to taste
1 tablespoon vegetable oil	splash of sherry
¾ teaspoon marjoram	
1 medium onion, chopped	
1 medium carrot, scraped and chopped	

Dredge the rabbit pieces in 2 tablespoons flour, which has been seasoned with salt and pepper, coating them well. Brown the rabbit in a large frying pan in 1½ oz (45 g) butter and the vegetable oil. When the pieces are browned, season them with the marjoram, and then transfer them to a casserole and keep them warm.

In the same frying pan fry the chopped onion and carrot for about 15 minutes, or until soft. Add the cooked vegetables to the rabbit.

In a medium saucepan melt the remaining ½ oz (15 g) butter and then add ½ tablespoon flour, whisking until smooth. Gradually stir in the chicken stock, stirring until the sauce is thickened. Then add the vinegar and the soured cream. Season with salt and pepper.

Pour the sauce over the rabbit and vegetables. Cover, bring to the boil and simmer for 1 hour.

Place the remaining tablespoon flour in a small bowl and add a little of the sauce to it to make a loose paste, then stir the paste back into the sauce and cook for a few minutes more, until the sauce has thickened. Add a splash of sherry.

Transfer to a serving dish and serve immediately.

Serves 4 to 6.

Halibut Steaks with Caviar Paltus po-astrakhanski

These halibut steaks topped with a delicate *mirepoix* are exquisite as they are, but the caviar garnish gilds the lily. The dish is named after the port city of Astrakhan on the Caspian Sea, where much of the caviar is processed.

4 halibut steaks (about ½ lb/225 g each)	1 carrot, scraped and finely chopped
8 fluid oz (225 ml) dry white wine	2 oz (60 g) mushrooms, finely chopped
6 peppercorns	salt, pepper to taste
2 cloves garlic	3 tablespoons flour
1 bay leaf	¼ pint double cream
½ teaspoon marjoram	4 teaspoons freshly squeezed lemon juice
2½ oz (75 g) butter	3 tablespoons black caviar
1 small onion, finely chopped	
2 oz (60 g) green beans, finely chopped	2 teaspoons black caviar

First prepare a *mirepoix*: Mix together the finely chopped onion, green beans, carrot, mushrooms, salt and pepper. Place the vegetables in an ovenproof dish and coat them with 1 oz (30 g) butter. Cover and bake at 180°C/350°F/Gas 4 for 30 minutes.

Put the halibut steaks in a large, shallow, ovenproof dish along with the white wine, peppercorns, garlic, bay leaf and marjoram. Cover and poach in a preheated 180°C/350°F/Gas 4 oven for 15 to 20 minutes, or until the fish is done.

Remove the halibut from the poaching liquid and keep it warm. Reserve the liquid.

In a medium saucepan melt the remaining 1½ oz (45 g) butter and stir in the flour. Cook over low heat for just a minute. Stir in the poaching liquid, whisking constantly, and cook until the sauce has thickened. Then stir in the double cream, lemon juice and 3 tablespoons of caviar.

Place the halibut steaks on a serving platter. Top each steak with some of the *mirepoix*, spreading it rather thickly over the top of each steak. Pour the sauce over the vegetables and fish, and garnish each steak with ½ teaspoon of black caviar. Serve immediately.

Serves 4 generously.

Sturgeon with Cherry Sauce Osetrina pod vishnyovym sousom

Early travellers to Russia had fantastic tales to tell of the abundant fish in the rivers and streams. More than one visitor to Siberia and the Ukraine wrote of fish so numerous, they were forced right out of the water by the sheer weight of their numbers. The fishermen had only to approach the shore and gather them up. Moreover, the fish were often so large that it took three or four men to carry a single one (or so the seventeenth-century journals claim). But by the nineteenth century the plentiful stocks had been so depleted that only the wealthy could afford to put sturgeon on their dinner table; yet it has remained a Russian favourite. The recipe below crowns the sturgeon with a tart cherry sauce.

4 sturgeon steaks (about ½ lb/225 g each)
8 fluid oz (225 ml) dry white wine
6 peppercorns
1 bay leaf
1½ oz (45 g) butter
3 tablespoons flour
6 oz (170 g) canned sour cherries

8 tablespoons cherry juice from the canned cherries
2 tablespoons freshly squeezed lemon juice
2 teaspoons sugar
salt, white pepper to taste
3 tablespoons Madeira
1 tablespoon capers

In a large, shallow ovenproof dish place the sturgeon steaks along with the white wine, peppercorns and bay leaf. Cover and poach in a 180°C/350°F/Gas 4 oven for 15 to 20 minutes, or until the fish is done.

Remove the fish from the poaching liquid and keep it warm. Reserve the liquid.

In a medium saucepan melt the butter and stir in the flour, cooking over low heat for just a minute. Then gradually stir in the poaching liquid, whisking constantly. Cook until the sauce has thickened.

Stir in the sour cherries and the cherry juice, lemon juice, sugar, salt and pepper to taste. Add the Madeira and capers.

Place the sturgeon steaks on a serving platter and pour the sauce over them. Serve immediately.

Serves 4.

Cod with Egg and Butter Sauce Treska s pol'skim sousom

In Russia, this method of preparing cod is popularly known as Polish-style. It is a very rich dish, especially nice when presented in small, deep casseroles for individual servings.

2 lb (900 g) cod (or other fish), cut into 2 in (5 cm) cubes	½ teaspoon thyme
salt and pepper to taste	1–2 lb (450–900 g) tiny new potatoes
6 fluid oz (170 ml) dry white wine	3 hard-boiled eggs
6 fluid oz (170 ml) fish or chicken stock	6 oz (170 g) butter
6 black peppercorns	6 tablespoons freshly-squeezed lemon juice
1 sprig parsley	6 tablespoons minced parsley
	½ teaspoon salt

Preheat the oven to 180°C/350°F/Gas 4. Season the cubes of fish with salt and pepper. Place them in an ovenproof dish and add the wine, stock and seasonings. Bring to a simmer over medium heat and then transfer the dish to the preheated oven. Poach for 15 minutes, or until the fish is flaky but still holds its shape.

Meanwhile, boil the tiny new potatoes in salted water. They do not have to be peeled. Cut them into quarters or halves.

Prepare the sauce. Hard-boil 3 eggs. Melt the butter and the lemon juice together over low heat. Chop the hard-boiled eggs coarsely and add them to the butter mixture along with the parsley and the salt.

To serve, place the potatoes in the bottom of a serving dish (or individual casseroles). Top with a layer of fish. Pour the sauce over all. Serve at once.

Serves 4.

Beef Stroganoff Bef-stroganov

In the nineteenth century Russians of gentle birth often spent the social season in Paris. Although they professed a reverence for all things French – to the extent of employing local cooks – the Russians secretly cherished a love for their own native cuisine. This led to the invention of many new dishes bearing the names of the Russian nobility: Veal Orloff, Salad Demidoff, Nesselrode Pie. Beef Stroganoff was born in a similar way, the brainstorm of the French chef to Count Pavel Stroganov, a popular society figure in Paris at the turn of the century. The Stroganovs were one of the oldest noble families in Russia; as far back as the sixteenth century, when they were still merchants, Tsar Ivan the Terrible had granted them the right to develop land in Siberia. As their enterprise grew, so did their wealth, and by Count Pavel's time the family had been flourishing for several generations.

In order to come up with a dish to please his benefactor, Count Stroganov's chef simply added some very Russian soured cream to a basic French mustard sauce and voilà! it was a success. He named the dish after his employer, and Beef Stroganoff soon became an international favourite. Unfortunately, it has suffered all too often from a liberal addition of tomato paste and even ketchup, but made according to the original recipe, it is a noteworthy dish. It must be made with top quality beef.

1½ lb (700 g) fillet of beef, trimmed and cut into strips 2 in (5 cm) long and ½ in (12 mm) thick	8 fluid oz (225 ml) rich beef bouillon*
2 oz (60 g) butter	4 tablespoons soured cream
1 small onion, sliced paper thin	salt, freshly ground black pepper to taste
1 tablespoon flour	
1 teaspoon dry mustard	parsley

Cut the beef into strips and set aside.

In a heavy frying pan melt 1 oz (30 g) butter; sauté the onion slices in it until they are soft and just barely golden. Add the meat all at once and cook over high heat for just a few minutes, until it is cooked through. Season with salt and pepper to taste. Set aside, but keep warm.

In a small saucepan melt the remaining 1 oz (30 g) butter. Mix together the flour and the dry mustard and whisk into the butter. Cook for a minute, then gradually add the rich bouillon, stirring constantly, until a fairly thick sauce has been formed. Stir in the soured cream, mixing well. Pour the sauce over the meat, check for seasoning, and heat through, but do not boil.

Spoon the meat and sauce on to a large platter (not a bowl) and garnish with parsley. Serve with straw potatoes mounded decoratively on top of the meat.

Serves 4 to 6.

Note: Mushrooms may be added to Beef Stroganoff if desired, although they are not strictly authentic.

Straw Potatoes Kartofel' solomkoi

4 baking potatoes	salt
vegetable oil for deep frying	

Peel the potatoes and cut them into julienne strips. (This is most easily done with the julienne disc of a food processor.)

Heat the vegetable oil to 185°C/365°F in a deep-fat cooker. Drop the potato strips a few at a time into the pot. Do not crowd them. Fry

---

* To make a rich bouillon, boil down ¾ pint (450 ml) basic bouillon to concentrate it, or else a commercial condensed broth may be used.

the potatoes until they just begin to turn golden, then remove them from the fat and drain on kitchen paper.

Just before serving the potatoes, heat the oil a second time to 186°C/370°F. Add the half-cooked potatoes a few at a time. They should cook through in just a few seconds and should be crisp and brown.

Drain the potatoes on kitchen paper; salt them to taste.

Serves 4 to 6.

Note: Potato baskets, often filled with new peas as a traditional garnish for Chicken Kiev, may be made by placing the raw julienne strips of potato in a commercial basket mould, and proceeding as directed above.

Hussar's Beef Myaso po-gusarski

Hussars were the elite of the Tsars' cavalry. Decked out in their smart uniforms of bright blue and red, astride the finest horses in the Empire, they were known for their high-living, often dandified ways. Interestingly, many of the Hussars were descended from Cossacks, who joined the guard in 1756, bringing with them a tradition of colourful language and daredevil style.

It is hardly surprising, then, to find such a showy dish as Hussar's Beef named after these guards. While admitting certain similarities to Beef Wellington and Saddle of Veal Orloff, Hussar's Beef uses native Russian methods and ingredients to achieve its splendid results – splendid enough to serve at a grand dinner party, yet hearty enough to feed a troop of hungry Cossacks.

2 tablespoons active dry yeast	3½ oz (105 g) finely grated stale black breadcrumbs
6 fluid oz (170 ml) warm water	
1 lb 3 oz (535 g) rye flour	¾ lb (350 g) mushrooms, trimmed
¾ pint (450 ml) water	
1 tablespoon salt	2 teaspoons soured cream
½ lb (225 g) plain flour	1 oz (30 g) grated Gruyère cheese
2 pieces 1 in (2.5 cm) thick top round of beef, each 1½ lb (700 g)	
	freshly ground black pepper
2½ oz (75 g) butter	1 oz (30 g) butter
8 fluid oz (225 ml) rich beef stock	2 tablespoons flour
1 large onion, quartered	minced parsley

First, prepare a sponge for the dough. Dissolve the yeast in the warm water. Stir in 3 oz (85 g) rye flour until well mixed, then cover and leave to rise in a warm place for 1 hour.

Meanwhile, start preparing the beef. In a large casserole brown the steak in 1 oz (30 g) butter. Then add the quartered onion and the beef stock. Cover the pot and simmer for 10 minutes, no more. Remove the meat to a board to cool. Reserve the stock.

Finely chop the quartered onion from the pot. Chop the mushrooms finely. Melt the remaining 1½ oz (45 g) butter in a large frying pan. Sauté the onions until golden, then stir in the mushrooms and the finely grated stale black breadcrumbs. Cook for 10 minutes more. Remove from the heat, then stir in the cheese and soured cream. Add freshly ground black pepper liberally. Set aside.

When the meat has cooled enough to handle, with a sharp knife cut each piece thinly on the diagonal, cutting all the way through, but keeping the shape of the steak intact by reassembling the pieces. The pieces should be ¼ in (6 mm) to ½ in (12 mm) thick.

By this time the sponge should be ready. Stir in the ¾ pint (450 ml) water, the salt, the remaining rye flour and plain flour. Turn out on to a board and knead until smooth and satiny. Place in a greased bowl, turning to grease the top, and leave to rise in a warm place until doubled in bulk, about 1½ hours.

Return to the meat. Spread some of the cooled mushroom filling between the slices of beef, reassembling each steak as you go. I find this easiest to do by spreading one slice of beef with the filling and placing it flat on the board. Spread the next slice with filling and place it flat on top of the preceding piece, continuing in this manner until 4 spread slices are stacked together. Then place this group of slices upright again, and proceed to the next. Continue filling the slices until the steaks have been completely reassembled again.

When the dough has risen, knock it back, and knead for just a minute. Then divide it in half. Working with one piece of dough at a time, divide the dough into two pieces, one slightly larger than the other. Roll out the slightly smaller piece to an oval ¼ in (6 mm) thick. The oval should be 1 in (2.5 cm) to 2 in (5 cm) larger than the reassembled steak on all sides.

Place this oval on a greased baking tray. Using two spatulas, carefully transfer the stuffed steak on to the oval of dough, centring it. Then roll out the second piece of dough and fit it on top of the steak, sealing the edges well by joining them with the bottom piece of dough. It helps to turn the bottom piece of dough up over the top piece at the edges, forming a rim, so that it won't come unsealed during baking. Use a little cold water if necessary to help the dough adhere.

Repeat this same procedure with the remaining ball of dough and the second steak. Leave the pies to rise until doubled, about 45 minutes.

Preheat the oven to 190°C/375°F/Gas 5. Bake the pies for about 40 minutes, or until the crust sounds hollow when tapped. Brush with melted butter to make the crust glisten.

While the pies are baking, prepare a sauce. Melt 1 oz (30 g) butter in a small saucepan and add the flour. Cook for a minute over medium heat, stirring constantly. Then pour in 8 fluid oz (225 ml) of the reserved beef stock to make a gravy. Keep warm over low heat.

When the bread is done, with a very sharp knife cut a large oval lid in the top crust, leaving an edge of only about 2 in (5 cm) on all sides. Drizzle some sauce over the neatly-sliced meat that is revealed inside, and sprinkle on some minced parsley. Bring to the table with the crust slightly ajar to reveal the meat. Pass the rest of the sauce separately.

Serves 10.

Beef Stew with Rum Tushonoye myaso s romom

Here is an unusual stew which my grandmother used to make. In Russia it was reserved for special occasions because rum, unlike the ubiquitous vodka, was a luxury item.

1 large onion, sliced
2 cloves garlic, crushed
2 tablespoons vegetable oil
3 lb (1.4 kg) lean stewing beef
salt, freshly ground black
  pepper to taste
1 tablespoon Worcestershire
  sauce
1 large bay leaf, crumbled
1 teaspoon ground savory
1 handful of parsley sprigs
8 fluid oz (225 ml) water
1 carrot, scraped and cut into
  ½ in (12 mm) rounds
2 parsnips, peeled and cut into
  ½ in (12 mm) rounds

¼ lb (120 g) mushrooms,
  trimmed and thickly sliced
1–1½ lb (450–700 g) tiny new
  potatoes, scrubbed but not
  peeled
1 tablespoon flour
2 heaped tablespoons green
  olives, minced
16 oz (450 g) jar whole spiced
  crab apples
2 tablespoons juice from the
  spiced apples
4 tablespoons Barbados rum

parsley

In a stewpot sauté the onion and garlic in the oil until golden. Add the beef and brown it on all sides over medium high heat. Season to taste with salt and pepper. Add the Worcestershire sauce, bay leaf, savory and parsley sprigs and pour the water over all. Cover, bring to the boil, and simmer for 1 hour.

After the stew has simmered for 1 hour, stir in the carrot, parsnips, mushrooms and potatoes. Continue to simmer, covered, until the meat and the vegetables are tender, about 45 minutes.

When the stew is ready, strain it, reserving the broth. Place the meat and vegetables in a deep serving dish and keep them warm. Return the broth to a saucepan and add the flour which has been made into a paste with a little of the broth. Cook over medium heat, stirring constantly, until the gravy has thickened.

Add the olives and the spiced apple juice. Stir to mix well; continue cooking for 1 minute. The gravy will turn a deep rose colour from the spiced apple juice.

Remove the sauce from the heat and then stir in the rum. Immediately pour the sauce over the reserved meat and vegetables, mixing well. Serve garnished with the whole spiced crab apples and parsley.

Serves 4 generously.

Veal Stew with Cherries Telyatina, tushonaya s vishnoi i fasol'yu

Anyone who has read Chekhov's *Cherry Orchard* knows of the Russians' fondness for cherries. Especially prized are the tart *more-livki*, Morello cherries, which flourish in the central heartlands of the Soviet Union. In this recipe, the cherries are combined with veal – a meat delicate enough to absorb their flavour – and the result is a beautiful wine-red stew with a subtly sweet taste.

6 oz (170 g) dried white beans	8 fluid oz (225 ml) juice from
2 lb (900 g) stewing veal, cubed	the cherries
1 tablespoon flour	8 tablespoons Madeira or port
2 oz (60 g) butter	1 teaspoon salt
4 large spring onions,	freshly ground white pepper to
including the green tops,	taste
chopped	a few grindings of fresh
12 oz (340 g) canned Morello	nutmeg
cherries	

Soak the beans overnight in water, and then cook them until just tender. Drain and set aside.

Dredge the veal cubes in flour, then brown them in the butter. Add the spring onions, cherries, cherry juice, Madeira, salt and spices to the veal. Bring to the boil and then simmer for 1½ hours. Fifteen minutes before serving, stir in the cooked beans.

Serves 4 to 6.

Note: This stew will taste even better if made a day ahead and allowed to chill overnight. Reheat to serve.

Roast Calf's Liver Zharenaya pechonka

Many years ago, in the first home I ever visited in the Soviet Union, I was offered some delicious baked liver, served cold in one large piece and sliced very thinly. I remember being struck not only by the delicious taste, but by the realisation that there is more to calf's liver than the pre-cut slices offered in the supermarket. Since that day I have served roast whole liver many times, and I think it tastes even better straight from the oven. A whole liver can be bought from any good butcher.

1 whole calf's liver
  (2–2½ lb/900–1125 g)
½ lb (225 g) bacon rashers
2 large onions, sliced
¼ pint (150 ml) olive oil
4 tablespoons dry red wine
4 tablespoons red wine vinegar

salt, freshly ground pepper to
  taste
2 bay leaves, crushed
1 teaspoon basil
½ teaspoon mace
¼ teaspoon ground cloves
½ teaspoon ground coriander

In a large, shallow, ovenproof dish place the liver, bacon rashers and onion slices. Mix together the remaining ingredients and pour the mixture over the meat. Marinate, covered, at room temperature for 4 hours, turning occasionally.

When ready to cook, lift the liver from the marinade and sprinkle with salt and pepper. Put some onion slices in a baking tin, put the liver on top, then place the remaining onion slices on the liver. Spread the bacon rashers crosswise across the top of the liver, covering it completely (the onion will be between the liver and the bacon).

Preheat the oven to 200°C/400°F/Gas 6. When the oven is heated, place the liver in it and immediately reduce the heat to 180°C/350°F/Gas 4. Bake for 1½ hours, according to size. Test after 1 hour. Serve warm, removed from the marinade and with the onions and bacon as garnish.

For a cold dish, chill the liver, slice thinly, then marinate for several hours in any leftover marinade from Marinated Mushrooms (see p. 44).

Serves 4.

Cold Stuffed Aubergine Baklazhan farshirovannyi

This stuffed aubergine looks spectacular and tastes every bit as good. As the slices fall away, the inside is revealed to be ribboned layers of aubergine and vegetable purée.

1 large unpeeled aubergine
  (2 lb/900 g), sliced lengthwise
2 oz (60 g) flour
2 eggs, beaten
2 oz (60 g) fine dry
  breadcrumbs
8 fluid oz (225 ml) olive oil

1 lb (450 g) carrots, scraped and
  finely chopped
2 lb (900 g) tomatoes, peeled
  and finely chopped
½ teaspoon salt
½ pint (300 ml) home-made
  tomato sauce (see p. 49)

First, prepare the filling. Heat 4 tablespoons of the olive oil in a large frying pan. Add the chopped carrots and tomatoes and cook, covered, over medium heat for 30 minutes, until the carrots are just barely tender; then simmer uncovered for 30 minutes until all moisture has evaporated.

While the vegetables are cooking, prepare the aubergine. Slice it lengthwise, into ½ in (12 mm) thick slices (you will need a very sharp knife to do this). Dip each slice in flour, then beaten egg, and then fine dry breadcrumbs until well coated. Try to keep the slices in their natural succession, since you will want to reassemble the aubergine.

Heat about 4 tablespoons of the olive oil in a large frying pan. Fry the breaded aubergine slices on both sides until golden. (The two end pieces should be fried on one side only – the skinless side. Leave the rounded end with the skin on it intact.) Repeat this process until all the slices have been browned, adding more oil to the pan as necessary. Drain on kitchen paper.

When the carrots and tomatoes are ready, purée them in a liquidiser or food processor until a coarse purée has been formed (do not make it fine and smooth – there should still be some lumps of carrot in it.)

Reassemble the cooked aubergine slices until the aubergine looks whole again. Then, taking one slice at a time, salt each slice and spread some of the vegetable purée between the slices. Tie a string around the reassembled aubergine to hold it together, and place it in a greased baking dish.

Preheat the oven to 180°C/350°F/Gas 4. Pour the rich tomato sauce over the aubergine. Bake it, uncovered, for 45 minutes, basting twice with the tomato sauce. Remove it from the oven and cool to room temperature, then chill it (preferably overnight) before serving.

To serve, cut the aubergine into crosswise slices to reveal the ribboned layers of vegetable purée.

Serves 6.

Mushrooms in Soured Cream Griby v smetane

A fortuitous marriage of two Russian favourites.

1 lb (450 g) mushrooms, sliced paper thin
1½ pints (900 ml) boiling salted water
juice of ½ lemon
¼ pint (150 ml) soured cream
4 tablespoons grated onion
dash of cayenne
freshly ground white pepper

Boil the mushrooms in the water with the lemon juice for 1 minute. Refresh them under cold running water and pat dry. Add the remaining ingredients, mixing well. Cover and chill for several hours in the refrigerator before serving.

Serves 4 to 6.

Kasha (Buckwheat Groats) with Mushrooms and Cream Dragomirovskaya kasha

Here homely kasha is embellished with mushrooms galore in a dish named after the nineteenth-century general Dragomirov.

2 lb (900 g) mushrooms, trimmed and minced
2 oz (60 g) butter
¼ pint (150 ml) double cream
salt, freshly ground black pepper to taste
4 tablespoons chopped parsley

1 recipe cooked kasha (see p. 135), which has been kept warm

Dried Mushroom Sauce (see p. 146)
cooked carrots

In a large frying pan cook the minced mushrooms in the butter until the pan juices have evaporated. Stir in the cream and seasoning and cook for 1 minute. Remove from the heat and stir in the parsley.

Grease a 1½ pint (900 ml) mould. Place one-third of the cooked kasha in the mould, pressing down with the back of a spoon. Make sure it covers the bottom completely. Place half of the mushroom mixture on top of the kasha, leaving about 1 in (2.5 cm) on all sides along the edges. Top the mushrooms with half of the remaining kasha, then add the rest of the mushrooms. The top layer will consist of the last third of the kasha.

Press down firmly with the back of a spoon, then turn out on to a serving plate. Serve with the dried mushroom sauce poured over it. Pass extra sauce in a gravy boat. Garnish with cooked carrots which have been cut into fanciful shapes.

Serves 8 to 10.

Soured Cream and Jam Pie Smetannik

Smetannik, whose name derives from the Russian *smetana* or soured cream, is a gloriously rich pie, its buttery crust holding copious amounts of soured cream, jam and nuts.

Pastry
8 oz (225 g) plain flour
pinch of salt
grated rind of 1 lemon

8 oz (225 g) unsalted butter, cut into pieces
2 egg yolks
1 tablespoon iced water

Mix together the flour, salt and lemon rind. With a pastry blender or your fingers, cut the butter into the flour mixture until it resembles coarse meal. Work in the 2 egg yolks and the water until the dough holds together, adding more water if necessary. Shape the dough into two balls. Wrap each in waxed paper, and chill in the refrigerator for 1 hour. Meanwhile, prepare the filling.

Filling

1 lb (450 g) raspberry jam
   (preferably seedless)
6 oz (170 g) pecans, ground
¼ pint (150 ml) soured cream

1 egg yolk
1 teaspoon cinnamon
¼ teaspoon almond essence

1 teaspoon sugar

Grind the pecans. Stir in the soured cream, egg yolk, cinnamon and almond essence.

Remove one ball of dough from the refrigerator. Roll it out to fit into a 9 in (22.5 cm) pie tin. Spread the raspberry jam evenly across the bottom of the pie crust. Top the jam with the pecan and soured cream mixture, spreading it with a spatula so that it covers the jam evenly.

Preheat the oven to 190°C/375°F/Gas 5. Roll out the remaining dough into a top crust and position it over the filling. Trim the crusts and crimp the edges together to seal. Prick the top of the crust with a fork in a decorative pattern, and then sprinkle it with the sugar. Bake the pie for 35 to 40 minutes, or until lightly browned. Cool on a rack before serving.

Serves 8 to 10.

Eugenia Torte Tort 'Evgenia'

New culinary creations were traditionally named in honour of family members and no doubt this delicate torte is a tribute to one long-forgotten Eugenia. I have adapted this recipe from a limited-edition cookery book published in the San Francisco Russian community in the 1930s.

4 eggs, separated
2 egg yolks
4 oz (120 g) caster sugar
grated rind of 1 large orange
4½ oz (135 g) sifted potato flour
2 teaspoons ground *unsalted* pistachio nuts
2 teaspoons ground blanched almonds

3 oz (85 g) thick apricot jam

1 oz (30 g) toasted sliced blanched almonds

Icing
2½ oz (75 g) finely chopped *unsalted* pistachio nuts
4 oz (120 g) icing sugar
1 teaspoon orange-flower water*
4 tablespoons double cream

Separate the eggs. Beat the 6 yolks together with the caster sugar until thick and lemon-coloured. Stir in the orange rind, potato flour and ground nuts.

Beat the egg whites until stiff but not dry. Fold into the cake batter.

Preheat the oven to 180°C/350°F/Gas 4. Prepare two 8 in (20 cm)

* Orange-flower water is available in delicatessens. Freshly squeezed orange juice may be substituted, but the flavour will not be as delicate.

round cake tins. Grease them lightly, then fit a round of greaseproof paper on to the bottom of each pan, and grease the greaseproof paper.

Pour the batter into the prepared tins and bake the cakes for 20 minutes. Let them cool in the tins for 10 minutes, then turn out on to racks. Peel off the greaseproof paper and leave to cool.

Meanwhile, toast the sliced almonds until just golden in a 150°C/300°F/Gas 2 oven for about 10 minutes.

When the cakes have cooled, spread one with apricot jam, sprinkle with the toasted almonds and sandwich with the other cake.

Prepare the icing. Mix together 2 oz (60 g) finely chopped pistachio nuts, the icing sugar, orange-flower water and double cream. Spread the icing over the top and sides of the cake, working quickly before it hardens. Sprinkle the remaining pistachio nuts over the top of the cake.

Serves about 12.

Queen Cake Korolevskii tort

Old Russian cookery books list several variations for this rich meringue-topped cake which is said to have been introduced by the Nordic Prince Rurik who was invited to rule over ancient Russia in 862 AD. Along with his retinue he brought the Scandinavian taste for meringue and fruit combinations.

Dough
5 egg yolks
4 oz (120 g) sugar
2 tablespoons Barbados rum
grated rind of 1 lemon
8 oz (225 g) plain flour

Filling
2 lb (900 g) tart apples, pared, cored and finely chopped
8 fluid oz (225 ml) dry white wine
4 oz (120 g) sugar

3 oz (85 g) sultanas
4 oz (120 g) black cherry jam
2 oz (60 g) coarsely chopped blanched almonds, toasted
¼ teaspoon ground cardamom (optional)
1 tablespoon flour

Meringue
5 egg whites
6 oz (170 g) sugar
pinch of cream of tartar

Prepare the filling: simmer the apples with the wine, 4 oz (120 g) sugar and sultanas for 20 minutes, uncovered. Remove from the heat and stir in the jam, the toasted nuts, the cardamom and the 1 tablespoon flour. Set aside to cool.

While the filling is cooling, prepare the dough. Beat the egg yolks with the 4 oz (120 g) sugar until thick and lemon-coloured. Stir in the rum, lemon rind and enough flour to make a fairly firm dough. With floured hands knead it until smooth. Divide the dough in half. Roll out each round to 9 in (22.5 cm) in diameter. Place one of the rounds in the bottom of a greased false-bottomed tart tin, spreading the dough with your fingers so that it comes up the sides of the tin.

Spread the cooled apple filling on the bottom round of dough in the tin. Cover the filling with the second round, sealing the edges of the crusts to keep the filling in. Prick the top in a few places.

Preheat the oven to 180°C/350°F/Gas 4. Bake the cake for 30 to 35 minutes, until golden. Allow the cake to cool on a rack.

A couple of hours before serving, prepare the meringue topping. Beat the egg whites with the sugar and cream of tartar until stiff but not dry. Spread the meringue over the top of the cake, covering the crust completely. Bake in a preheated 170°C/325°F/Gas 3 oven for about 15 minutes, until golden. Cool the cake slightly, then remove the rim of the tin. Serve the cake at room temperature. (Do not prepare the meringue too much in advance as it does not hold well.)

Serves 10 to 12.

Baba au Rhum Romovaya baba

Although the *romovaya baba* has been adopted into the classical French cuisine, its roots are Slavic, as it was created at the court of the deposed Polish king Stanisław Leszczyński. The word *baba* is a pejorative term for "old lady" (the original shape of the cake was said to resemble an old woman in skirts), but the dessert's whimsical moniker belies its true elegance.

4 tablespoons warm water
1½ tablespoons dried yeast
3 eggs, well beaten, at room
    temperature
2 oz (60 g) unsalted butter, at
    room temperature
scant ¼ teaspoon salt
1 oz (30 g) sugar

9 oz (250 g) strong white flour
2 oz (60 g) currants

Syrup
6 fluid oz (170 ml) water
10 oz (280 g) sugar
juice of ½ lemon
6 fluid oz (170 ml) light rum

Dissolve the yeast in the warm water until bubbly. Beat in the eggs, butter, salt, sugar and flour, mixing well. Stir in the currants. Leaving the dough in the bowl, work it with your hands for about 10 minutes, until it loses some of its stickiness and is pliable. Transfer the dough to a greased bowl, turning it to coat the top. Cover the bowl and leave the dough to rise in a warm place for 1 hour.

Liberally grease 8 baba moulds (2½ in/6 cm high). Fill them about one-third full with the dough. Then place in a warm place to rise until the dough comes just to the tops.

Preheat the oven to 190°C/375°F/Gas 5. Bake the babas for 15 to 20 minutes, or until lightly browned. Turn the cakes out on a wire rack.

Now prepare the syrup. Bring the water, sugar and lemon juice to the boil in a small pan, stirring until the sugar dissolves. Boil for about 5 minutes, until a thin syrup is formed. Then stir in the rum.

Place the warm cakes in a large dish. Spoon the hot syrup over them, covering the tops and sides of the cake. Spoon up any excess syrup in the dish and continue to pour syrup over the cakes until it has all been absorbed.

Makes 8 small cakes.

Charlottes Sharlotki

Here are two recipes for charlottes, one to be served hot, the other cold. Hot apple charlotte is an old dessert with variations in many national cuisines. The cold version is a more recent creation, the brainchild of the great French chef Carême, who dreamed up the luxurious *charlotte russe* or Russian charlotte while cooking for Tsar Alexander I around the time of Waterloo. Carême's *charlotte russe* is made of sponge fingers filled with a thick Bavarian cream. The recipe became so popular that it crossed the Atlantic with the waves of immigrants to the New World, where it was hawked in the streets of New York at the turn of the century.

The cold charlotte I am presenting here is even tastier than the original, I believe. It too bears a Russian sobriquet, Charlotte Malakoff, having most likely been named to commemorate the French victory at Malakoff Hill during the Crimean War. In this version, the basic *charlotte russe* is rendered lighter and more delicate by substituting whipped cream for the Bavarian cream.

Baked Apple Charlotte Sharlotka yablochnaya

1 lb (450 g) loaf stale white bread
6 fluid oz (170 ml) Barbados rum
2 oz (60 g) sugar
3 oz (85 g) unsalted butter

Filling
4 lb (1.8 kg) tart cooking apples
grated rind and juice of 1 lemon
4 tablespoons sweet white wine

2 oz (60 g) sugar
1 oz (30 g) unsalted butter
1 teaspoon cinnamon
15 oz (420 g) thick apricot jam

Sauce
¼ pint (150 ml) double cream
1 oz (30 g) icing sugar
¼ pint (150 ml) soured cream
grated rind of ½ lemon
¼ teaspoon almond essence
½ teaspoon vanilla essence

Trim the crusts from the bread and cut into slices ½ in (12 mm) thick. Cut each piece lengthwise into thirds. There will be about 2 dozen pieces.

Preheat the oven to 130°C/250°F/Gas ½. Dip each piece of bread lightly in the rum to moisten on both sides, and then into the sugar, coating it lightly. Place the bread fingers on a rack in the oven and bake them for 10 minutes, or until just barely dry to the touch. Do not allow the bread to harden.

Melt the 3 oz (85 g) butter in a heavy frying pan. Lightly fry the bread slices until golden, on one side only.

Butter a 3 pint (1.7 litre) charlotte mould and dust it lightly with sugar. Arrange a few of the bread slices to cover the bottom, fried side down. Then position the other bread fingers vertically around the sides of the mould, fried side out. The fingers should overlap slightly. Reserve a few for the top.

Next, prepare the filling. Peel, core and coarsely chop the apples. Place them in a large frying pan with the lemon rind, lemon juice, wine, sugar, butter and cinnamon. Cover; simmer until tender, about 20 minutes. Then stir in the apricot jam, mixing thoroughly, and continue to cook uncovered until the mixture resembles a thick purée (it will remain lumpy, though).

Preheat the oven to 190°C/375°F/Gas 5. Allow the apple mixture to cool slightly, then pack it into the bread-lined mould. Top with the reserved fingers of bread, fried side up. Cover the mould. Bake the charlotte for 45 minutes.

Remove the charlotte from the oven and let it cool in the mould for at least 30 minutes. Then invert it on to a plate and serve it warm with the soured cream sauce.

To prepare the sauce, beat the double cream until it holds soft peaks. Beat in the icing sugar, then fold in the remaining ingredients. Chill until serving time.

Serves 6 to 8.

Charlotte Malakoff Sharlotka Malakova

15 sponge fingers
  (approximately)
4 oz (120 g) unsalted butter
4 oz (120 g) icing sugar
4 oz (120 g) almonds, ground
4 tablespoons framboise
  (raspberry eau-de-vie)

1 oz (30 g) dark chocolate,
  grated
1 pint (600 ml) double cream
1 tablespoon icing sugar

Lightly butter a 3 pint (1.7 litre) charlotte mould. Place a round of greaseproof paper on the bottom and line the sides with sponge fingers. Set aside.

Cream the butter; beat in the icing sugar and continue beating until light. Grind the almonds and grate the chocolate finely. Stir the almonds and chocolate into the butter mixture. Whip ¾ pint (450 ml) double cream until it stands in firm peaks, beating in the framboise towards the end.

Gently fold the whipped cream into the butter mixture, making sure that it is well incorporated. Pour into the prepared mould. Cover and chill for at least 2 hours.

Just before serving, whip the remaining double cream with the icing sugar until stiff. Unmould the charlotte on to a serving platter, and pipe rosettes of whipped cream on top of the dessert.

Serve with fresh or frozen raspberries.

Serves 6 to 8.

Guriev Kasha Gur'evskaya kasha

This classic Russian dessert is as full of calories as it is of panache. It was named after Count Dimitri Guriev, Tsar Alexander II's Minister of Finance, well known for his high-living ways. Guriev Kasha may be served warm from the oven or chilled.

2¾ pints (1.6 litres) single cream*
5 oz (150 g) semolina
pinch of salt
6 oz (170 g) sugar
1½ teaspoons vanilla essence
½ lb (225 g) walnuts, coarsely chopped

1 teaspoon freshly squeezed lemon juice
12 oz (340 g) brandied fruit, drained and coarsely chopped

2 teaspoons sugar

Bring the cream to the boil in a deep saucepan, and then slowly pour in the semolina, stirring constantly. Add the pinch of salt. Cook over medium heat, uncovered, until thick. Then stir in 2 oz (60 g) sugar and the vanilla essence. Keep warm.

While the semolina is cooking, caramelise the nuts. Put 4 oz (120 g) sugar and the lemon juice in a large frying pan. Carefully heat until the sugar begins to melt, stirring constantly. Continue to cook until the sugar turns golden brown and syrupy; do not let it burn. Immediately stir in the chopped walnuts and coat them well. Keep warm.

Grease four 8 oz (225 g) glass serving bowls. In the bottom of each bowl place a layer of the cooked semolina, then top it with a layer of caramelised nuts. Top the nuts with some drained brandied fruit, and then repeat the layering. The top layer should be semolina.

Decorate the tops of the desserts with extra nuts and fruits. Sprinkle each with ½ teaspoon sugar and brown under the grill. For a more flamboyant touch, top the Guriev Kasha with spun sugar.

Serves 4.

Spun Sugar

½ lb (225 g) cube sugar
⅛ teaspoon cream of tartar

6 tablespoons water

* Traditionally, the layers of Guriev Kasha are separated by skins formed from cooked milk. To make these milk skins, use half single cream and half milk in the amount called for above. Pour the mixture into a large, shallow pan and bake at 200°C/400°F/Gas 6 until a skin forms on top. Carefully transfer the skin to a buttered plate. Make five or six skins in this manner. Measure the remaining milk, adding more single cream if necessary to bring it to 2¾ pints (1.6 litres). Then cook the cream of wheat in it as directed above. When Guriev Kasha is made with milk skins, it is usually prepared in one large dish. The skins are layered with the kasha, fruit and nuts.

Take a dowel or broomstick 1 in (2.5 cm) in diameter and support it between two chairs, or between the kitchen counter and a chair. It should be at about waist height. Grease the dowel liberally with vegetable oil.

Place the sugar, cream of tartar and water in a small, deep saucepan. Bring to the boil, stirring. When the crystals have dissolved, wash down the sides of the saucepan with a small brush dipped in water, until no sugar crystals remain.

Boil the syrup rapidly until it reaches 156°C/312°F on a sugar thermometer. (You must watch carefully, as this happens rather quickly.) Just at this point remove the syrup from the heat and, working as quickly as possible, take a wire whisk and dip it into the sugar. Throw the thick sugar syrup across the dowel, letting it drip down and turn into strands of spun sugar. Continue throwing the hot sugar on to the dowel until it is all used up, heating the sugar gently if necessary.

Gather the spun sugar from the dowel and gently shape it into a mound (or several) of caramel-coloured strands. The sugar does not keep well, especially in damp weather, so it is best to prepare it no more than a few hours before serving time.

Note: For ease in cleaning up, it is best to spread newspaper on the floor underneath the dowel to catch any sugar syrup that drips on to it.

The Tsarina's Cream Krem tsaritsy

Even the Tsarina, Empress of All Russia, seems too lowly an eponym for this exquisite dessert. Some people call it *pishcha bogov* or 'Food of the Gods'. It is a perfect ending to a rich meal.

1 packet gelatine (¼ oz/10 g)	5 tablespoons maraschino
4 tablespoons water	2 oz (60 g) *unsalted* pistachios,
¾ pint (450 ml) double cream	chopped, *or* 2 oz (60 g)
2 oz (60 g) icing sugar	lightly toasted blanched
¼ teaspoon almond essence	sliced almonds
1¼ teaspoons rose water	green food colouring

Soak the gelatine in the water, then heat gently until the gelatine dissolves.

Whip the cream until it just begins to form soft peaks. Beat in the dissolved gelatine (which has cooled somewhat), the icing sugar, the almond essence, rose water and maraschino. Fold in the nuts. Add 2 to 3 drops of green food colouring, to tint the mixture pale green. If, with all the beating and folding, the cream is still not in stiff peaks, give it a few more turns with the whisk.

Turn the mixture into a 1½ pint (900 ml) mould or into 6 individual moulds. Sprinkle chopped pistachio nuts on the top.

Chill for several hours before serving.

Serves 6.

Berries and Cream Yagody

The Russians have a penchant for berries, the glorious fruits of a summer season all too brief in the northern climate. During the summer they flock to the countryside for wild strawberries, raspberries, blackberries, cloudberries, lingonberries, and other berries too numerous to name. Perhaps the best way to enjoy berries is straight from the bush, but a popular Russian combination is berries and cream. Here are two variations on that theme.

In the first recipe, soured cream gives the berries a Slavic twist. The second recipe, for Strawberries Romanov, is now an international dish. The dessert was no doubt dubbed Romanov – the name of the Tsarist dynasty which ruled over Russia for several centuries – because of its spendthrift use of rich ingredients. But don't expect to find Strawberries Romanov in the Soviet Union today: Romanov is no longer a name to be commemorated there, not even in a dessert.

Berries with Soured Cream Yagody so vzbitoi smetanoi

8 fluid oz (225 ml) soured cream	1 oz (30 g) sugar ¼ teaspoon vanilla essence

Mix together the soured cream, sugar and vanilla essence in a medium-sized bowl, and beat with an electric mixer for 10 to 15 minutes, until the cream has doubled in bulk. Spoon the beaten cream over berries, and serve.

Note: In order for the cream to attain the greatest volume, both the bowl and the beaters should be well chilled before the whipping begins.

Strawberries Romanov

¾ pint (450 ml) strawberries, hulled	5 oz (150 g) sugar 2 egg whites
4 tablespoons Cointreau or Triple Sec	⅛ teaspoon cream of tartar ¼ pint (150 ml) double cream
2 tablespoons freshly squeezed orange juice	1 tablespoon icing sugar

Hull the strawberries. Place them in a bowl and toss them with 1 oz (30 g) sugar. Mix together the Cointreau and orange juice, pour over the berries, and leave to macerate for 2 hours at room temperature.

Beat the egg whites with the cream of tartar till they begin to hold soft peaks. Gradually beat in the remaining sugar, beating until a thick meringue has been formed.

Preheat the oven to 140°C/275°F/Gas 1. Line a baking tray with foil and grease the foil. With a spoon make 8 rounds of meringue on the foil, flattening the centres slightly with the bowl of the spoon. Bake the meringues for 1 hour or until lightly browned. Remove to a rack to cool.

To serve the dessert, whip the double cream with the icing sugar. Place a generous portion of macerated strawberries on top of each meringue round. Top with the whipped cream.

Serves 4.

Rhubarb Mousse Muss iz revenya

Improbable as it sounds, rhubarb belongs to the same family as buckwheat, that perennial Russian favourite. It was first introduced to England from the Volga region of Central Russia. Prepared here with a judicious amount of sugar and sweet cream, it makes an exquisite dessert.

2 to 3 large stalks of rhubarb, cubed	8 fluid oz (225 ml) double cream
12 oz (340 g) sugar	¼ teaspoon almond essence
½ teaspoon cinnamon	½ teaspoon vanilla essence
1 tablespoon cornflour	

Put the rhubarb cubes in a heavy saucepan with the sugar and cinnamon; stir to mix well. Cover and simmer over low heat until the rhubarb is just tender, about 5 minutes. Strain the juice from the cooked rhubarb into a measuring cup. There should be about ½ pint (300 ml). Reserve the cooked rhubarb.

Rinse out the saucepan and return the rhubarb juice to it. Mix the cornflour with a small amount of the juice in a bowl, then add it to the saucepan. Cook the mixture over medium heat for about 15 minutes, or until it has thickened and is reduced by half.

Stir the thickened juice into the reserved rhubarb. Set aside to cool to room temperature.

Whip the cream until stiff, beating in the almond and vanilla essences. Fold in the cooled rhubarb carefully until it is well blended with the cream. Chill until serving time.

Serves 4 to 6.

Frosted Cranberries Klyukva s sakharom

In many Soviet restaurants these beautiful frosted berries may be ordered for dessert. They arrive at the table mounded high in a glass bowl, sparkling and festive.

1 lb (450 g) cranberries	12 oz (340 g) sugar
1 egg white	

Beat the egg white until foamy, but not stiff. Pour the cranberries into the foamy egg white, stirring gently until the berries are completely coated.

Put the sugar in a large bowl and add the cranberries. Toss until the berries are completely coated with sugar.

Preheat the oven to 65°C/150°F/Gas ⅛. Spread the cranberries in a shallow pan (about 12 in (30 cm) × 18 in (45 cm)) in a single layer. Place in the oven for about 12 minutes, or until the sugar has melted.

Turn the berries out on to a large sheet of greaseproof paper (about 2 feet/60 cm long) and separate them so that the frosting can harden. Leave the berries to dry overnight at room temperature. Store in an airtight container. The cranberries will keep in the refrigerator for about two weeks.

Holiday Celebrations

Russians are a celebratory people, always eager for an excuse to make merry – and the merrymaking usually revolves around food. When Russians celebrate, it's a lavish affair; there's no stinting on ingredients or proportions. A holiday feast is not just for family, it's a *pir na ves' mir*, a feast for all the world. (Russians are as given to hyperbole as they are to extravagance.) Under the old Russian Orthodox calendar, there were plenty of holidays, each an excuse to celebrate. And around these excuses developed traditional meals, accruing ritual as years went by.

The Russian holidays evolved from the pagan, pantheistic festivals of ancient Slavic tribes, coinciding with the natural change of seasons and the harvest cycle. After Prince Vladimir accepted Christianity for Russia in 988 AD, the pagan rites were gradually assimilated by the clergy, until the springtime merrymaking celebrating the start of a new planting season came to glorify the Orthodox Easter, and the winter festivities, once celebrating the rebirth of light into the world after the winter solstice, became Christmas.

The Orthodox calendar was based on a succession of feasts and fasts, the presence of food or the lack of it thus playing a central role in worship. Everyone took part in the feasting, of course, but except for the major fasts, like Lent, most Russians just went on eating. After the fall of the Romanovs in 1917, the traditional Russian religious holidays were either abolished or reformed to become secular occasions. What had been the elaborate Christmas festival became the New Year's celebration; Easter was superseded by International Workers' Day on 1 May. The other holidays are only rarely observed in the Soviet Union today, although émigré communities continue to celebrate them.

All of the old Orthodox feast days were associated with special dishes, often made from foods unavailable at other times of the year. Russians love to regale one another with delicacies. They love to eat.

The newer Soviet holidays have yet to produce ritual dishes, consequently the holidays described in this chapter are those celebrated
by the Russian Orthodox Church, in which the role of food bears
great significance.

Easter (Paskha)

By far the most important holiday in the Russian Orthodox Church
is Easter, a time of great feasting and rejoicing, falling as it does after
the six-week Lenten fast when no meat or dairy products are
allowed – a considerable deprivation in a climate where vegetables
are often scarce. During the week preceding Easter, known as
Passion Week (*strastnaya nedelya*), the foods for the feast are prepared. One can only imagine the extremes of temptation the cooks
are subjected to, preparing delicacies from the finest available
ingredients after six long weeks of denial. Finally, on Easter Eve the
table is set with an abundant spread, featuring the traditional *paskha*,
kulich and decorated eggs. This custom of decorating eggs can be
traced back to the pagan spring festivals when eggs were painted
with bright colours to symbolise the blossoming of the plant world.
Today egg-painting is considered an art form, especially in the
Ukraine, where the intricate designs are applied by a complex
process of dipping in beeswax and dye baths. These spectacular
Ukrainian eggs are known as *pisanki*.

Once the table has been set with the ritual foods, the Russians
throng to the cathedral where a midnight Mass is celebrated. This
Mass is so meaningful that even today, in the provincial cities of the
Soviet Union, the populace makes an effort to attend. When I was in
Rostov-on-the-Don police were called out to control the large crowd
trying to make its way into the cathedral. The police would allow
only the *babushki* – women over sixty, for the most part – to go in, but
the crowd continued to mill around the square outside, hoping for
a glimpse of the procession of the cross. The same crowds are
attracted, halfway around the world in San Francisco. The entire
block around the Orthodox cathedral is closed to traffic on Easter
Eve. Even that enormous cathedral cannot accommodate everyone, and people spill off the cathedral steps, crowding into the
street. Traditionally, the women arrive at the cathedral carrying
baskets filled with Easter foods to be blessed – *kulich*, *paskha* and
dyed eggs. The church itself is redolent with the heavy scent of
incense wafting from ornate censers. The crowd presses close
together as the midnight service begins. Soon it is time for the most
dramatic part of the service, the *krestnyi khod* or procession of the
cross. As the cathedral doors are swung open, the priest intones
several times '*Khristos voskrese*', the congregation responding with
'*Voistine voskrese*': 'Christ is risen; truly He is risen', words from the
Church Slavonic which are still spoken in Easter greeting today
among the older generation. Holding the cross on high, the priest,

followed by altar boys and much of the congregation, proceeds through the main doors of the church and circles the building three times.

After the service people return to their homes where the Easter breakfast – in its most literal sense – is enjoyed. The table has been set like a *zakuska* table, only on a grander scale, decorated with flowers and greenery to celebrate the arrival of spring. In the centre is usually the *barashek iz masla*, a lamb moulded out of butter, its body textured by rubbing with cheesecloth to resemble fleece. The lamb holds a sprig of greenery in its mouth, and sometimes its neck is adorned with a parsley collar. Flanking the butter lamb are the two most symbolic Easter dishes, the *paskha* and the *kulich*. *Paskha* is perhaps the most glorious version of cheesecake to be found in any national cuisine. This dessert evolved from the ancient Slavic custom of eating curd cheese (*tvorog*) with honey at the onset of spring, but nowadays the cheese is sweetened with sugar. Traditionally the *paskha* is moulded in a pyramid-shaped form indented with the Cyrillic letters *XB*, which stand for 'Christ is Risen'. If the form does not already bear these letters, they are applied by careful decoration with currants or glacé fruits.

The *paskha* is sliced and spread on its companion, *kulich*, a tall loaf of saffron-scented bread, topped with a mushrooming crown. To serve the *kulich*, the crown is first cut off from the top and then the loaf is sliced horizontally. (The crown is always replaced after serving so the bread will retain its moistness as well as visual appeal.) Around the table other sweets and confections also proclaim *XB*. Typical Russian Easter desserts include *mazurki* (rich biscuits), *krendel'ki* (boiled, pretzel-shaped biscuits), and *babki* (sweet, yeast-raised cakes which often exceed the *kulich* in height, attaining up to 19 inches, but not decorated as elaborately as *kulich*). More substantial fare is provided by roast ham or suckling pig. And of course the table is laden with baskets of brightly dyed and decorated eggs displayed on beds of green leaves or grass.

The Easter table, in all its glory, remains set for at least a week, with replacement delicacies constantly coming in from the kitchen to welcome hungry guests. The visiting begins on Easter Sunday. On this first day only the men go out visiting while the women stay at home to receive guests and regale them with the abundance of their table. After the first day the women go visiting, too, and guests roam from house to house, bringing greetings to all with 'Christ is Risen', accompanied by three kisses on alternate cheeks. The usual meal hours are suspended, as people eat whenever guests arrive or they themselves go visiting. Easter is the height of the religious year, a time when the best foods are offered and enjoyed, the occasion of much indulgence.

In fact, the Russian Easter is such an occasion that it became the object of irreverent satire from the pen of Teffi in 1912. In her *Easter Advice to Young Homemakers*, a spoof on the leading cookbook of the time, Teffi makes fun of all the ritual Easter foods in turn, reaching finally the chicken:

Besides what's been mentioned above, you must put either a turkey or a chicken on the Easter table, depending on what terms you and your grocer are on. But no matter what kind of bird it is, you are bound to dress its stumps with pantaloons of frilled paper if you have any couth at all. This will immediately raise the bird in the esteem of your guests . . .

Under one of the bird's wings you must tuck its own liver; under the other – its kidney. A chicken decked out this way will look as if it's about to rise into the air and take off on a long journey with all its essentials in hand, having forgotten only its head . . .

Butter Festival (Maslenitsa)

The closest rival to the Easter feast is found in the gorging that precedes the great Lenten fast. This revelry is known as the Butter Festival, and since it offers the last chance to eat dairy products for a long six weeks, the Russians make the most of it. *Maslenitsa* (from the word *maslo* or 'butter') is a carnival time akin to *mardi gras*. Young people used to build ice hills and send burning effigies of Winter crashing down their slopes; they constructed large bonfires (fire signified the pagan worship of the sun); they hired *troikas* for gay rides in the country.

But the favourite pastime, providing the best entertainment of all, was (and still is) the eating of *blini*. *Blini* are thin pancakes made with buckwheat flour and leavened with yeast. They are round, as the ancient Slavs made them in the image of the sun. *Blini* are served with a wide choice of condiments: they can be spread thickly with butter, then topped with red or black caviar, or smoked sturgeon, salmon or herring; they can be served sweet, spread with sour cream and jam. The Russians eat large numbers of these light pancakes, at one time in anticipation of the rigorous fast ahead, but now simply out of pure pleasure. Even though *Maslenitsa* is no longer officially recognised, Russians are always on the lookout for an excuse to eat *blini*. The pancakes are so popular that they have even worked their way into speech: an expression meaning 'to live high off the hog' has come down in contemporary language as 'This isn't everyday life, it's Butter festival!' And of flatterers it is said, 'He tries to slip like a buttery *blin* into your mouth.'

Arrival of Spring (Zhavoronki)

The only other springtime festival worthy of note is by custom celebrated on 9 March, the day the skylarks or *zhavoronki* are said to return from their winter migration. Young girls used to go out into the fields to toss breadcrumbs to the birds, wishing them welcome as the harbingers of spring. Bakers' shops were full of sweet rolls made in the form of larks, and even today these confection larks are prepared in early March, although their significance has been lost.

Christmas (Rozhdestvo)

Just as the spring solstice is greeted with celebration, so winter brings festivities too. Like Easter, the Orthodox Christmas ends a period of fasting, which is broken on Christmas Eve; and like Easter, the Christmas customs are elaborate. Before sitting down to the ritual meal, the head of the household goes out into the street, seeking any wayfarers who might not have a home for Christmas and inviting them inside to share in the breaking of the fast. On Christmas morning young girls bring boughs of cherry blossoms to the church to place before the icons. The boughs are cut on St Catherine's Day (7 December) and kept in water so they will bloom at Christmas. Other gifts are offered as well, such as home-made *ledentsy*, fruit-flavoured hard sweets wrapped in bright papers. Amusements include *kolodovanie* or carolling, when groups of young people go from house to house singing in exchange for small gifts. Another favourite custom is mummery (wonderfully described in Volume II of Tolstoy's *War and Peace*), for which the young people dress in exotic costumes and travel by sleigh from house to house, spreading mirth and good cheer.

Christmas means feasting in all lands; in Russia the holiday fare centres around *kut'ya*, a dish of steamed, sweetened wheat with fruit and raisins, and *vzvar*, stewed dried fruits. In the Ukraine a fancy braided loaf or *kolach* is served, sometimes adorned with candles. Other foods which might enhance the Christmas Eve meal include hot soups, especially rich with fats for the occasion; *pirozhki* filled with meat or cabbage or mushrooms; fish, usually carp, served hot or sometimes cold in aspic; and roast goose stuffed with fruit. Most homes are decorated with a Christmas tree, introduced by Tsar Peter the Great, Russia's first westeriser. In tsarist Russia, among the gentry, it was often a matter of great pride to have the largest and most ornate tree. Today, in the Soviet Union, the custom of having a holiday tree still prevails, only now it is considered a New Year's tree.

The New Year (Novyi God)

Strictly speaking, the New Year is a Soviet holiday, a time of partying and drinking, but since the occasion has acquired folkloric aspects, it deserves mention here. Some of the Russian New Year's customs are similar to western tradition: the erstwhile Christmas tree is put up and decorated with tinsel and ornaments; and *Ded Moroz* or Grandfather Frost makes a holiday appearance. *Ded Moroz* is a character out of old Russian folklore, a tall, bearded figure encrusted in snow and ice who lives in an ice cave and chats with the creatures of the forest. Resurrected to play a refreshingly whimsical role in contemporary socialist life, *Ded Moroz* can be ordered by telephone to pay a visit to the children on New Year's Day. He is accompanied on his rounds by another folk figure, *Snegurochka*, the

Snow Maiden, a princess dressed in shades of white and blue, sparkling with snowflakes. She and Grandfather Frost distribute biscuits or *pryaniki*, which symbolise a sweet new year for the children. Since the New Year is a family holiday in the Soviet Union, a large meal featuring roast goose or chicken is usually prepared. This meal is eaten after midnight when the first vodka toasts to the New Year have been made.

Name Day (Imeniny)

Finally, food plays a significant role in the Russian Name Day festivities. The Name Day was celebrated in old Russia more than the actual birthday. Before the Revolution only the names of saints recognised by the Russian Orthodox Church were deemed suitable for a newborn child. Each day on the Orthodox calendar was named for a saint, as was each child, and the Name Day was celebrated according to the saint's day on which it fell. The Name Day celebrant customarily held a party, inviting friends and family to share in the traditional treat of *krendel'*, a large, rich, pretzel-shaped loaf of sweet bread. Along with the *krendel'* there might be *khvorost*, thin, deep-fried twists of dough sprinkled with powdered sugar. These sweets were often washed down with thick hot chocolate fortified with beaten egg yolks.

Although all of the recipes in this chapter are closely associated with specific holidays, they can easily be adapted to the English lifestyle and made at any time. *Blini* are excellent for brunch. *Krendel'* and *kulich* are good breads to serve at teatime. *Kut'ya* should please one's vegetarian friends. And it's a shame to eat *paskha* only once a year!

Russian Easter Cheesecake Paskha

Here are recipes for three different kinds of *paskha* – evidence of my own weakness for this rich cheesecake. *Paskha* may be boiled or unboiled. The boiled version requires more effort, but it remains fresh longer, which was an important consideration in the days before refrigeration. My favourite is the unboiled *paskha* in the first recipe, lighter than the others since whipped sweet cream is used in place of soured cream. The recipe was given me by Maria Nikolaevna, a Russian émigré of the first wave who still loves to cook in the traditional style. The other two recipes have been adapted from Elena Molokhovets' renowned nineteenth-century cookbook.

Maria Nikolaevna's Paskha

20 oz (570 g) sugar (preferably vanilla sugar)	3 lb (1.4 kg) *tvorog* (see p. 171) or curd cheese
5 large egg yolks	1 whole vanilla pod, scraped
1 lb (450 g) unsalted butter	¾ pint (450 ml) double cream

Beat the sugar and the egg yolks together until light and thick. In a separate bowl, cream the butter until smooth, and then add the beaten sugar and egg yolks, mixing well.

Press the *tvorog* through a fine sieve, then mix it in well with the butter mixture, beating until the mixture is completely smooth. Slit the vanilla pod lengthwise and scrape the seeds out into the mixture. Stir in the double cream.

Line a 5 pint (3 litre) *paskha* mould or large clay flowerpot with muslin. Pour the cheese mixture into the mould, folding the muslin over the top. Set it in a bowl in the refrigerator. Place a saucer on top of the mould, and weight it with tins to force the liquid out through the drainage hole in the bottom.

Let the *paskha* drip overnight in the refrigerator, until all excess liquid has dripped out. Turn out.

Decorate the sides of the *paskha* with the letters XB in currants or nuts. Serve with *kulich*.

Variations: Add 10 oz (280 g) finely chopped, *unsalted* pistachio nuts to the cheese mixture.

Add 10 oz (280 g) stoned raisins, 1 oz (30 g) finely chopped blanched almonds, and finely chopped mixed peel to taste to the cheese mixture.

Notes: In all of these *paskha* recipes, *unsalted* butter must be used.

Always make sure that the *tvorog* is well sieved and thoroughly blended with the butter and other ingredients, otherwise the *paskha* will turn out lumpy and unstable.

Royal Paskha Paskha tsarskaya

3 lb (1.4 kg) *tvorog*, sieved (see p. 171)	1 lb (450 g) caster sugar
5 whole eggs, lightly beaten	2 oz (60 g) finely chopped blanched almonds
8 oz (225 g) unsalted butter	3 oz (90 g) currants
¾ pint (450 ml) soured cream	1 vanilla pod, scraped

In a large frying pan stir together the sieved *tvorog*, lightly beaten eggs, butter and soured cream. Heat the mixture just to boiling point, stirring until smooth and creamy. *Do not allow it to boil.* When the mixture is completely smooth, remove from the heat and set the frying pan over ice to stop the cooking. Stir the mixture until it cools to lukewarm.

Stir in the remaining ingredients (to scrape the vanilla pod, see footnote to *kulich* recipe, p. 109). Then chill the mixture in a bowl in the refrigerator until it is slightly thickened.

Line a 5 pint (3 litre) *paskha* mould or flowerpot with muslin. Pour the cheese mixture into it. Proceed as in the above recipe, weighting the cheese mixture and allowing it to drip overnight.

Pink Paskha Rozovaya paskha

4 oz (120 g) unsalted butter
6 oz (170 g) caster sugar
3 whole eggs
2 lb (900 g) *tvorog* (see p. 171)

¾ pint (450 ml) soured cream
8 oz (225 g) seedless raspberry
jam

Cream the butter and the sugar until light and fluffy, then beat in the eggs.

Put the *tvorog* through a fine sieve, then mix it with the butter mixture, beating until completely smooth. Stir in the soured cream, then the jam.

Line a 3 pint (2 litre) *paskha* mould or flowerpot with muslin. Pour the cheese mixture into it and proceed as directed above.

Note: This pink *paskha* should always be served alongside the more traditional white one.

Russian Easter Loaf Kulich

Many Russian families still treasure an heirloom recipe for *kulich*. The traditional loaf is saffron-flavoured and somewhat dry in texture, but it may also be made rich in butter and cake-like, as in the second recipe below. Old-fashioned cooks still treat their *kulichi* very gently upon removal from the oven. They turn the bread out on to a large down-filled pillow and carefully roll it from side to side until it is completely cool, so that the loaf does not lose its shape. *Kulich* may be decorated with silver or coloured dragees or, for a dramatic effect, crowned with a large red rose.

Traditional Kulich

1 tablespoon active dry yeast
4 tablespoons lukewarm water
2 oz (60 g) sugar
8 tablespoons milk
4 oz (120 g) plain flour

4 oz (120 g) unsalted butter, at
  room temperature
4 oz (120 g) sugar
8 egg yolks
1 vanilla pod, seeds scraped
  out

½ teaspoon saffron threads,
  crumbled
1 tablespoon rum
pinch of salt
12 oz (340 g) plain flour
2 oz (60 g) candied orange peel
2 oz (60 g) currants
1 oz (30 g) sliced blanched
  almonds
2 egg whites, beaten

Dissolve the yeast in the warm water. Stir in the sugar and the milk which has been heated to lukewarm. Then stir in the 4 oz (120 g) flour. Cover and leave to rise in a warm place for 1 hour. This is the sponge mixture.

Cream the butter with the 4 oz (120 g) sugar and then beat in the egg yolks. Stir the sponge mixture in, then add the scraped seeds from the vanilla pod.*

Put the saffron to infuse in the rum for 10 minutes and then add it to the mixture. Stir in the salt and enough flour to make a soft dough. Add the candied orange peel, currants and almonds.

Beat the egg whites until stiff but not dry, then carefully fold them into the dough. Turn the dough out on to a lightly floured board and knead gently until pliant. Place in a greased bowl, turning to grease the top of the dough. Cover and leave to rise until doubled, 1½ to 2 hours.

Grease a tall, 4 pint (2.3 litre) mould. If no mould is available, then use a 2 lb (900 g) coffee or other tin. Grease the tin and then line it with brown paper, turning the edges of the paper out over the top. Grease the paper so that the *kulich* will not stick.

Knock back the dough and knead lightly, then place it in the prepared mould or tin. Leave it to rise until it comes just to the top of the tin, no more. (The unrisen dough should come no further than two-thirds of the way up the sides of the mould; otherwise you will have to use 2 tins.)

Preheat the oven to 200°C/400°F/Gas 6. Bake the loaf for 10 minutes, then reduce the heat to 180°C/350°F/Gas 4 and continue baking for 35 to 40 minutes.

Turn the loaf out of the tin, and while it is still slightly warm, glaze with the following icing:

6 oz (170 g) icing sugar   2–3 tablespoons hot water
¼ teaspoon almond essence

Sift the icing sugar, then stir in the almond essence and enough hot water to make a pourable icing that is not too thin.

Decorate the iced loaf as desired.

Note: To serve the *kulich*, cut off the mushroom crown and set it aside. Then slice the *kulich* horizontally, replacing the crown after serving to keep the bread moist and its symmetry intact.

---

* To scrape a vanilla pod, slit it lengthwise along one edge. Then, with a fine, sharp knife, scrape out the moist insides of the pod and add them to the dough. Some cooks then chop the pod itself finely and add it as well.

Cake-like Kulich

An easy, no-knead loaf which will not, however, mushroom like the previous one.

1 tablespoon active dry yeast	3 oz (85 g) sugar
6 fluid oz (170 ml) double cream	4 egg yolks
	½ teaspoon salt
1 oz (30 g) sugar	½ teaspoon vanilla essence
4 oz (120 g) plain flour	8 oz (225 g) plain flour
	2 oz (60 g) raisins
5 oz (150 g) unsalted butter, at room temperature	1 oz (30 g) sliced blanched almonds

Heat the double cream to lukewarm, then stir in the yeast, 1 oz (30 g) sugar and 4 oz (120 g) flour, mixing well. Cover the bowl and leave to rise in a warm place for 45 minutes to 1 hour. This is the sponge mixture.

Cream the butter with the 3 oz (85 g) sugar. Then beat in the egg yolks, salt and vanilla essence. Stir in the sponge mixture, then add enough flour to make a soft dough. Stir in the raisins and almonds. Turn into a greased bowl, turning to grease the top of the dough, and leave to rise, covered, until doubled in bulk, 1½ to 2 hours.

Knock back the dough. Prepare a 4 pint (2.3 litre) mould or 2 lb (900 g) coffee tin as described in the previous recipe. Place the dough in the mould and leave to rise until it just reaches the top.

Preheat the oven to 190°C/375°F/Gas 5. Bake the bread for about 1¼ hours or until the loaf sounds hollow when tapped. If necessary, cover the top with foil to prevent excessive browning. When done, turn out and decorate as described above.

Ham Cooked with Hay Buzhenina

Hay may be had from local stables or farms, but if it is not available, then simply skip the first step, though the boiled meat will lose a certain subtlety of taste.

1 Uncooked ham (12–14 lb/5.4–6.3 kg)	1 large carrot, scraped and cut into chunks
4 large handfuls of hay	2 onions, quartered
2 dozen black peppercorns	1 parsley root, peeled and coarsely chopped
16 allspice berries	
4 teaspoons crushed dried thyme	6 pints (3.5 litres) black bread kvass or dark beer
2 bay leaves	

Rinse the meat. Place it in a very large stockpot with the hay and enough cold water to fill the pot. Bring the water to a rolling boil, then remove the pot from the heat and leave it to stand for 15 minutes. Return the pot to the heat and bring to the boil again, then leave it to stand off the heat for 15 minutes more.

Repeat the procedure one more time, bringing the water to the boil a third time. This time simmer the ham for 10 minutes. Then drain and rinse the meat.

Place the ham in a clean pot with the remaining ingredients, adding enough kvass or beer to cover it. Bring to the boil and skim the foam from the surface. Then simmer, covered, until done, about 20 minutes to the pound, or until the ham reaches an internal temperature of 150°F (66°C) to 160°F (71°C).

Remove the ham from the pot. Prepare a mixture of

> 2 oz (60 g) Barbados sugar
> 1½ tablespoons Russian
>   mustard

Score the fat on the meat and then rub the sugar–mustard mixture over it.

Preheat the oven to 220°C/425°F/Gas 7. Bake the ham until glazed, about 8 minutes. Serve hot or cold, with chestnut purée. Garnish with Spiced Cherries (see p. 167) or other pickled fruits.

Serves about 20.

Chestnut Purée

1 lb (450 g) roasted and shelled whole chestnuts	2 tablespoons soured cream
¾ pint (450 ml) chicken stock	salt, freshly ground white pepper to taste
1 oz (30 g) butter	freshly grated nutmeg

Simmer the chestnuts in the chicken stock for 30 minutes, then put them through a vegetable mill. Stir the remaining ingredients into the purée, mixing well. If the purée seems too thick, whisk in a little more stock. Serve hot.

Russian Pancakes Blini

Blini are one of the oldest Slavic foods, dating back to the heathen tribes who worshipped the sun and created pancakes in its image. These earliest pancakes were called *mlini*, from the verb *molot'* ('to grind'), and the word is still preserved in the Ukrainian, Serbian and Croatian tongues.

Although many kinds of pancakes exist in the world, Russian *blini* are unique, for, unlike any other liquid batters, they are leavened with yeast. The result is a light, porous pancake designed to soak up lots of butter.

Traditionally, one is expected to gorge oneself on *blini*. Literary and actual precedents are numerous in Russian life: Gogol's Chichikov finishes off nearly fifteen of the pancakes while visiting the widow Korobochka, gobbling them three at a time and dipping them repeatedly in melted butter; while the downfall of the nineteenth-century gourmand Lyapin was in the two dozen *blini* he once consumed before dinner.

To ensure perfect *blini*, Russian cooks use a special pan. Once seasoned, this pan is never washed, just wiped out with salt. The old-fashioned *blini* pan was clever indeed: four to six small, indented pans were joined by a long central body with a handle, so that mounds of *blini* could be turned out very quickly. A good cast-iron frying pan will work just as well (8 in/20 cm is a good size). Be sure to add more butter to the pan after each *blin* so that the next one won't stick. (Russian cooks use an onion half or a raw potato or a stale crust of bread to daub on the butter.) If the first *blin* you make turns out badly, don't despair. The Russians have a saying for this – as for every – eventuality: *Pervyi blin komom* – 'The first *blin*'s a lump.' I myself like to consider this first *blin* the cook's prerogative and pop it right into my mouth.

1 tablespoon active dry yeast	4 tablespoons soured cream
¾ pint (450 ml) milk	¾ teaspoon salt
1 teaspoon sugar	6 oz (170 g) plain flour
4 oz (120 g) buckwheat flour	3 eggs, separated
1 oz (30 g) butter	¼ pint (150 ml) double cream

Dissolve the yeast in 4 tablespoons of the milk, heated to lukewarm. Then stir in the sugar and ½ pint (300 ml) more of the milk. Add the buckwheat flour and stir briskly to mix. There should not be any lumps. Cover the sponge mixture and leave to rise in a warm place for 1 hour.

Melt the butter and mix it with the egg yolks and the soured cream. Add this mixture to the sponge, along with the remaining milk, the salt, and the plain flour. Cover the bowl and leave to rise in a warm place for 2 hours. (Make sure you have beaten the flour in well; there should not be any lumps.)

Beat the cream until stiff. Beat the egg whites until stiff but not dry and fold them into the cream. Fold this mixture into the batter. Then leave the latter to rest for 30 minutes more. If the batter seems too thick at this point, a little warmed milk may be added carefully.

Heat one or several cast-iron pans. Spread them with butter (and a little vegetable oil, if desired), and when the butter is hot the pans are ready.

Take 2 tablespoons of the batter for each *blin*, taking it from the top of the batter each time so that the rest doesn't fall. Pour it on to the prepared pan and swirl the pan to make a pancake about 5 in (12.5 cm) in diameter. Cook the *blin* for just a few minutes until bubbles appear on the surface, then turn and cook the other side just until faintly browned. The *blini* are best served hot from the pan, but if they must be held, pile them in a deep dish, brushing each one with butter, and cover the top of the dish with a large linen napkin.

Serve the *blini* with a choice of garnishes.
Serves about 6.

Note: Should there be any *blini* left over, they may be used to make *blinchiki*. Spread the cooked *blini* with any desired filling (cream cheese, minced meat, creamed mushrooms, jam, etc.) and fold the pancake around the filling like an envelope. Fry in butter until browned on all sides.

Garnishes for blini:
Melted butter
Soured cream
Black caviar
Red caviar
Chopped pickled herring
Chopped onion
Chopped hard-boiled egg
Smoked salmon
Jam

Lark Buns Zhavoronki

In old Russia larks were seen as the harbingers of spring, and sweet buns (*zhavoronki*) were baked in their image to welcome in the new planting season and the prosperity people hoped it would bring. In Ivan Goncharov's novel *Oblomov*, the hero Oblomov has a famous dream in which scenes of his childhood are replayed. He recalls the flurry of springtime activity as the lark buns are baked in the kitchen. Each year his mother supervised their preparation, asserting that she'd have to renounce spring entirely if she didn't prepare *zhavoronki* for her darling boy. The buns, symbolic of spring, become symbolic of a golden childhood for Oblomov.

Prepare Sweet Raised *Pirozhki* Dough (Variation 1 to Basic Raised *Pirozhki* Dough, p. 62).

Knock back the risen dough and divide it into 24 pieces. Out of each piece fashion a lark-shaped bun:

Separate each ball of dough into thirds. With one third of the dough make an oval body for the lark. With a sharp knife make a diagonal slash part way through the dough, extending from the bottom of the oval about two-thirds of the way up. This will represent a wing.

Flatten the second piece of dough slightly. Cut it into a broad triangle. Attach the triangle to the underneath side of the oval on the righthand side, so that the point of the triangle is hidden. These are the tail feathers. With a sharp knife make a few horizontal cuts in the tail part way through the dough.

Take the last third of dough and shape it into a circle which is elongated at one end. This is the head. Attach it to the upper lefthand side of the oval body, with the elongated part sloping downwards. Place a currant in the head for an eye.

Transfer the 'lark' to a greased baking tray. Repeat the process with the remaining 23 pieces of dough.

Leave the buns to prove, covered, for about 20 minutes or until doubled in bulk.

Brush them with beaten egg yolk; decorate them with sugar crystals and blanched sliced almonds.

Bake in a preheated 180°C/350°F/Gas 4 oven for 20 minutes, or until golden. Transfer to a rack to cool.

Makes 24 buns.

Note: If the pieces of dough do not adhere well, brush them with a little cold water to make them stick.

Compote of Dried Fruits Vzvar

This compote of dried fruits is a speciality of southern Russia and the Ukraine (where it is known as *uzvar*). In Ukrainian families, the compote is always served alongside *kut'ya* at the yearly Christmas dinner celebrating the breaking of the fast. Preparations for *vzvar* are begun months in advance, in late summer, when fresh fruits are gathered and hung to dry in large bunches in pantries, storerooms, or along the wattle fences of rural homesteads – a picturesque sight.

1¼ pints (750 ml) boiling water	3 oz (85 g) dried pears
¾ lb (340 g) honey	3 oz (85 g) dried apple slices
2 allspice berries (or ⅛	3 oz (85 g) prunes
teaspoon mixed spice)	3 oz (85 g) dried peaches
1 stick cinnamon	3 oz (85 g) dried apricots
½ small lemon, sliced	3 tablespoons brandy

In a saucepan combine the water and honey, stirring until the mixture is smooth. Add the allspice, cinnamon stick and sliced lemon. Add the dried pears and apples. Bring to the boil, cover, and simmer for 10 minutes.

Stir in the prunes and the dried peaches. Bring to the boil again, cover, and simmer for 10 minutes more.

Finally, add the apricots, bring to the boil a third time, cover, and simmer the fruits until tender, about 15 minutes.

Remove the compote from the heat. Discard the cinnamon sticks and allspice berries. Stir in the brandy. Cover the pan and allow the fruit to steep until lukewarm. Then refrigerate if desired.

The compote may be served warm or chilled. Spoon the fruits

along with some of the liquid into glass serving bowls so the orange, yellow and brown of the mixture can be seen.

Serves 4 to 6.

Note: The fruits in the compote should be cooked only until tender and not overcooked to a pulp.

Wheat Berries with Honey and Nuts Kut'ya

Kut'ya is strongly associated with ritual. An ancient dish, it was served at funerals to send off the dead. In some areas of Russia, people ate the grain right at the graveside, tossing a handful on to the coffin where it might 'moisten the dry lips of the dead'. This funereal connotation appears in Fyodor Sologub's novel, *The Petty Demon*. Sologub's hero is the provincial schoolteacher Peredonov, one of whose essential traits is paranoia. Peredonov imagines the threat of poisoning everywhere. He is equally afraid to take a wife and to drink his evening coffee. When Pavlushka, an old acquaintance, comes for a visit, the conversation quite naturally turns to food, specifically *erly*, a wheat and honey dish from Pavlushka's village. Because Peredonov has never tasted *erly*, Pavlushka explains that it's like the funeral porridge *kut'ya*. At the mere mention of *kut'ya*, Peredonov becomes suspicious. 'Funeral fare,' he thought. 'Pavlushka wants to send me to my grave.'

But this dish of wheat and honey has more pleasant associations as well, since it is traditionally served on Christmas Eve to help in breaking the fast. Some families arrange the *kut'ya* on a bed of hay in remembrance of Christ's birth in a manger; others toss a spoonful of the honey-soaked grain up to the ceiling. If it sticks, the bees will swarm and the harvest be bountiful. If not . . .

Kut'ya is delicious and bound to delight vegetarian friends. For the sake of tradition, serve it with *vzvar* or else as an accompaniment to roasted meat.

8 oz (225 g) wheat berries	1 oz (30 g) poppy seed
¼ lb (120 g) almonds	3 tablespoons honey
¾ pint (450 ml) water	2 oz (60 g) chopped toasted
½ teaspoon salt	almonds

Soak the wheat berries in ample water to cover overnight.

The next day, make almond milk: place the almonds in a saucepan with the water. Bring to the boil, then remove the pan from the heat and leave the almonds to steep until the water comes to room temperature.

Drain the wheat. Drain the almonds, reserving the milk. Pour the almond milk over the wheat and stir in the salt. Bring to the boil and then simmer slowly until the wheat is tender, about 2 hours.

Meanwhile, soak the poppy seed in water for 30 minutes to soften. Then drain and grind it.

Toast the chopped almonds at 170°C/325°F/Gas 3 for 10 minutes, until golden brown.

When the wheat is tender, stir in the poppy seeds. Add the honey, mixing well. Transfer the wheat to a serving dish and sprinkle it with the toasted almonds.

Serves 8.

Roast Goose with Apples Gus' zharenyi s yablokami

As the goose roasts, the apples in the stuffing are transformed into a thick sauce: meat and condiment in one. This goose makes an excellent holiday meal when served with baked sugared apples and kasha.

6 lb (2.7 kg) goose	¼ pint (150 ml) chicken or beef
salt	stock
thyme	tart apples
3 to 4 large tart apples, peeled,	sugar
cored and chopped	
olive oil	kasha (see p. 135)

Rub the inside of the goose with salt and thyme. Leave to rest for 30 minutes.

Preheat the oven to 230°C/450°F/Gas 8. Stuff the goose with the chopped apples and rub the skin lightly with olive oil. Place the goose on a rack in a roasting pan, breast side up.

Roast the goose at 230°C/450°F/Gas 8 for 15 minutes. Then reduce the heat to 170°C/325°F/Gas 3 and pour the stock into the roasting pan. Prick the skin of the goose and then roast for about 2½ hours more, or until done (it should take about 25 minutes per pound). Baste the goose every half hour or so.

About 1 hour before the goose is done, prepare the baked apples: slice each apple into eighths and place the slices in a greased shallow baking dish. Sprinkle the apples lightly with sugar and baste them with some of the goose fat from the pan. Cover and bake at 170°C/325°F/Gas 3 for 50 minutes.

Serve the roast goose with the sugared baked apples and kasha.

Serves 4 to 6.

Deep-fried 'Twigs' Khvorost

Khvorost are a popular Christmas treat. These biscuits came to Russia by way of Scandinavia, where similar treats, *klenäter*, are still prepared for the Swedish Christmas table. In Russian, *khvorost* means 'twigs', and the gnarled shape and crisp texture of the biscuits do seem to resemble small branches. When they are sprinkled with a goodly amount of icing sugar and mounded high on a plate, one can easily imagine forest twigs covered with snow.

While *khvorost* are usually made from a sweet noodle dough, rolled out thinly and cut into intricate shapes, some cooks pour a liquid batter into the hot fat, and the biscuits assume free-form shapes. Even more spectacular are the Tatar-style *khvorost*. The dough is deep fried in a single large piece to form an elaborate edible rose. *Khvorost* should always be served with a hot drink, as they lend themselves to dunking, especially in hot chocolate.

10 oz (280 g) plain flour	3 oz (85 g) icing sugar
2 egg yolks plus 1 whole egg	pinch of salt
2 tablespoons rum	1 heaped teaspoon cinnamon
½ teaspoon vanilla essence	
4 tablespoons single cream	vegetable oil for deep frying

Put the flour in a mixing bowl and make a well in the centre. Into the well pour the egg yolks, whole egg, rum, vanilla essence, and single cream. Using a fork or your hands, mix well. Then stir in 1 oz (30 g) icing sugar and the salt. Knead the dough lightly until it holds together, then place it under an overturned bowl and leave it to rest for 30 minutes.

On a floured surface roll out the dough at least 1/16 in (1.5 mm) thick, and with a fluted pastry cutter, cut out strips 1 in (2.5 cm) wide and 5 in (12.5 cm) long. With a sharp knife make a slit in the centre of each strip.

Preheat the oil in a deep-fat fryer to 185°C/365°F. Working with one strip of dough at a time, slip one end of the strip through the slit in the centre, forming a half-bowknot.

Drop the biscuits into the hot fat, a few at a time, and cook until golden all over, turning once. Remove from the fat with a slotted spoon and drain on kitchen paper.

Mix the remaining icing sugar with the cinnamon. Sprinkle the *khvorost* liberally with the sugar mixture and mound them on to a serving platter.

Makes about 4 dozen biscuits.

Variation: To make four Tatar 'roses', roll out the dough into four long rectangles. Along both sides of one rectangle, make alternating diagonal slashes radiating out from the centre of the rectangle (a knife may be used, but a fluted pastry cutter is nicer). After the rectangle has been slashed, make 3 or 4 inch (2.5 cm) long slits along the edge of each strip. Take a rolling pin, and starting at a narrow end, carefully roll the rectangle of dough on to the pin. Immerse the dough (still on the rolling pin) into the hot fat, spinning the rolling pin constantly so the flaps of dough created by slashing it will open up like a rose. Drain on kitchen paper and sprinkle with icing sugar mixed with cinnamon before serving. Repeat with the other rectangles.

Russian Gingerbread Pryaniki

Pryaniki are the oldest Russian sweet, older than Christianity itself in Russia. The earliest biscuits were rather coarse and heavily spiced and baked without any leavening at all, but over the ages their texture and flavour have been refined. Many different varieties of *pryaniki* can be found, according to region and local method, but the most classic of all are those resembling a chewy, spicy gingerbread, cake-like instead of crisp. Such *pryaniki* are still baked in the city of Tula, south of Moscow, a city renowned as well for its beautifully crafted samovars.

Pryaniki are either cut free-form in whimsical shapes (*siluetnye*) or pressed with a wooden stamp to imprint a design on the surface (*pechatnye*). They are often frosted or filled with thick jam, as in the recipe below. The biscuits keep well; in fact, some of the most beautiful examples, in the shapes of reindeer, horses and cocks, are still preserved in the Ethnographic Museum in Leningrad.

1 oz (30 g) butter	1 tablespoon crushed blanched
6 oz (170 g) honey	almonds
1 egg	6 oz (170 g) thick jam (plum is
7–8 oz (200–225 g) plain flour	especially good)
¼ teaspoon bicarbonate of	
soda	2 oz (60 g) icing sugar
¼ teaspoon each ground	2 tablespoons freshly squeezed
cardamom, ginger, mace	lemon juice
and cinnamon	

Cream the butter and the honey, and then beat in the egg. Stir in the bicarbonate of soda, spices and almonds, mixing well. Add enough flour to make a soft dough. Wrap the dough in greaseproof paper and chill in the refrigerator for 1 hour.

Preheat the oven to 180°C/350°F/Gas 4. On a floured board roll the dough out ⅛ in (3 mm) thick. Cut out rounds with a 2½ in (6 cm) biscuit cutter. Spread a generous teaspoon of jam on half of the rounds. Top each jam-covered round with a plain round, sealing the edges with your fingers, then crimping them decoratively. Place on a greased baking tray.

Bake the biscuits for 10 minutes at 180°C/350°F/Gas 4, then reduce the heat to 170°C/325°F/Gas 3 and continue baking for 8 to 10 minutes more. Cool the biscuits on a rack.

Prepare the glaze: mix together the sifted icing sugar and the lemon juice. Pour over the cooled biscuits.

Makes 18 biscuits.

Mint Biscuits Myatnye pryaniki

In Leningrad on the Nevsky Prospect there is a bakery and coffee shop that used to be known as Filippov's. The walls are panelled in mahogany, the ceiling is mirrored, the floors are marble. Entering the shop is almost like entering another era. An enticing array of biscuits and cakes beckons from behind large glass-enclosed cases, and the speciality of the house is mint biscuits, sold by the gram weight and offered to the buyer in paper cones. Because of the cost of peppermint essence, these chewy biscuits were traditionally reserved for special occasions. But they can be had every day now in Leningrad. They are light and refreshing and hard to resist.

8 tablespoons water	generous ¼ teaspoon
10 oz (280 g) sugar	peppermint essence
12 oz (340 g) flour	1 egg, beaten
½ teaspoon bicarbonate of soda	

In a small saucepan bring the sugar and water to the boil. Bring the syrup to just below the soft ball stage (to about 110°C/230°F on a sugar thermometer), to the point where it will spin a thick thread. Immediately remove the syrup from the heat and cool to lukewarm.

Meanwhile, mix together the flour and the bicarbonate of soda. (The biscuits will be even lighter if the flour is sifted first.) Stir in the cooled syrup, the peppermint essence, and the egg.

With your hands, knead the dough until it is a uniform mass which holds together. This will take several minutes. The dough will be sticky.

Preheat the oven to 180°C/350°F/Gas 4. Lightly grease two baking trays.

Pinch off pieces of dough the size of walnuts, roll them into balls between your palms, and place them on the baking trays. Then, with a glass or a decorative biscuit stamp, lightly flatten the balls.

Bake them for 10 to 12 minutes, or until they are just faintly golden. They should not brown. Remove to wire racks to cool.

Makes 30 biscuits.

Name Day Bread Krendel'

Krendel' is a pretzel-shaped loaf of sweet bread. Both the name and the shape of the loaf originated with the German bakers who were numerous in Russia from the late thirteenth century, especially in the merchant town of Novgorod. *Krendel'* is a corruption of the German *Kringel*, a round biscuit. The *krendel's* pretzel shape inspired the guild signs that hung over bakeries, symbolic of the baker's art. *Krendel'* dough is similar to the dough used for *kulich*, and in fact some cooks use the same recipe interchangeably, altering only the shape of the final loaf.

1 tablespoon dried yeast
8 tablespoons milk
4 oz (120 g) sugar
4 oz (120 g) flour

4 oz (120 g) unsalted butter, at
  room temperature
3 whole eggs
½ teaspoon salt
¾ teaspoon ground cardamom

½ teaspoon nutmeg
¼ teaspoon ground anise
12 oz (340 g) flour
2 oz (60 g) blanched sliced
  almonds
2 oz (60 g) sultanas

1 egg yolk
1 tablespoon cold water
sugar crystals

Make a sponge by dissolving the yeast in the milk which has been heated to lukewarm. Add the sugar and 4 oz (120 g) flour. Cover and let rise in a warm place for 1 hour.

Stir in the butter, cut into small pieces, and the eggs, beating well after each addition. Add the salt and spices and then stir in enough flour to make a soft dough. Stir in the almonds and sultanas.

Turn the dough out on to a floured board and knead until smooth and elastic. Place the dough in a greased bowl, turning it to grease the top. Cover and leave to rise for 1½ to 2 hours, until doubled in bulk.

Grease a large baking tray. Knock back the risen dough. Knead it for a minute or two on the floured board. Then shape it into a long roll, about 3½ feet (1 metre) long, which tapers at the ends.

Bring the tapered ends of the roll up and around to the centre of the roll, overlapping them to form a large pretzel shape. (This is easiest to do once the roll is already on the baking tray so that it does not have to be transferred.) Cover the *krendel'*. Leave it to rise for 30 to 40 minutes.

Preheat the oven to 190°C/375°F/Gas 5. Brush the loaf with a glaze made from the egg yolk beaten with the cold water. Sprinkle generously with sugar crystals. Bake for 30 to 35 minutes, until the loaf is nicely browned and sounds hollow when tapped.

Doughnuts Ponchiki

Doughnuts are a great favourite in the Soviet Union, especially in Moscow where they are rarely prepared at home since it's so easy to run to the nearest doughnut stand and get them piping hot from a large vat of fat, over which an equally large woman usually presides. Russian doughnuts are traditionally fried in oil and lard, with a few tablespoonfuls of vodka added to keep them from absorbing too much grease. Here I've opted for pure vegetable oil. These *ponchiki* may well be the lightest doughnuts you've ever tasted.

1 tablespoon dried yeast
¼ pint (150 ml) milk
1½ oz (45 g) sugar
2 egg yolks
1½ oz (45 g) butter, at room
  temperature
¼ teaspoon salt
1 tablespoon Barbados rum

¼ teaspoon cinnamon
1 2 in (5 cm) piece of vanilla
  pod, split and scraped
8 oz (225 g) plain flour

vegetable oil for deep frying
icing sugar

Dissolve the yeast in half the milk which has been heated to lukewarm. Then add the remaining milk, sugar, egg yolks and butter. Stir in the salt, rum, cinnamon and the vanilla seeds which have been scraped from the pod. Stir in the flour. The dough will be very soft and sticky. Leave it in the bowl to rise, covered, in a warm place until doubled in bulk, 1½ to 2 hours.

Generously coat your hands with flour and turn out the dough on to a well-floured board. Since the dough is so sticky, it will be necessary to coat the surface of it with flour in order to roll it out, but be careful not to use more than is necessary, or else the doughnuts will not be light.

With a floured rolling pin roll out the dough to ½ in (12 mm) thickness. Cut out rounds with a doughnut cutter. Set them aside to rise again, covered, for 20 to 25 minutes, or until doubled in bulk.

Preheat the vegetable oil in a deep fat fryer to 185°C/365°F. Drop in the risen doughnuts, not more than 2 or 3 at a time, and cook them until golden brown, turning only once. The cooking time will be about 5 minutes.

Remove the doughnuts from the fat and place on kitchen paper to drain. Sprinkle with sifted icing sugar and serve warm.

Makes about 1 dozen doughnuts.

Blueberry Ice Cream Morozhenoye s chernikoi

Legend has it that ice cream was introduced to Russia in the sixteenth century by the Italian workmen who came to Moscow at Ivan the Terrible's behest. He wanted them to build a cathedral, the likes of which the world had never seen. Alas, the world was not to see anything similar again. Once they had finished, Ivan blinded the Italians to prevent them from duplicating their feat. But they left behind two great legacies for the Russian people, which are beloved to this day: the spectacular St Basil's Cathedral on Red Square, and ice cream. Russian ice cream is excellent, and it is eaten year-round, no matter what the temperature. Commercially-prepared ice cream is mainly vanilla, but at home it is often flavoured with fruit, as in the recipe overleaf.

¾ pint (450 ml) fresh
   blueberries
8 oz (225 g) sugar
1 tablespoon vodka
2 teaspoons freshly squeezed
   lemon juice

4 egg yolks
¾ pint (450 ml) scalded milk
(½) pint (150 ml) soured cream
½ pint (300 ml) double cream
pinch of salt

In a large bowl crush the blueberries. Add half the sugar, the vodka and the lemon juice. Set aside.

In the top part of a double boiler put the remaining sugar, the salt and the egg yolks. Beat until light and fluffy. Gradually add the scalded milk, mixing well. Cook until just thickened, about 5 minutes (do not cook any longer or the mixture will curdle). Set aside to cool.

Meanwhile, in the large bowl of an electric mixer beat the soured cream at high speed for about 10 minutes, until nearly doubled in volume. Whip the double cream until stiff.

Carefully fold the beaten soured cream and double cream into the cooled custard mixture. Then stir in the sweetened blueberries. Pour into an ice-cream freezer and freeze according to manufacturer's instructions.

Makes about 3 pints (1.7 litres).

Russian Hot Chocolate   Kakao s yaichnym zheltkom

Russian hot chocolate is so rich that it has come to symbolise the good life – at least for the great Soviet satirist Mikhail Zoschenko. In his story, *The Lilacs are Blooming*, Zoshchenko targets the social climber Volodin, whose only aspiration in life is to better his position. Accordingly, Volodin marries for status, not for love, and he is thrilled to find that weekly hot chocolate is part of the bargain: 'Now he could eat all kinds of respectable foods: soups, meat, tomatoes, meatballs, and the like. In addition, once a week he drank cocoa with the whole family; he was amazed and delighted at this rich drink, the taste of which he'd forgotten over the eight or nine years of his bleak camp life.'

This is the perfect drink to serve after a winter outing.

¾ pint (450 ml) milk
2 tablespoons unsweetened
   cocoa powder

2 oz (60 g) caster sugar
1 egg yolk

In a saucepan heat the milk and cocoa powder together, stirring with a whisk until the cocoa has dissolved.

In a small bowl mix together the sugar and the egg yolk.

When the milk is hot, whisk a small amount of it into the sugar and egg yolk mixture, stirring rapidly so that the yolk doesn't cook. Then pour the yolk mixture back into the milk, stirring constantly.

Heat the hot chocolate, but do not boil. Serve immediately, with sweetened whipped cream, if desired.

Serves 2.

Wine Bowl Kryushon

In *Pnin*, Vladimir Nabokov's classic portrait of a Russian émigré living in America, one of the few things Professor Pnin manages to do right is to make this aromatic punch, which he serves at a faculty party. Were one to follow Pnin's prescription exactly, the punch should be served from an aquamarine crystal bowl, and the Sauternes should be Château d'Yquem. But since few of us have aquamarine crystal bowls at hand, and since Château d'Yquem is so expensive, I have found it economical and not at all detrimental to substitute a lesser wine, as well as a lesser bowl. This is a sensational punch.

1 bottle Sauternes, well-chilled	8 tablespoons maraschino
5 tablespoons freshly squeezed grapefruit juice	liqueur

Mix together the above ingredients and serve over ice in a crystal bowl.

Serves 10 to 12.

Note: As the sweetness of the Sauternes varies with each bottle, the punch may take more or less of the other ingredients for a perfect balance.

At the *Dacha*
Russian Home-Cooking

The October Revolution caused an upheaval in Russian life and society like no other. One thing that did not change, however, is the Russians' deep love for their countryside. Under the old order, the gentry would migrate every summer to their country estates, escaping the heat of the cities. Each of these large estates comprised a manor house, vast meadows and fields and woods, and a village stocked with peasants who lived there year round and worked the estate for the mostly absentee owners. A few landowners chose to dwell on their property, but more often than not they were considered provincial for doing so. Today, of course, the large estates no longer exist, but a yearly summer exodus from the cities still takes place. And the scale is even larger now that the bulk of the Russian population is urban.

Every summer the Russians flock to the countryside to feel renewed by the lush rural life after their winter's confinement, and they remember it fondly throughout the ensuing year. Each time they serve sweet wild strawberries or pickled field mushrooms, or salted forest mushrooms, or tart lingonberries and currants in whose dusky flavour the scent of late summer still lingers, the host is likely to proclaim, 'We picked these ourselves at the *dacha* last summer!' There follows a sigh and a silence, as all present indulge in nostalgic reverie of those halcyon summer days.

Dacha means 'summer house' in Russian, but the term has come to be more loosely applied to just being in the countryside, even for a picnic. The *dachas* of old were large, comfortable wooden houses, often brightly painted and adorned with intricate wood carvings on shutters and gables. Sometimes the *dachas* were fairly isolated; in other instances whole villages were made up of summer homes. One such picturesque village is Repino, named after Ilya Repin, the great Russian painter of the *Peredvizhniki* ('Wanderers') school, famous for his natural landscapes and historical portraits. Repino is just north of Leningrad, in what was formerly Finnish Karelia. Its streets are narrow and winding, lined on both sides with two-storey wooden houses. The village borders on a pine and birch wood which yields abundant wild berries and mushrooms in the summer and early autumn and provides wonderful cross-country ski trails in the winter. Now the houses are neglected and in need of repair, but the village still retains its storybook charm.

Russians today rarely own their own *dachas*; more often they rent a room or a floor of one of the large old houses to use as their summer base. Frequently there is no indoor plumbing, but the accommodation is not meant to be luxurious. Simplicity only contributes to the charm of the *dacha* and to the sense of closeness to nature. Gazing out on to a birch wood or frolicking in the tall meadow grass or catching the scent of a wood stove in the chilly late summer air – these are some of the moments Russians wax nostalgic about when they think of time spent at the *dacha*.

Not only is the accommodation rudimentary, but the very pace of life is slowed down. Food preparation is simplified, too. The recipes in this chapter are typical of the Russian fare which might be enjoyed at the *dacha*. There are no complicated preparations, no time-consuming labours, no pretension to elegance or expense: just the simple food of the Russian folk, what they ate a hundred years ago and what they are still eating today; the 'meat and potatoes' of the Russian cuisine.

A meal in a peasant home could hardly have differed more from the banquets served to the gentry and nobility. The first, most obvious limitation was the peasant cottage itself, whose only implements consisted of a few pots and pans and the huge Russian stove – a stove, however, perfectly geared to the long slow cooking which produces the best soups and stews and porridges, the mainstays of the peasant diet. Instead of a parade of dishes, the peasants sat down to a single course: soup, *kasha* and bread. Yet this was no mean meal; the bread was rye, the loaves coarse and heavy but full of such nutrition and flavour that the peasants rightly believed that 'a table with bread is an altar; without it, a plank'. The variety of rye breads was great, each loaf taking its name from the region or village where it originated. White bread (*bulka*, from the French *boule*) was not known to the peasantry, since it was available only through the French and German bakers in the cities.

The peasant family's table usually stood in the icon corner of the cottage, and at mealtime a large bowl of steaming soup was placed in the centre. Each member of the family had his own personal spoon – often ornately carved or lacquered with the bright yellow, red and black flourishes of the Russian *khokhloma* style – and everyone ate from the communal pot together. Today an expression used to convey grief or strong experience shared in common is *my s odnoi miski khlebovali*, 'we have shared food from the same bowl'. A guest was honoured to be asked to partake of the communal meal.

In Russian fairy tales, peasant food makes frequent appearances, often as the key motivation for the story. One of the first tales Russian children read concerns a round loaf of rye bread, *kolobok*, the flour for which an old *babushka* just barely manages to scrape together from the corners and cracks in her flour bin. She mixes the flour with sour cream, shapes the loaf, lovingly cooks it, and sets it on the window sill to cool. After hopping off the sill, *kolobok*'s further adventures rival the western gingerbread man's, until he is eaten up by a wily, hungry fox. In other folk tales, no matter how brave the exploits of a handsome prince or how bitter the tribulations of a fair maiden, the characters always take the time to eat something – whether a simple repast in the forest hut of the witch Baba Yaga or a royal feast at the Tsar's palace. The tales tell too of the wondrous *samobranka*, a tablecloth that not only spreads itself, but causes the table under it to groan from the weight of so much food.

The Russians are both a superstitious and a thankful people; they do not forget the source of their daily bread: they love the soil and the rain and the summer sun, which nurture the grain and promise a rich harvest. Nor do they neglect the stove which transforms the grain into breads and porridges. In Vasily Shukshin's story, *In Profile and Full Face*, a young boy (already in the Soviet period) decides to leave his village to seek his fortunes in the world, but before he leaves, his mother admonishes him, as she has in the past, to say farewell to the stove in the corner. The boy kisses the stove three times (the magical number) and intones: 'Mother Stove, bless me on my long journey as you have blessed me with food and drink.' When the boy leaves, his mother feels relieved to know that her son is travelling with the blessing of the stove, the symbol of home and warmth and family.

For city dwellers, summers at the *dacha* are long and languorous, with days spent wandering through the woods and fields picking berries and mushrooms. The variety is extensive. Russians like the tiny sweet wild strawberries, the red- and black-currants that over-run the kitchen garden, the tart lingonberries and cranberries in the swamps of the lowlands, the black bilberries and golden cloudber-ries. Mushrooms, too, are ubiquitous, and just as colourful as the berries, ranging in hue from the saffron *ryzhik* to more exotic shades of lilac and green. All are delicious when expertly chosen and prepared, and many, if not most, Russians still possess this exper-tise. All lands except army training grounds are open to gatherers. Throughout the summer the riches of the earth are enjoyed to their fullest. Fresh fruits, greatly lacking during the long winter months, are plentiful, and in general the feeling is one of abundance, even excess. The bounty is a source of pride to those who dwell on the land. In Sologub's novel *The Petty Demon*, an argument starts as to whose farmyard produces the most eggs. The boasting goes on until finally one maid silences her neighbours by claiming that not only does her chicken lay two eggs a day, but a spoonful of butter besides! The boasting is not pure vanity, though; by custom the plenty is meant to be shared. The wealthy peasants of the Volga region used to host lavish fêtes for their less fortunate compatriots, thereby showing off their own well-being, as well as enhancing the lives of the poorer peasants.

The aspiration towards displays of excess was also reflected on the country estates of the gentry. The food may have been more simply prepared than in the city, but still it was a source of pride to the estate to serve food in endless quantities and transformations. One such country estate preoccupied with food is Oblomovka in Goncharov's novel *Oblomov*. Oblomov dreams of Oblomovka, fondly recalling his idyllic childhood there, the pampering, and the food:

The first and foremost vital concern at Oblomovka was food. What calves were fattened there for the holidays! What fowl were raised! How many subtle considerations, how many pursuits and worries there were in taking care of them! The turkeys and chickens intended for name-days and other celebrations were fed on nuts; the geese were deprived of any exercise at all and hung motionless in a sack for several days before the holiday, so they would swim in their own fat. What stores of jams and pickles and biscuits there were! What honeys! What kvasses were brewed, and what pies were baked at Oblomovka!

The pies baked at Oblomovka were indeed wonderful. Baked on Sunday, they were large enough to last throughout the week until Friday, when the last stale crumbs were given to beggars as charity.

In this chapter you will find recipes for the most basic foods of the Russian cuisine, some of which the Slavic peoples have been preparing (with ever greater refinement) for nearly a thousand years. You will find hearty soups such as *borshch* (beetroot) and *shchi* (cabbage); grains cooked into kasha (buckwheat groats) or robust rye bread; stews that are guaranteed to stick to your ribs; desserts as simple and sweet as baked apples with jam. You may even be surprised to find yourself exclaiming, in true Russian fashion, 'I can't take another bite – but I will have a pie!'

Cabbage Soup Shchi

In Gogol's *Dead Souls* the scoundrel Chichikov is invited to dine with the landowner Manilov. As they sit down to table, Manilov says, 'Excuse us for not serving a dinner like they would in the elegant salons of the capital. Here we simply have *shchi*, in the Russian tradition – but it's straight from the heart. Please help yourself.'

Shchi is the most Russian of soups, and coupled with *kasha* it represents basic Russian fare, straightforward in both preparation and spirit. Russian folk wisdom advises, 'If the *shchi*'s good, you don't need anything else.' And it's true that a bowl of this hearty soup is enormously satisfying, begging only a chunk of black bread with garlic to round out the meal.

There are several different kinds of *shchi*. The original soup was made exclusively from fermented cabbage (sauerkraut), hence the name *kislye shchi* or sour cabbage soup. *Kislye shchi* is still very popular in the Soviet Union. It is a wintertime soup, harking back to the days before mass production, when the soup could not be prepared until the sauerkraut, put up in the early autumn, had fermented. At some point an inventive cook decided to make cabbage soup in the summer as well, and resorted to using fresh cabbage. Thus *lenivye shchi* or 'lazy' cabbage soup was born: the cook was able to avoid the laborious process of souring the cabbage before turning it into soup.

The *shchi* offered here is slightly unorthodox, as it combines both the summer and winter variations, but the small dose of sauerkraut adds a nice tang without making the soup overly heavy. This version of *shchi* can be served year-round with equanimity.

1 oz (30 g) butter	(¾ lb/340 g), coarsely
1 medium onion, coarsely	shredded
chopped	4 oz (120 g) sauerkraut
1 small leek, white part only,	1 tomato, peeled and cut into
thinly sliced	chunks
1 small carrot, scraped and	salt, freshly ground black
thinly sliced	pepper to taste
2 pints (1.2 litres) rich beef	
stock	soured cream
1 small head white cabbage	fresh dill (optional)

Melt the butter in a stockpot. Add the onions, leeks and carrots and sauté them until they just begin to soften. Pour in the beef stock and bring to the boil. Stir in the shredded cabbage, sauerkraut and tomato.

Simmer the soup, covered, for about 50 minutes, or until the cabbage is tender. Check for seasoning. To serve, top each portion with a dollop of soured cream and a sprinkling of fresh dill, if desired.

Serves 4 to 6.

Note: As with most Russian soups, the *shchi* tastes best when prepared a day ahead and refrigerated overnight before serving.

Ukrainian Borshch   Borshch ukrainskii

Native to the Ukraine, *borshch* is one of the great soups of the world. Well over a hundred variations exist – rather a startling total when one considers the relatively small size of the Ukraine. Although as many as twenty different ingredients may go into a *borshch*, the common component is beetroot, lending the soup its characteristic taste and colour. (The sole exception to this rule is the so-called 'green' *borshch* made with spinach and sorrel.) Each region of the Ukraine boasts its own preparation of *borshch*, and the best of these have transcended local boundaries. There is Kiev *borshch* made with lamb and mushrooms, *borshch* from Poltava with poultry and dumplings. The Galician soup is heavy with potatoes, while Chernigov cooks add marrow to the broth. Lvov has a version with small, mild frankfurters, but in Konotop three different meats make up the soup. Other varieties of *borshch* appear throughout Russia: Moscow *borshch*, rich with tomato, 'navy' *borshch* made with bacon, and the ever-popular 'soldiers' *borshch*, designed to assuage grumblings both verbal and intestinal.

As a general rule, the further west one goes, the more beetroot is added to the soup. But even here the possibilities are numerous: it may be added raw in cubes or in julienne strips; it may be baked first or boiled. Some cooks add raw beetroot to water and make a strong broth, then set it aside for a few days to ripen. Others add beetroot along with its kvass, as in the recipe below. A sour tang can be had from soused apples, sauerkraut, even prunes. It all depends on the resources and imagination of the cook.

Ukrainians often eat *borshch* with *ushki*, their tiny ear-shaped dumplings, while Muscovites prefer unsweetened *vatrushki* or *pirozhki*. But I find that a thick slice of black bread tastes best of all. Make this soup a day ahead for best results.

3½ pints (2 litres) water	½ celeriac, peeled and diced
1¼ pints (750 ml) beetroot kvass (see p. 175)	¾ lb (340 g) potatoes, peeled and cubed
4 lb (1.8 kg) beef shin or chuck with bone	1 small head of white cabbage, shredded
2 oz (60 g) dried beans, soaked overnight	1 small tart apple, peeled, cored and diced
2 large beetroot, peeled and cut into julienne stripes	3 tablespoons tomato paste
3 tablespoons red wine vinegar	1½ tablespoons salt
½ lb (225 g) smoked pork shoulder or knuckle	freshly ground black pepper to taste
1 oz (30 g) butter	1 oz (30 g) salt pork
1 carrot, scraped and diced	4 tablespoons minced parsley
1 onion, chopped	1 bay leaf

Put the water and the beetroot kvass in a large stockpot. Add the beef. Bring to the boil, skimming the foam from the surface of the soup. Simmer for 1 hour.

Meanwhile, cook the dried beans in salted water until almost tender. Keep warm.

Sprinkle the raw beetroot with 2 tablespoons of vinegar. Then add it to the soup along with the smoked pork. Cook for 10 minutes.

Sauté the onion, carrot and celery root in the butter until softened, then add to the soup. Stir in the potatoes, shredded cabbage, and apple.

Drain the beans and add them to the soup, along with the tomato paste, salt, pepper, and remaining tablespoon of vinegar. Cook the soup for 20 minutes more.

Mince the salt pork together with the parsley, then carefully stir it into the soup, mixing well. Stir in the bay leaf. Boil for 15 minutes longer. Leave to cool to room temperature and then refrigerate overnight. Reheat to serve.

Makes 6 pints (3.5 litres).

Moscow Borshch Borshch moskovskii

Here is *borshch* as prepared by a born-and-bred Muscovite, Klara Leivovna.

(3½) pints (2.75 litres) water
2 lb (900 g) beef shin or chuck with bone
3 medium beetroot, peeled and cut in half
1½ tablespoons salt (or less, to taste)
2 medium potatoes, peeled and cubed
1 small carrot, scraped and grated
½ medium head of white cabbage (¾ lb/340 g), shredded

1 ripe tomato, coarsely chopped
6 tablespoons tomato paste
4 black peppercorns
freshly ground black pepper to taste
2 tablespoons wine vinegar
1 teaspoon sugar
1 bay leaf

soured cream

Simmer the meat in the water for 30 minutes. Then add the beetroot and the salt. Boil for 10 minutes more.

Remove the beetroot from the broth and grate them coarsely. Then return them to the pot along with the remaining ingredients, except for the bay leaf and the soured cream.

Simmer the soup until done, about 1½ hours. Remove it from the heat and add the bay leaf. Leave to cool to room temperature, then chill overnight. Next day, skim the fat from the soup and reheat to serve. Put a slice of meat and a dollop of soured cream in each bowl.

Makes 4½ pints (2.6 litres).

Mixed Meat and Tomato Soup Solyanka sbornaya myasnaya

Yet another type of slightly sour Russian soup, *solyanka* is great fun to eat, as each spoonful surprises the diner with a new taste sensation.

2½ pints (1.5 litres) water
2½ lb (1.4 kg) beef shin or chuck with bones
¼ lb (120 g) cooked ham
¼ lb (120 g) frankfurters
1 veal kidney, sliced
flour
2 medium onions, chopped
1 oz (30 g) butter
2 medium dill pickles, cut into julienne strips
1 tablespoon capers

2 oz (60 g) olives, sliced
2 tomatoes, peeled, seeded and chopped
1 teaspoon tomato paste
4 oz (120 g) marinated mushrooms (see p. 44)
1 teaspoon salt
freshly ground black pepper to taste
1 bay leaf
2 lemon slices 1 in (2.5 cm) thick

Cook the beef in the water for 1½ hours to make a rich broth (or substitute 2½ pints (1.5 litres) prepared beef stock).

Chop the ham and the frankfurters. Dredge the kidney slices in flour and brown in ½ oz (15 g) butter. Brown the chopped onions in the remaining butter. Stir the ham, frankfurters, kidney and onions into the beef stock. Cook for 15 minutes.

Then add the pickles, capers, olives, tomatoes, tomato paste, mushrooms, salt, pepper, bay leaf and lemon slices. Cook 10 minutes more.

This soup tastes best when made a day ahead and allowed to stand overnight.

Makes 3 pints (1.7 litres).

Note: As with most Russian soups, a dollop of soured cream tastes good in *solyanka* too.

Mushroom and Barley Soup Pokhlyobka

Pokhlyobka is a typical, hearty peasant soup. In true rustic style it is usually eaten with black bread generously rubbed with raw garlic. Real garlic lovers simply eat the garlic straight: take a whole peeled clove of garlic and dip it in salt before biting into it. This kind of garlic-eating is best done among friends, however. It wasn't until I got to know my Russian hosts well that we ate the pungent cloves together.

3 oz (60 g) butter
2 onions, chopped
2 cloves garlic, crushed
2½ pints (1.5 litres) rich beef stock
1 large potato, coarsely chopped
2 carrots, scraped and sliced
2 bay leaves
1 tablespoon fresh dill *or* ½ teaspoon dried dill

1 teaspoon salt
freshly ground black pepper to taste
4 oz (120 g) raw pearl barley
1 lb (450 g) mushrooms, trimmed and sliced
1 tablespoon freshly squeezed lemon juice
soured cream (optional)

In a stockpot sauté the onions and garlic in 1 oz (30 g) butter until soft. Pour in the beef stock, stirring well, then add the potato, carrots, bay leaves, dill, salt, pepper and barley. Bring the soup to the boil and then simmer, covered, for about 1 hour, or until the barley is tender.

Sauté the mushrooms in the remaining butter for 3 minutes. Stir them into the soup. Simmer for 10 minutes.

Just before serving, stir in the lemon juice. Test for seasoning. Pour the soup into bowls and garnish with a spoonful of soured cream, if desired.

Serves 6 to 8.

Variation: For a more strongly flavoured soup, 1½ oz (45 g) dried mushrooms may be substituted for the fresh mushrooms. Soak them in water to cover for 20 minutes, then drain and slice. Add to the beef stock along with the potato, carrots and barley.

Two Summer Soups   Svekol'nik i khlodnik

These two cold soups revitalise even as they nourish – perfect refreshment for languid summer days. The first is a standard cold beetroot soup, the second an import from Poland. Both put the beetroot to good use, the *svekol'nik* relying on the root's colour and flavour while the *khlodnik* capitalises on the subtle taste of the greens. Serve both soups well chilled.

Cold Beetroot Soup   Svekol'nik

2 pints (1.2 litres) rich chicken stock (see p. 159)
1 small onion, chopped finely
½ a large carrot, scraped and julienned
1 small parsnip, peeled and julienned (optional)
½ lb (225 g) beetroot, peeled and julienned
2 cloves garlic, crushed

salt, freshly ground pepper to taste
2 tablespoons tomato paste
4 teaspoons sugar
2 tablespoons freshly squeezed lemon juice

soured cream (preferably home-made)
parsley

In a large stockpot bring the chicken stock to the boil with the vegetables and the garlic, salt and pepper. Simmer for 10 to 15 minutes. Then stir in the tomato paste and sugar. Continue cooking for 30 minutes more.

Leave the soup to cool to room temperature, then stir in the lemon juice. Taste for seasoning. Chil the soup for several hours or overnight before serving.

This soup is best served in a glass bowl so that its colour can be seen to advantage. Garnish with minced parsley and soured cream.

Serves 4 to 6.

Khlodnik

½ lb (225 g) fresh beetroot tops
1¼ pints (750 ml) rich chicken stock (see p. 159)
½ pint (300 ml) kvass (see p. 173)
¼ pint (150 ml) soured cream
2 tablespoons fresh snipped dill *or* 1 teaspoon dried dill
1 tablespoon chives
½ lb (225 g) cooked veal, cubed
2 large radishes, trimmed and sliced

1 small dill pickle, diced
1 small cucumber, diced
1 small beetroot, cooked, peeled, and diced
salt, freshly ground pepper to taste
2 teaspoons sugar

2 hard-boiled eggs, chopped
ice cubes

Cook the beetroot greens in boiling salted water for 25 minutes. Drain, squeezing out any excess liquid, and chop.

In a large bowl mix together the chicken stock, kvass and soured cream. Stir in the cooked beetroot tops. Then add the dill, chives, cooked veal, radishes, pickle, cucumber and beetroot. Season with salt and pepper to taste. Stir in the sugar. Mix all the ingredients together well.

Cover the soup and chill for at least 4 hours.

To serve, place 1 or 2 ice cubes in each soup bowl, and pour the soup over. Garnish each portion with chopped hard-boiled egg.

Serves 6 to 8.

Cold Meat and Vegetable Soup Okroshka

Okroshka is Russia's most popular cold soup and one of the easiest to prepare. The basic recipe calls only for chopped meats and vegetables doused with a liberal amount of kvass. But since such a sour taste is not always to Western liking, I have opted instead for a version of *okroshka* as prepared by the Russians living in Central Asia. There, a mixture of kefir (a yogurt-like substance) and water is substituted for the kvass, making an attractive, refreshing soup.

2 hard-boiled eggs
1 teaspoon prepared mustard
generous ¼ pint (150 ml)
   soured cream
1 tablespoon sugar
¼ teaspoon salt
1 pint (600 ml) plain kefir
   (p. 172)
¾ pint (450 ml) cold water

¾ lb (340 g) mixed cooked
   meats, in julienne strips
   (beef, chicken, tongue,
   turkey, etc.)
2 spring onions, chopped
6 red radishes, thinly sliced
1 small unpeeled cucumber,
   finely chopped
2 tablespoons fresh snipped
   dill

Mash the egg yolks and mix them with the mustard. Then stir in the soured cream, sugar and salt till well blended. Gradually beat in the kefir and then the water, until the mixture is well blended and frothy.

Stir in the meats, prepared vegetables and dill. Chill the soup well before serving.

Serves 8.

Variation: a more authentic *okroshka* is made with kvass: for the kefir and water mixture substitute 1½ pints (900 ml) bread kvass. Just before serving, stir in ¾ pint (450 ml) sparkling water. Place an ice cube in each plate before ladling out the soup.

Cold Fruit Soup with Dumplings Kholodets iz vishen, grush i sliv

Unlike the usual clear fruit soups thickened with cornflour, *kholodets* is a well-textured purée. Served with light apple dumplings, it makes an excellent first course in hot weather.

1 lb (450 g) each apples, pears
   and plums
¾ pint (450 ml) cold water
1 tablespoon freshly squeezed
   lemon juice
grated rind of 1 lemon
½ teaspoon cinnamon
1 oz (30 g) soft fresh
   breadcrumbs

3 oz (85 g) seedless raspberry
   jam
4 oz (120 g) sugar
¼ pint (150 ml) sweet white
   wine
½ pint (300 ml) cranberry juice

Peel and core the apples and pears. Stone the plums but do not peel them. Put the prepared fruit, the water, lemon juice, lemon rind, cinnamon and breadcrumbs in a large saucepan. Bring to the boil and simmer for 20 minutes, until the fruit is soft. Then put through a vegetable mill to purée.

Stir in the remaining ingredients. Chill well before serving, garnished with apple dumplings.

Serves 6 to 8.

Apple Dumplings Kletski

2 medium apples, peeled, cored and finely chopped	1 whole egg, lightly beaten
juice and rind of 1 lemon	3 oz (85 g) fine dry breadcrumbs
2 oz (60 g) sugar	

Pour the lemon juice over the apples to keep them from turning brown. Then gently squeeze them dry. Mix the apples with the lemon rind, sugar, lightly beaten egg and breadcrumbs. Chill in the refrigerator for 20 minutes.

Form the mixture into walnut-sized balls. Bring a large pan of lightly salted water to the boil. Drop the dumplings into the water and boil until they rise to the surface, about 5 minutes. Remove with a slotted spoon.

Cool to room temperature before serving in the soup.

Makes 2 dozen dumplings.

Kasha (Buckwheat Groats) Grechnevaya kasha

Besides cabbage soup, no food is more Russian than *kasha*. As one saying goes, 'Cabbage soup and *kasha* – that's our fare.' And this statement is made with affection rather than irony or scorn. (While in English the word 'kasha' refers to the cooked groats of buckwheat so closely associated with Russian cuisine, *kasha* in Russian applies to any grain cooked to porridge consistency.)

The eating of *kasha* goes back many centuries. The early Slavic tribes used to boil their porridge with so much liquid it resembled soup. This practice gradually died out, and by the twelfth century the preparation of *kasha* had become so refined that it was considered fitting provender for feasts. In fact, the word *kasha* was used synonymously with the word 'feast' for a good two hundred years. Later, when the vast expanses of Siberia were first opened up for exploration in the sixteenth century, adventurers and traders carried with them huge sacks of buckwheat, since this hearty grain is easily prepared even under the most primitive conditions. At about the same time, the peasants began cooking *kasha* at home in their large Russian stoves, whose constantly falling temperatures ensured a perfect *kasha*, one that never burned, even when baked for long hours. Today the cooking process has been greatly simplified, and more often than not *kasha* is boiled on top of the range like rice. But it still tastes best when made in the traditional manner, baked in an earthenware pot in a moderate oven.

8 oz (225 g) kasha (coarse-cut buckwheat groats)	¾ pint (450 ml) boiling water
½ teaspoon salt	1 oz (30 g) butter

In a large frying pan stir the kasha over medium high heat for about 5 minutes, until each grain begins to brown. Preheat the oven to

180°C/350°F/Gas 4. Grease a 2 pint (1.2 litre) earthenware casserole with a lid. Put the kasha in the greased casserole and add the salt. Pour the boiling water over it. Dot with the butter, cover the casserole and bake for 45 minutes.

Serves 4 to 6.

Note: Kasha is available in fine, medium and coarse grades. For the best flavour and texture, always choose the coarse variety.

Variations:
1. Place the grains in a large frying pan and crack 1 large egg over them, stirring well to coat each grain. Cook the kasha over medium high heat for about 5 minutes, or until all the moisture from the egg has evaporated. Then proceed as above.
2. Replace the boiling water with ¾ pint (450 ml) liquid in which dried mushrooms have soaked. Add the soaked dried mushrooms (or fresh ones, sautéed in a little butter) to the kasha before baking.
3. For a creamy consistency, boil 8 oz (225 g) kasha in ¾ pint (450 ml) water over high heat, uncovered, until the water is absorbed. Then stir in ¾ pint (450 ml) milk and cook the kasha slowly, covered, over low heat until done, about 20 minutes. This kind of kasha is often served as a breakfast porridge.
4. Add 1 tablespoon fresh snipped dill to the boiling water before pouring it over the kasha.
5. Add a little chopped onion which has been sautéed in butter to the kasha before baking it.
6. A good use for leftover kasha is to make *croûtons* (*grenki*). Spread leftover kasha in a greased pan, levelling the top with a knife dipped in cold water. Place in the refrigerator and chill until firm. Then cut the kasha into cubes. Dredge the cubes in flour, egg yolks and breadcrumbs. Fry in plenty of butter until crisp and brown. These *croûtons* taste quite good in *shchi*.

Russian Black Bread Chornyi khleb

In pre-Revolutionary days, the best black bread in Russia was baked at Filippov's bakery on Tverskaya Boulevard, now Gorky Street. Filippov claimed that his secret lay in the flour he used. He shipped his grains in from the Tambov Province, then ground them in his own mills before sieving to eliminate all the chaff. Filippov's loaves were so good that a shipment was sent daily to the court in St Petersburg – and this before the advent of railways!

Today, in a less extravagant era, there is still great bread in Moscow. To my way of thinking the best is 'Borodinsky', made of rye and wheat flours and scented with coriander. Although it's impossible to recreate this bread exactly outside of Moscow, the recipe given here makes a valiant attempt, yielding a dark loaf with a good sour tang.

14 oz (400 g) dark rye flour
1¼ pints (750 ml) flat beer
2 tablespoons active dry yeast
½ oz (15 g) butter
1½ oz (45 g) honey
1 tablespoon instant coffee
1 oz (30 g) plain dark chocolate
3 oz (85 g) bran flakes (available

at health-food stores; do not
use bran cereal)
2 teaspoons crushed coriander
seed
1½ tablespoons salt
10–14 oz (280–400 g) strong
white flour

Five days before breadmaking, prepare the following starter: Mix 4 oz (120 g) rye flour with 8 fluid oz (225 ml) beer. Stir well. Leave to stand, covered, at room temperature for 5 days, stirring once a day.

On breadmaking day, dissolve the yeast in 4 tablespoons of beer, which has been heated to lukewarm. Leave for 5 minutes.

Meanwhile, heat the butter, honey, coffee and chocolate together in a small saucepan, just until the chocolate melts. Set aside to cool to lukewarm.

Stir the starter mixture into the yeast. Then stir in the remaining beer, rye flour, bran flakes, salt and coriander and chocolate mixture, beating well.

Gradually beat in 10 oz (280 g) plain flour, mixing well to form a soft dough which will be slightly sticky.

Turn the dough out on to a floured board and knead until smooth and elastic, adding up to 4 oz (120 g) more of plain flour. Shape into a ball and place in a deep, greased bowl, turning to grease the top of the dough. Cover and leave to rise in a warm spot until doubled in bulk, about 1½ hours.

Knock the dough back and knead it briefly on a floured board. Divide it in half and shape into 2 round, free-form loaves. Place the loaves on a baking tray which has been sprinkled with cornmeal.

Cover the loaves and leave to rise until doubled in bulk, about 30 minutes.

Preheat the oven to 200°C/400°F/Gas 6. Bake the loaves at 200°C/ 400°F for 10 minutes, then reduce the heat to 180°C/350°F/Gas 4 and continue to bake for 50 minutes more, until the loaves are browned and sound hollow when tapped.

Prepare the following glaze:

1 teaspoon cornflour   5 tablespoons water

Dissolve the cornflour in 1 tablespoon of the water. Place the remaining water in a saucepan and stir in the dissolved cornflour. Bring to the boil, stirring constantly. Boil for 1 minute, until thickened.

Brush the baked loaves with the glaze, covering them evenly on all sides. Return them to the oven for 3 to 4 minutes, until the glaze is set.

Cool on racks before serving.

Rye Bread Rzhanoi khleb

The Soviet Union still boasts the cheapest bread in the world, with a standard loaf costing 20 kopecks or 12p. The Russians love their bread, and the government encourages its consumption by keeping prices low. No wonder the average Russian eats a pound of bread a day! Although bread comes in many varieties, the favourite remains the basic rye loaf. Here is another recipe for rye bread, this one faintly sweet and aromatic.

2 rounded tablespoons black tea leaves (preferably fruit-scented, such as black-currant or peach)	1 oz (30 g) Barbados sugar
	2 oz (60 g) day-old black breadcrumbs
¾ pint (450 ml) boiling water	1 tablespoon salt
4 oz (120 g) sugar	12 oz (340 g) dark rye flour
4 tablespoons boiling water	6–8 oz (170–225 g) strong plain flour
2 tablespoons dried yeast	1 egg white
4 tablespoons warm water	1 tablespoon cold water

Pour ¾ pint (450 ml) boiling water over the tea leaves and leave until lukewarm. (Cooled leftover tea may be used instead, but the tea should be strong.) Strain.

Meanwhile, make the caramel colouring. In a large frying pan melt the sugar, stirring constantly until it turns a deep golden brown. Gradually pour in 4 tablespoons boiling water (it *must* be boiling) and stir until well mixed. Cool to lukewarm.

Dissolve the yeast in the 4 tablespoons warm water. Stir in the cooled, strained tea and the cooled caramel. Then add the Barbados sugar, breadcrumbs, salt and rye flour, mixing well. Gradually stir in enough strong plain flour to make a firm dough.

Turn the dough out on to a floured board and knead until smooth and elastic. Place it in a greased bowl and turn to grease the top. Cover; leave to rise in a warm spot for 2 hours, or until doubled in bulk. Knock back and shape the dough into 2 free-form loaves.

Sprinkle a baking tray with cornmeal and place the loaves on it. Cover and leave them to rise until doubled, about 45 minutes.

Preheat the oven to 190°C/375°F/Gas 5. In a small bowl lightly beat the egg white; mix in the cold water. Brush the loaves with this mixture, then place them in the oven and bake for 30 to 35 minutes, until nicely browned.

Sourdough White Bread Khleb iz pshenichnoi muki

The earliest leavened bread baked by the Slavs was a type of sourdough. A lump of dough was reserved from each bread baking and allowed to ferment, then used as the starter for the next batch. Even today classic recipes for yeast-raised dough begin with an *opara*, or starter, to add that faint taste of sour the Russians so love. This bread is especially aromatic as it bakes, reminding one of early accounts of St Petersburg, where the stirring odour of freshly baked bread drifted down the Nevsky Prospect at dawn.

8 oz (225 g) strong plain flour	8 fluid oz (225 ml) milk
8 fluid oz (225 ml water	

Mix the above ingredients together and let sit, covered, at room temperature for about 5 days. The sponge will give off a strong, sour smell.

2 teaspoons dried yeast	1 tablespoon caraway seed
4 tablespoons warm water	(preferably Russian black
1 teaspoon sugar	caraway)
2 teaspoons salt	1 lb (450 g) strong plain flour

Once the sponge is ready, prepare the bread. Dissolve the yeast in the warm water along with the sugar. Stir the sponge, which will have separated, and then add it to the dissolved yeast. Stir in the salt, caraway seed and flour, adding the latter gradually until a fairly firm dough has been formed.

Turn the dough out on to a floured board and knead until smooth and elastic, about 10 minutes. Place it in a greased bowl, turning to grease the top. Cover and leave to rise until doubled in bulk, about 1½ to 2 hours.

Knock back the dough and then knead it again for a minute or two. Sprinkle a large baking tray with cornmeal. Shape the dough into one large, round loaf and place it on the baking tray.

Cover the loaf and leave it to rise until doubled, about 45 minutes.

Preheat the oven to 200°C/400°F/Gas 6. With a sharp knife slash an X in the top of the loaf. Brush it with cold water and bake for 45 minutes until the loaf is nicely browned and sounds hollow when tapped.

Note: If you can get the dark, aromatic Russian black caraway, by all means use it.

Beef Stew with Horseradish Sauce Tushonoye myaso s podlivkoi iz khrena

Don't be alarmed at the large amount of horseradish called for in this recipe. Over a low fire it marries well with the beef to produce a rich, hearty, one-dish meal, which tastes equally good served cold.

3 lb (1.35 kg) stewing beef
3 oz (85 g) butter
2 large onions, finely chopped
4 cloves garlic, crushed
2 medium carrots, scraped and
   finely chopped
¾ pint (450 ml) beef broth
¾ pint (450 ml) dry white wine
2 bay leaves
3 tablespoons (20 g) flour

5 oz (150 g) prepared
   horseradish (or more, to
   taste) (see p. 170)
2 tablespoons prepared
   mustard
4 tablespoons soured cream
salt, freshly ground black
   pepper to taste

minced parsley

Brown the stewing beef in 2 oz (60 g) butter, then remove it from the pan and keep it warm. Cook the onions, garlic and carrots in the pan for 15 minutes over medium low heat. Then smooth the vegetables into an even layer over the bottom of the pan and place the browned meat on top of them. Pour the beef broth and wine over the meat; add the bay leaves. Cover and simmer for 1½ hours, until the meat is tender.

Strain the broth, reserving the meat and vegetables. Return the broth to a saucepan and reduce it by half.

In a medium saucepan make a roux of the remaining butter and the flour. Stir in the reduced beef broth. Stir until thickened, then add the horseradish and mustard. Gradually stir in the soured cream; do not allow the sauce to boil. Check for seasoning. Pour the sauce over the meat and vegetables and warm through.

Serve garnished with minced parsley.

Serves 4 to 6.

Russian Hamburgers Bitki

For a lively variation on the hamburger motif, try adding beetroot and caraway seed to minced beef. These patties are best served rare, and never in buns.

1 medium beetroot
1 lb (450 g) minced beef (good
   quality)
6 spring onions, including the
   green tops
1 teaspoon salt

1 teaspoon caraway seed
½ oz (15 g) butter
1 tablespoon oil

tiny new peas

Boil the beetroot in salted water until tender. Slip off its skin and mince the beetroot. Mince the spring onions. Mix the minced beetroot and spring onion into the beef along with the salt and caraway seed. Shape into 6 oval patties.

In a large frying pan heat together the butter and oil. Fry the patties over medium high heat until they are just done, about 6 to 8 minutes.

Serve garnished with tiny new peas.

Serves 3 to 4.

Note: These patties are also nice when topped with a sauce of dried mushrooms (see p. 146).

Baked Fish with Horseradish Pechonaya ryba s khrenom

Three Russian favourites – fish, horseradish and soured cream – are combined here in an excellent dish that's easy to prepare. Use horseradish flavoured with beetroot for a rosy glow under the cream.

8 white fish fillets (2 lb/900 g)	5 oz (150 g) prepared
½ teaspoon salt	horseradish (see p. 170)
½ teaspoon thyme	1 oz (30 g) butter
freshly ground black pepper to taste	¼ pint (150 ml) soured cream

Preheat the oven to 190°C/375°F/Gas 5. Grease an ovenproof dish. Season the fish fillets with the salt, pepper and thyme.

Place four of the fillets in the baking dish. Spread half the horseradish over them. Dot with half the butter. Spread on half the soured cream.

Place the remaining four fillets on top and repeat the procedure, spreading on the remaining horseradish, butter and soured cream.

Cover the dish and bake for 30 minutes. Remove the cover and continue baking for 15 minutes more, or until the fish is flaky.

Serves 4 generously.

Variation: Place a layer of sliced sour apples between the two layers of fish fillets. Bake as directed.

Potato and Herring Casserole Kartofel's selyodkoi

The Baltic Sea has been so thoroughly fished that herring is growing scarce, and this wonderful fish, once considered so plebeian, is now a delicacy in the Soviet Union. Here, a single herring is economically stretched into a filling meal for four in a dish that is common to both Northern Russia and Estonia.

1 salt herring (about ¾ lb/340 g)	1 large onion, sliced
milk	1 oz (30 g) grated Parmesan
4 bacon rashers	cheese
4 medium potatoes	butter
freshly ground black pepper	

Rinse the herring and soak it overnight in milk. Discard the milk; skin the herring. Split it and remove the backbone. Cut it into 1 in (2.5 cm) pieces.

Grease an 8 in (20 cm) ovenproof casserole. Fry the bacon rashers until just barely crisp. Leave them to cool, then crumble them. Peel the potatoes and slice them thinly.

Preheat the oven to 190°C/375°F/Gas 5. Place one-third of the potatoes in a layer in the bottom of the casserole. Pour on half of the bacon grease, then sprinkle on half of the crumbled bacon, half of the sliced onions, and half of the herring. Pepper liberally. Top with *half* of the remaining potatoes, then cover the potatoes with the rest of the bacon grease, bacon, onion and herring. Again pepper liberally and make a top layer with the remaining potatoes.

Dot the potatoes with butter and sprinkle them with the grated Parmesan cheese. Bake uncovered for 30 minutes, then cover the dish and bake for 30 minutes more. Serve hot.

Serves 4.

Stuffed Cabbage Leaves Golubtsy

Stuffing cabbage leaves is an art in the Soviet Union, where each region and ethnic group claims its own expertise. One finds Central Asian cabbage stuffed with lamb, Baltic cabbage layered with bacon, and a sweet-and-sour cabbage attributed to Russian Jewish cookery. When cabbage leaves are stuffed and rolled into packets they are called *golubtsy* or 'little doves', as the rolls resemble the small birds at rest with wings folded under. Sometimes, though, the head of cabbage is left whole, as in the second recipe below, a typically Russian preparation, and a splendid one.

Stuffed Cabbage Leaves (Jewish Sweet-and-Sour) Golubtsy

1 head of white cabbage (about 2 lb/900 g)
2 large onions, coarsely chopped
3 tablespoons olive oil
¾ lb (340 g) minced beef (or half beef and half veal)
1½ oz (45 g) uncooked rice
1 large carrot, scraped and grated
1 large clove garlic, crushed
¼ teaspoon crushed fennel seed
2 tablespoons minced parsley
1¼ teaspoons salt
freshly ground black pepper to taste (use it liberally)
1 large egg, beaten
2 lb (900 g) ripe tomatoes, peeled and cut into chunks (or a 28 oz (790 g) tin, drained)
¼ pint (150 ml) fresh lemon juice
4 oz (120 g) Barbados sugar

Core the cabbage. Blanch it in boiling water for about 5 minutes. Remove from the pot and gently peel off the outer leaves. If the inner leaves are still too stiff to remove, return cabbage to the boiling water for another minute or so. Continue until all the leaves have been removed. Use the small inner leaves or any damaged ones to line the bottom and sides of a 5 pint (3 litre) casserole.

Prepare the onions: in a heavy-bottomed frying pan mix the 2 chopped onions with the olive oil. Pour over enough of the hot water from the cabbage pot to just cover the onions. Bring to the boil and simmer slowly, uncovered, for 45 minutes to 1 hour, or until the water has evaporated and the onions are golden. Stir occasionally to make sure the onions don't stick to the pan.

While the onions are simmering, prepare the filling. In a large bowl thoroughly mix together the minced beef, raw rice, grated carrot, garlic, fennel seed, parsley, 1 teaspoon salt and the pepper. Stir in the egg, blending well.

Now, starting with the largest leaves, take a cabbage leaf and place a mound of the filling along the centre of it. Tuck up the bottom edge of the leaf first, then roll and tuck until the filling is completely enclosed in the leaf. Continue until all the filling has been used. There will be about 12 rolls.

Place half of the rolls in the cabbage-lined pot in a single layer. Cover with half of the prepared onions, and then top with the remaining cabbage rolls and the rest of the onions.

In a medium saucepan heat the peeled tomatoes, pressing with the back of a spoon until they begin to give off juice. Stir in the lemon juice, sugar and ¼ teaspoon salt. Bring to the boil. Pour over the cabbage rolls. The chunks of tomato will form a layer on top.

Cover the pot and simmer for 1½ to 2 hours.

Serves 4.

Note: These cabbage rolls are even better reheated the second day.

Stuffed Whole Cabbage   Kapusta farshirovannaya

1 head white cabbage (about
   2¼ lb/1 kg)
1 lb (450 g) minced beef
4 slices stale white bread,
   crusts removed
8 tablespoons milk
1½ teaspoons salt
freshly ground black pepper to
   taste

½ teaspoon crushed hot dried
   pepper
¼ teaspoon caraway seed
1 tablespoon fresh dill *or* ½
   teaspoon dried dill
2 oz (60 g) butter, melted
½ pint (300 ml) rich beef broth
½ pint (300 ml) soured cream

Core the cabbage and place it in a large pot with a tightly-fitting lid. Add some boiling salted water and steam the cabbage until it is just barely tender, about 25 minutes. Remove from the water and drain; set aside to cool.

Soak the stale bread in the milk. Squeeze out the excess milk and then mix the bread with the minced beef, salt, pepper, hot pepper, caraway seed and dill, blending well.

When the cabbage is cool enough to handle, carefully pull back each of the leaves, one at a time, being careful not to tear them from the base of the cabbage. Continue pulling back the leaves until only the tiny inner leaves remain in a point. Starting from the inside, brush some melted butter on each leaf as you work with it, then sprinkle it with salt. Place some filling on each leaf, and then carefully reposition the leaf as if you were putting the head back together again. Continue until all the leaves have been filled. Pour any extra butter over the cabbage.

Place the cabbage in a round 9 in (22.5 cm) ovenproof dish. The dish should be just large enough to hold the cabbage comfortably and retain its shape. Preheat the oven to 190°C/350°F/Gas 4.

Pour the beef broth around the edges of the cabbage and place the dish in the oven. Bake, uncovered, for 40 minutes, basting occasionally with the broth if the cabbage looks dry on top. After 40 minutes spread the top of the cabbage with the soured cream, masking it completely. Return to the oven and continue baking for 20 minutes more.

Serve the cabbage by cutting it into thick wedges and ladling the pan juices over it.

Serves 4 generously.

Cabbage with Noodles and Poppy Seed Kapusta s lapshoi i makom

As advertisements are rare in the Soviet press, I was surprised to see in a recent edition of the Leningrad *Pravda* a half-page spread for none other than cabbage. 'Dear housewives,' it exhorted, 'there are 137 different and delicious ways to prepare cabbage! Try them all . . . cabbage is not only tasty, it's good for you.' I don't know who determined the 137 variations, but this recipe for cabbage with noodles and poppy seed is no doubt one of them. And just as the advertisement claims, it's both tasty and nutritious.

1 small head white cabbage (1–1½ lb/450–700 g)	salt, freshly ground black pepper to taste
1 onion	3 oz (85 g) fettucine or similar pasta
2 small, tart apples	
4 oz (120 g) butter	2 tablespoons poppy seed

Coarsely chop the cabbage and onion. Peel, core and coarsely chop the apples. In a large frying pan melt 3 oz (90 g) butter. Stir in the chopped vegetables, coating them well with the butter. Add salt and freshly ground pepper to taste. Cover the pan; simmer the vegetables for about 20 minutes, or until they are soft, adding a tiny bit of water if necessary to keep them from burning.

Cook the pasta in boiling salted water until barely tender. Drain. Stir in the remaining butter and coat the noodles well. Stir the cooked vegetables into the noodles. Add the poppy seed, and check for seasoning.

Serves 6.

Note: This dish improves upon standing, and tastes best when made ahead of time, refrigerated, and then reheated.

Casserole of Creamed Potatoes Kartofel'naya zapekanka

Potatoes are so much a part of the Russian diet that they are fondly called the *vtoroi khleb* or 'second bread' of the people. But they were not always so popular. When the potato was first introduced to Russia in the early eighteenth century, the Russians were reluctant to cultivate this strange tuber. Under Catherine the Great attempts were made to popularise the vegetable, but the people still felt suspicious of it, as the Europeans did of the tomato at first. The Government's determination to impose the potato on the populace led to conflict in the early nineteenth century, when there were numerous 'potato rebellions', culminating in the so-called Potato Mutiny of 1842. This rebellion, a downright refusal by the peasants to sow potato crops, was the largest popular uprising of the nineteenth century in Russia. It was only after Tsar Nicholas I issued a harsh edict enforcing cultivation that the peasants submitted to his will, and by 1844 prizes were being offered for the best potato cultivation.

Of course, life in Russia today is unthinkable without the potato, and a favourite way of preparing this 'second bread' is in *zapekanka*. This Russian version of creamed potatoes is often made livelier with a sauce of dried mushrooms, but if the pungent flavour of wild mushrooms is not to your liking, the casserole may be served plain or with a milder sauce made with cultivated mushrooms.

2 lb (900 g) potatoes	3 large onions, thinly sliced
1½ oz (45 g) butter, melted	1 oz (30 g) butter
½ pint (300 ml) milk	2 tablespoons vegetable oil
1 teaspoon salt	¼ pint (150 ml) soured cream
2 eggs, lightly beaten	

Boil the potatoes in salted water until tender; then peel and cream them. Stir in the 1½ oz (45 g) melted butter, the milk and the salt. Beat in the eggs.

While the potatoes are boiling, fry the onions until golden in the 1 oz (30 g) butter mixed with the oil.

Grease a 3 pint (1.7 litre) casserole. Pour half of the creamed potatoes into it; smooth the top. Spread the onions in an even layer over the potatoes, and top the onions with the remaining potatoes. Spread the soured cream over the top.

Bake the casserole in a preheated 180°C/350°F/Gas 4 oven for 30 minutes, or until lightly browned on top.

Serves 4 to 6.

Dried Mushroom Sauce Gribnoi sous

2 oz (60 g) dried black mushrooms	2 tablespoons finely chopped spring onion
¾ pint (450–600 ml) water	¼ teaspoon salt
1½ oz (45 g) butter	freshly ground black pepper to taste
1 tablespoon flour	

Soak the dried mushrooms in the water for 1 hour. Drain, reserving the liquid.

In a saucepan melt ½ oz (15 g) butter. Stir in the flour and cook for a minute or two, until the flour begins to turn golden. Gradually stir in ¾ pint (450 ml) of the reserved mushroom liquid. Bring to the boil; cook over medium heat for 15 minutes, or until the liquid is reduced by almost half.

Meanwhile, melt 1 oz (30 g) butter in a frying pan. Sauté the spring onion and the drained and finely chopped mushrooms.

Add the spring onion and chopped mushrooms to the sauce, along with the salt and pepper to taste.

Serve over the potato *zapekanka* or Russian-style hamburgers.

Sauerkraut with Mushrooms and Soured Cream Kislaya kapusta s gribami i smetanoi

Should any sauerkraut be left at the bottom of the barrel, put it to good use in this vegetable mélange, a perfect accompaniment to pot-roasted meat.

¼ lb (120 g) mushrooms	4 fluid oz (120 ml) soured
¼ pint (150 ml) water	cream
1 lb (450 g) sauerkraut, slightly	freshly ground black pepper to
drained	taste
1 small tomato, coarsely	
chopped	

Chop the mushrooms finely. Place them in a saucepan with the water and bring to the boil. Add the sauerkraut (do not squeeze it dry) and the coarsely chopped tomato. Simmer for 5 minutes.

Stir in the soured cream. Season to taste, and serve at once.

Serves 4.

Ukrainian Curd Cheese Machanka

In the Ukraine, *tvorog* is often dressed up with rich cream and spring onions. I like to serve this cheese spread thickly on black bread or as part of a mixed salad plate.

½ lb (225 g) dry *tvorog* (curd	2 spring onions, chopped
cheese) (see p. 171)	1 tablespoon fresh snipped dill
½ pint (300 ml) (approx.)	salt to taste
double cream	

Mix together the above ingredients. Use right away or chill.

Serves 6 (or more as a sandwich spread).

Cucumbers in Soured Cream Ogurtsy v smetane

Because there were no other green vegetables to be had the summer I spent in Leningrad, I virtually lived on this salad. It's so good that I never grew tired of it and still find myself making these creamy cucumbers quite often.

2 cucumbers	freshly ground white pepper to
½ pint (300 ml) soured cream	taste
2–3 tablespoons cider vinegar	2 teaspoons salt
4 tablespoons snipped chives	
2 tablespoons snipped fresh	
dill *or* 2 teaspoons dried dill	

If the cucumbers have been waxed, peel them; otherwise, wash them well but leave the peel on. Slice the cucumbers very thinly and pat them dry with kitchen paper. Mix together the remaining ingredients, adding vinegar to taste. Then stir in the cucumbers. Leave to sit at room temperature for 30 minutes before refrigerating. Serve well chilled.

Serves 4 to 6; more as a *zakuska*.

Variation: Add freshly grated horseradish to the soured cream mixture before stirring in the cucumbers. Use 1 to 2 tablespoons of the peeled root, to taste.

Beetroot Salad Svekol'nyi salat

A delectable salad, good on the *zakuska* table or as a complement to roasted meat.

1 lb (450 g) beetroot	2 oz (60 g) chopped moist
3 large cloves garlic	prunes (or more, to taste)
4 tablespoons mayonnaise	salt
1 oz (30 g) chopped walnuts (or	
more, to taste)	

Scrub the beetroot and remove the green tops. Place the whole beetroot in a baking dish and bake at 190°C/375°F/Gas 5 for 1 to 1½ hours, until soft. When cool enough to handle, slip off the skins and shred the beetroot coarsely.

Finely mince the garlic and add to the beetroot along with the chopped nuts and prunes. Stir in the mayonnaise and mix well. Season to taste.

Serves 6.

Carrot Salad Salat 'Zdorov'ye'

This combination of carrots, garlic and mayonnaise is known as 'Health Salad' in the Soviet Union, for Russians believe that carrots thicken the blood – an asset in their harsh northern climate. This is a nice change from the usual sweet carrot salad with fruit.

½ lb (225 g) carrots, scraped	3 tablespoons mayonnaise
1 teaspoon freshly squeezed	salt to taste
lemon juice	parsley
4 cloves garlic	

Grate the carrots. Pour the lemon juice over them, mixing well. Mince the garlic finely and add it to the carrots. Stir in the mayonnaise and salt to taste. Chill several hours before serving, garnished with parsley.

Serves 4.

Radishes in Soured Cream Rediska v smetane

The radish is all too often relegated to the salad bowl. For a change, try preparing it as the Russians sometimes do, blanched and then mixed with soured cream and spring onions.

1 lb (450 g) red radishes	1 tablespoon soured cream
¾ pint (450 ml) boiling water	2 tablespoons chopped spring
salt	onion

Wash and trim the radishes. Bring the water to the boil with salt and cook the radishes in it for about 4 minutes, until tender but still firm. Drain. Stir in the soured cream, spring onion, and salt to taste, mixing well. Serve immediately.

Serves 4.

Celeriac Salad Vinagret iz sel'dereinogo kornya

This salad is cousin to the more familiar potato salad.

1 celeriac (about 1¼ lb/570 g)	4 tablespoons white
6 black peppercorns	wine vinegar
1 small onion, quartered	1 teaspoon hot mustard
2 chicken bouillon cubes	1 tablespoon minced parsley
1 bay leaf	salt, freshly ground black
4 tablespoons olive oil	pepper to taste

Trim the ends of the celeriac and peel it. Boil it until tender in salted water to which the peppercorns, onion quarters, bouillon cubes and bay leaf have been added. This will take about 45 minutes.

Drain the celeriac and cut it into cubes. While still hot, pour over it a dressing made from the remaining ingredients which have been well blended. Let the salad sit at room temperature for 1 hour, and then chill. Serve cold.

Serves 4.

Baked Apples Pechonye yabloki

Russians are known to wax poetic at the mere mention of apples, of which they have many indigenous varieties. By consensus the favourite is the *antonovka*, a winter apple and the theme of the Nobel Prize winner Ivan Bunin's story, *Antonov Apples*. His narrative opens on a hot September day when the air is heavy with the fragrance of Antonov apples ripening for the harvest. Throughout the story this particular autumnal smell evokes memories of bygone days on the estates of the Russian landed gentry, when the country houses were imbued with the smell of Antonov apples, a smell greeting the visitor as soon as he crossed the threshold. Those who knew and loved the country life maintained that 'if the apples are good, the year will be, too'. Here are two simple recipes for baked apples, both catering to the Russian sweet tooth.

Baked Apples with Jam Pechonye yabloki s varen'em

Bramley apples   butter
seedless raspberry jam

Use one apple per person.

Preheat the oven to 190°C/375°F/Gas 5. Peel each apple 1 in (2.5 cm) down the sides. Remove the core, leaving a generous hollow, to within ½ in (12 mm) of the bottom, being careful not to pierce the bottom of the apple.

Fill each cavity with seedless raspberry jam. Dot the top of each apple with butter.

Place the apples in a baking dish. Pour in 1 in (2.5 cm) of boiling water. Cover with foil. Bake for 30 minutes, or until tender but still intact.

Serve warm with sweet cream.

Souffléed Baked Apples Yabloki so smetanoi

2 lb (900 g) tart apples, peeled,   ½ pint (300 ml) soured cream
    cored and sliced   4 eggs, separated
¾ pint (450 ml) cold water   ¼ teaspoon almond essence
2 tablespoons lemon juice   ¼ teaspoon ground cardamom
6 oz (170 g) seedless raspberry   1 tablespoon flour
    jam   5 oz (150 g) sugar

In a saucepan mix together the water and lemon juice. As each apple is peeled, cored and sliced, drop it into the water. Then bring the water to the boil and simmer the apples for 3 to 5 minutes, until tender. Drain.

Preheat the oven to 170°C/325°F/Gas 3. Grease a 9 in (22.5 cm) × 13 in (32.5 cm) glass baking dish. Mix together the poached apples and the jam, coating each slice. Spread the apples in an even layer in the dish.

In a small bowl combine the soured cream, egg yolks and flavourings. Stir in the flour and 4 oz (120 g) sugar.

Beat the egg whites until stiff but not dry and gently fold them into the soured cream mixture. Spread over the apples. Sprinkle the top with 1 oz (30 g) sugar. Bake the apples for about 30 minutes, or until puffed and golden. Let the dessert sit 10 minutes before serving so that it can be cut easily into squares.

Serves 4 to 6.

Apple Fritters Olad'i

These apple fritters are made by the old Russian sponge method,
yielding light and puffy pancakes suitable for brunch or dessert.

1½ teaspoons active dry yeast	1 oz (30 g) butter, softened
8 fluid oz (225 ml) milk	3 apples, peeled, cored and
3 oz (85 g) sugar	chopped
pinch of salt	2 tablespoons rum
8 oz (225 g) flour	vegetable oil for frying
2 eggs, separated	

Dissolve the yeast in 2 tablespoons of the milk, then stir in the
remaining milk, 1 oz (30 g) sugar, salt and 4 oz (120 g) flour. This is
the sponge. Cover it and leave to rise in a warm place for 1 hour.

Stir in the egg yolks, butter and remaining flour. Cover and leave
to rise for 1½ hours.

Meanwhile, mix the apples with the remaining sugar and the
rum. Leave to stand for 1 hour. When the batter has risen, stir in the
apple mixture, including the liquid from the apples and rum.

Beat the egg whites until stiff but not dry and fold them into the
batter.

Heat the vegetable oil in a large frying pan. It should be 1 in
(2.5 cm) deep in the pan. Drop the batter by tablespoonsful into the
hot oil and cook over medium high heat until puffed and brown,
turning once. They take only about 4 minutes to cook.

Dust with icing sugar and serve immediately.

Makes 18 to 24 fritters.

Russian Fruit Pudding Kisel'

Kisel' is the traditional Russian fruit pudding. Its name is derived
from the word *kislyi* or 'sour', since the pudding has a delightfully
tart taste. *Kisel'* is also one of the oldest Russian foods. As early as the
tenth century Slavic tribes were making primitive puddings, but
these precursors of *kisel'* were made from grains instead of fruit.

Controversy rages as to the perfect consistency for *kisel'*. It can be
as thin as soup or as thick as moulded jelly. I think the best
consistency is somewhere in between: a slightly thickened pudding
that can still be poured, as in the recipes below.

Strawberry Kisel'

¾ pint (450 ml) fresh	1 tablespoon freshly
strawberries	squeezed lemon juice
8 fluid oz (225 ml) water	drop of almond essence
4 oz (120 g) caster sugar	
2 teaspoons potato flour	

In a heavy saucepan simmer the strawberries, uncovered, with the water for 15 minutes. Put through a vegetable mill, then stir in the sugar and the potato flour which has been dissolved in the lemon juice.

Rinse out the saucepan and return the purée to it. Cook for just 2 to 3 minutes, until thickened. Stir in the almond essence, then pour into a bowl and leave to chill in the refrigerator. Serve well chilled in a deep glass bowl with fresh cream.

Serves 4 to 6.

Blueberry Kisel'

Substitute ¾ pint (450 ml) fresh blueberries for the strawberries Proceed as above.

Cranberry Kisel'

½ lb (225 g) cranberries	1 tablespoon freshly squeezed
6 oz (170 g) sugar	orange juice
8 fluid oz (225 ml) water	
2 teaspoons potato flour	

Proceed as in the recipe for strawberry *kisel'*, substituting the cranberries and using 6 oz (170 g) sugar. After the cranberries have been put through the vegetable mill, force the purée through a fine sieve to remove all seeds. Then continue as directed above.

Serves 4 to 6.

Note: If a *kisel'* thick enough to mould is desired, substitute 1 tablespoon potato flour for the 2 teaspoons called for in the recipes.

Russian Cheese Pancakes Syrniki

The name *syrniki* derives from the Russian word *syr* or 'cheese'. Although these cheese pancakes are standard fare in mediocre Soviet cafeterias, they can be quite delicious, providing a pleasant diversion from the usual griddle cakes for a Sunday-morning brunch or a late-evening supper.

2 lb (900 g) *tvorog* (see p. 171) or curd cheese	3 oz (85 g) flour
2 egg yolks	butter for frying
1 whole egg	soured cream
¼ teaspoon salt	sugar (optional)
1 tablespoon sugar	

If the *tvorog* is wet, press and drain until it loses all excess moisture. Then mix in the remaining ingredients, blending well. Form the cheese mass into 2 sausage-shaped rolls. Chill them for 30 minutes (or up to a couple of days).

When ready to serve the pancakes, cut the rolls into 1 in (2.5 cm) thick rounds, gently shaping the cheese mass into nice patties with your hands. Fry them in plenty of butter over medium high heat until browned, turning once. Serve hot with soured cream and, if desired, sugar.

Serves 4 to 6.

Variations:
1. To make *tvorozhniki* or sweetened *syrniki*, to the basic recipe above add the grated rind of ½ lemon and 1 teaspoon vanilla essence; use 4 tablespoons sugar instead of 1 tablespoon. Proceed as directed above.
2. To make *lenivye vareniki* or 'lazy' dumplings, shape the chilled cheese mixture into walnut-sized balls. Bring a large pan of salted water to the boil, and gently boil the cheese balls until they rise to the surface, about 3 minutes. Serve with plenty of melted butter and soured cream.

Russian Cottage Pudding Drochona

Drochona, one of the oldest Russian foods, is a simple batter pudding often spiked with grated potatoes, fruits, caviar. But even in its plain state, *drochona* is still satisfying: its name stems from the archaic verb *drochit'*, to pamper or coddle.

2 oz (60 g) unsalted butter	4 oz (120 g) cranberries,
2 oz (60 g) sugar	chopped
4 eggs	
4 oz (120 g) plain flour	jam
pinch of salt	double or single cream
4 tablespoons milk	

Cream the butter and the sugar. Add the eggs one at a time, beating well after each addition. Gradually add the flour, then stir in the salt and the milk. Beat on the high speed of an electric mixer for 5 minutes, or by hand until the mixture is light and frothy. Then stir in the cranberries.

Preheat the oven to 180°C/350°F/Gas 4. Grease an 8 in (22.5 cm) deep-dish pie tin well, then dust it with flour. Pour the batter into the prepared tin, and bake the pudding for 40 minutes, until lightly browned.

Serve warm with jam and cream.

Serves 4.

Egg Toddy Gogol'-mogol'

The word *gogol'-mogol'* sounds as funny in Russian as it does in English. It is a whimsical name thought up to entice children to drink this nourishing, egg-rich custard as fortification against colds and other ailments – but many children need no enticement at all. This recipe has been handed down through my mother's family under the name of 'guggle-muggle', an even stranger appellation.

4 egg yolks	2 tablespoons rum
2 oz (60 g) soft brown sugar	nutmeg
4 tablespoons hot milk	

Beat the egg yolks until light. Gradually add the sugar and continue beating until the mixture is fluffy. Slowly stir in the hot milk and the rum. Continue beating for 5 minutes more, then pour into glasses and serve. If desired, grate a little fresh nutmeg on the top.

Serves 2.

From the Pantry

The Russian pantry of old was a wonderland of sights and smells. In the cool air the pungent odour of smoked meats and pickled vegetables blended with the nutty scent of milled grains and the sweet fragrance of dried apricots and apples and pears. Shimmering jars of fruit preserves and brandies reflected all manner of conserves displayed on shelves along the facing wall. In a rear corner stood large oaken tubs brimming with *mochonye yabloki*, apples soaked in brine, and sauerkraut, put up with caraway and other spices. Deep vats held cucumbers and mushrooms in various guises: salted heavily or lightly; pickled in vinegar; marinated in aromatic oils. Wild field mushrooms were strung on ropes and hung to dry in orderly profusion, accompanied by garlands of dried cherries and plums and other summer fruits. Coarse, heavy sacks of salt and wheat flour were in easy access by the door, as were sparkling cones of crystal sugar. There were bins of buckwheat groats for *kasha* and hulled wheat for *kut'ya*; bins of buckwheat flour for *blini* and rye meal for black bread. Bags of dried beans clustered in one section of the room. Butter was stored in a glazed tub in the 'dairy corner', along with a variety of home-made cheeses, both hard and soft. The curd cheese, *tvorog*, was hung in muslin bags to solidify over drip pans. Whole sides of ham and home-cured bacon were suspended from the rafters, as were sausages in fanciful shapes – links, rounds and tubes. Ropes of garlic and onions dangled in the air. Sometimes whole salted watermelons were piled high on the floor. Root vegetables such as turnips and horseradish lay buried in sand in a long, low box to remain fresh throughout the winter. A special area was set aside for preparations of fish, especially of sturgeon: *balyk*, the cured fillet; and *vesiga*, the gelatinous backbone, necessary for the perfect *kulebyaka*. Sturdy wooden shelves lined the room, providing great appeal. Row upon row of fruit preserves, jams and jellies greeted the eye, each jar beckoning, promising delight. There were strawberries from the field and from the garden, simmered over a slow fire to rich thickness or suspended in brandy. Golden peaches floated in their own syrup or in a compote with other fruits. Bright tomatoes and peppers kept each other company in jars of *baklazhannaya ikra*. There were sweet, viscous syrups to use in baking and fruit drinks; home-made brandies and liqueurs glistening garnet and amber; vinegars and mustards steeped with wild herbs. This well-stocked larder was integral to every household in the days when a party of twenty or more might unexpectedly drop in for a refreshing meal. From such bounteous stores a delectable meal could easily be prepared.

The stores were replenished yearly with the fruit of the harvest, a harvest imbued with ritual and folk belief. In common parlance, for instance, 4 August was known as *Avdot'i-malinovki* or *Yevdokii-ogurechnitsy*, plays on the peasant girls' names Avdot'ya and Yevdo-kiya, to signify the day the raspberries (*malina*) and cucumbers (*ogurets*) would ripen. Other days bore quaint names as well.

Once the fruits and vegetables were harvested, each household set itself to the arduous task of gathering, sorting and preserving the newly-picked produce. If their own harvest was lean, the land-owners flocked to the district *yarmarka* or fair, where they found tradesmen, merchants and peasants, and where goods could be bought, traded or sold. The country *yarmarka* was a festive event. The roads for miles around were jammed with all sorts of conveyances transporting people and their wares to the fair: rickety wooden carts piled high with produce and pulled by lethargic, withered nags; hand-wagons dragged by peasants in gaily-coloured shirts and skirts; sturdy carriages peopled with the well-to-do. Masses of vill-agers made their way to the fair on foot, carrying baskets of birch bark or bast filled to overflowing with the berries and mushrooms they had gathered with the early morning dew. The more enterpris-ing among them made the rougher journey to city centres such as Moscow or Kiev, where their fresh country produce commanded high prices among urbanites eager for fruits and vegetables to put up for the winter. At the *yarmarka* the din of clattering cart wheels was rivalled only by the squawking of chickens and the honking of geese and the comical songs of hawkers peddling their goods. Mounds of orchard fruits sparkled in the midday sun; the sweet heavy scent of honey in combs and in jars pervaded the air, as did the buzzing of the bees hovering over the honey; barrels of tiny, knobby cucumbers stood awaiting the pickling brine; boxes upon boxes of root vegetables begged not to be overlooked. And what apples there were! Russia had long been famed for the succulence and variety of its apples. In the late nineteenth century over three hundred varieties of apples were exported to the United States alone. Tales of record harvests circulated from season to season, and there was hardly a landowner who did not boast of apples the size of a dinner plate or watermelons as big as a beer barrel.

At the summer's end each household was caught up in frenetic activity – carting, chopping, stoking, stirring – all in order to ensure a plentiful and tasty winter season. Other chores and duties were temporarily suspended as the frantic pace gathered momentum: the produce had to be processed as soon as possible to taste its best, and the more that was processed, the better. Most of the activity took place out of doors. A large fire was built under the heavy copper pans hung from tripods, used for making jam. Another fire burned almost continually under odd-looking retorts which distilled vodka and fruit brandies. For several weeks the yard had the appearance of a mad alchemist's laboratory. But the transformation of raw fruits into jams, confections and syrups and of vegetables into preserves was carried out in an orderly way. In a well-run household nothing was allowed to go to waste. (Even the strong brine from pickles was – and is – commonly used as a cure for morning hangover, second in effect only to another swig of vodka.) Fruits were washed, but not peeled, to retain as many vitamins as possible. Not all fruits were stoned, but any available stones were used to flavour vodka. Mushroom scraps were cooked into mushroom caviar. Odd bits of vegetables were turned into summer soups. One must assume that most households were reasonable in their thriftiness. But in the case of the Golovlev family in Saltykov-Shchedrin's novel, *The Golovlevs*, thriftiness turned into miserliness. The family matriarch, Arina Petrovna, had endless storerooms at her disposal, and each year she made her servants put up far more preserves than the family could eat. Naturally, after standing untouched for several seasons, some of the food began to spoil, but still Arina Petrovna could not bear to waste a thing:

. . . With renewed zeal Arina Petrovna turned to her interrupted house-hold duties. The summer preserving was drawing to a close. As the clatter of cooks' knives in the kitchen died down, activity in the office, barns, pantries and cellars redoubled. The preserving, salting, and stocking up were in full swing. Stores for the winter were gathered from all over; from all of Arina Petrovna's family estates dried mushrooms, berries, eggs, vegetables and the like were brought in by the cartload. All of these were measured, processed, and added to the stores from previous years. It wasn't for naught that a whole series of cellars, pantries and barns had been built for Arina Petrovna, the lady of the estate; they all were filled to bursting and in spite of the servants' frequent pilferings, contained quite a lot of spoiled material, which one didn't dare approach because of the rotten smell. Spoiled and unspoiled were separated at the end of the summer. Whatever seemed unreliable was given to the servants.

'These pickles are still good, they're just a little slimy on top, and they smell a bit off. I'm sure the servants will enjoy them,' said Arina Petrovna as she ordered this or that tub left untouched, whether for her own use or to go rotten later on.

This passage is not intended to discourage the would-be preser-ver. The Golovlevs are the comical exception, and as a rule the pantries on most estates were orderly, the quantities realistic. Summer preserving was anticipated by all as a time of pleasure as well as of work. Away from the heat of the fires in the yard, massive wooden tables were set up in the shade of leafy poplar and lime trees. Here the cleaning and sorting and chopping of the produce took place. The servants shredded endless heads of cabbage for sauerkraut and snapped bushels of beans. They chopped small marrows and aubergines for 'poor man's caviar', picked sunflower seeds from the flower's dried head. Berries were sorted, fruits washed, mushrooms strung up to dry. If rain threatened, the tables were moved inside into the summer kitchen, a pleasant, well-scrubbed structure separate from the main house. (During the summer all of the cooking was carried on in this kitchen so as not to overheat the living areas.)

The interest in preserving was shared by servant and mistress alike. Many of the gentry prided themselves not only on their excellent produce, but on the special recipes and methods they applied. In *Anna Karenina*, the ladies make sure to supervise the cook's jam-making, lest she not conform to their new method of boiling the fruit without any water at all.

The ladies gathered on the terrace. Generally they liked to sit on the terrace after dinner, but today they had work to do there as well. Besides sewing baby shirts and swaddling wraps, tasks which occupied all of them, they were supervising the preparation of jam, which was being made by a method new to Agafia Mikhailovna, without the addition of water. It was Kitty who had introduced this method; she used it at home. The jam-making had earlier been entrusted entirely to Agafia Mikhailovna, who firmly believed that nothing done at the Levins' could be bad. But nevertheless she had added water to both the wild and the cultivated strawberries, because that was the way she'd always made jam. When she'd been caught in the act, she insisted that it was impossible to do otherwise; so now the raspberry jam was being made in the presence of everyone. Agafia Mikhailovna was to be taught that jam could turn out very well even without the addition of water.

Agafia Mikhailovna, looking flushed and distressed, with her hair tangled and her thin arms bared to the elbows, was gently shaking the pot in a circular motion over the fire, staring gloomily at the raspberries, hoping with all her heart that they would clump and not set well. The Princess, sensing that Agafia Mikhailovna's anger must be directed chiefly at her, as the one responsible for the raspberry jam-making, tried to act as though she were busy with other things and not at all interested in the jam; she talked only about extraneous issues, all the while glancing at the fire from out of the corner of her eye . . .

'Isn't it time to skim it now, dear?' asked the Princess, turning to Agafia Mikhailovna. 'You needn't do it, Kitty, it's too hot for you,' she added.

'I'll do it,' said Dolly. Getting up, she began carefully to skim the surface of the frothing sugar with her spoon; in order to release the jam clinging to it, she tapped the spoon from time to time against a plate already covered with yellowish-red foam and blood-red syrup. 'How they'll lick this up at teatime!' she said, thinking of her children and remembering herself as a child, how amazed she'd been that the grownups didn't like the best part of all – the skimmings from the jam.

'I think it's done now,' said Dolly, testing the syrup by dropping it from the spoon.

'When it starts to set as it drops it will be done,' said the Princess. 'You can cook it a little longer, Agafia Mikhailovna.'

Jam-making was of particular importance because a well-laid tea table offered several varieties of jam, each shimmering translucently against the stark white backdrop of a linen tablecloth. In Ivan Bunin's tale *Sukhodol*, so many different kinds of jam are offered at a fancy tea that it is impossible for the guests to taste them all at one go; they must repeatedly approach the table in order to sample the vast assortment.

In *Anna Karenina* the Princess again admonishes Agafia Mikhailovna, this time to pour the finished jam into jars and to cover them with paper moistened with a little rum to prevent the jam from growing mouldy. This practice is still followed in most Soviet homes, although today the moistening agent is more often vodka. Of jams, only the commercially-prepared are hermetically sealed. But vegetables and other highly perishable preserves must be sealed in glass jars, even at home. This is accomplished by a rather cumbersome capping process requiring both patience and strength, as no Kilner jars are available. The prepared foods are then hidden away in the most unlikely places – under tables and beds and chairs, in all available nooks and crannies – to be triumphantly pulled out and proffered to guests almost as soon as they walk through the door.

Even though the scale of entertaining has diminished since Tolstoy's time – now two jams are more likely to be served at tea than a dozen – the spirit has remained the same, and were it not for a lack of space and available produce, the larders of the modern Soviet family would be just as copious as they were in old Russia.

Basic Bouillon Bul'yon

Soup is a mainstay of the Russian cuisine, and the comforting smell of broth simmering on the back burner is encountered in virtually every Russian home. The recipe below is for a basic meat stock, to be served alone as a first course or used as the basis for other, more intricate concoctions. Beef stock, like fish stock, is a staple item in Russian cookery, one which should always be ready for unexpected guests.

2 lb (900 g) meat*	2 large onions, quartered
1½ pints (900 ml) cold water	2 bay leaves
12 black peppercorns	6 carrots, scraped
6 sprigs parsley	1 tablespoon salt

* If a beef broth is desired, use shin or chuck with some bone left in; for a chicken broth, use a boiling fowl, adding all of the giblets except the liver.

Place all of the ingredients, except the salt, in a large stockpot and bring to the boil, skimming any scum that rises to the surface. Reduce the heat to low and stir in the salt.

Simmer, covered, for 2 to 3 hours, until the meat is tender and the liquid has been reduced by half. Strain the broth. Cut the meat and the carrots into serving-sized pieces and divide among the soup bowls. Pour the broth over to serve.

Makes about ¾ pint (450 ml).

Note: If the stock is going to be frozen, do not return the meat and carrots to it after straining.

Basic Fish Stock Krepkii bul'yon iz ryby

This fish stock is sometimes served with tiny pies for the soup course, but more often than not it forms the base for Russia's famous fish soups. It's a good idea always to keep some on hand in the freezer.

2 lb (900 g) fish, including trimmings (at least one fish head is recommended for flavour)
1¼ pints (750 ml) cold water
8 fluid oz (225 ml) dry white wine
½ oz (15 g) butter
1 small onion, coarsely chopped
1 carrot, scraped and coarsely chopped
2 oz (60 g) mushroom trimmings
2 sprigs parsley
2 sprigs dill
1 bay leaf
6 white peppercorns
¾ teaspoon salt
1 tablespoon freshly squeezed lemon juice

Sauté the onion, carrot and mushroom trimmings in the butter.

Put the remaining ingredients in a large stockpot; add the sautéed vegetables. Bring to the boil, skimming off any foam that rises to the surface.

Cook partially covered over medium heat for 30 to 40 minutes. Strain through muslin.

Makes 1½ pints (900 ml).

Cranberry Juice Klyukvennyi mors

A refreshing cold drink which is also good mulled.

1 lb (450 g) cranberries	zest of half a lemon, in a long
1½ pints (900 ml) water	spiral
8 oz (225 g) sugar	
4 tablespoons freshly squeezed lemon juice	

Rinse the cranberries. Place them in a large saucepan with the water and bring to the boil. Boil for about 5 minutes, or until the skins have burst.

Meanwhile, line a colander with muslin. When the cranberries have burst, strain the juice through the colander, letting it drip into a bowl for a few minutes. Then gently press the berries to extract the remaining juice. If a very clear juice is desired, strain once again through clean muslin.

Return the juice to a clean saucepan and bring to the boil with the sugar. Simmer for just a minute or two, stirring to dissolve the sugar. Leave to cool.

When the juice has cooled, stir in the lemon juice and the lemon spiral. Chill and serve.

Makes about 1½ pints (900 ml).

Spiced Honey Drink Sbiten'

Sbiten' is an ancient Russian drink. I first tasted it in Azov, a sleepy town on the Don River delta. Azov was once a strategically important city guarding the entrance to Russia's waterways, the site of a great battle against the Turks in the eighteenth century. Stone ruins still stand overlooking the water, and a charming restaurant, 'The Fortress Ramparts', has been built on the promontory. The restaurant is decorated in the Old Russian style, with ornately carved shutters and long wooden benches. In keeping with its decor and the history of the town, 'The Fortress Ramparts' serves old Russian specialities, including this spicy, hot drink.

1½ pints (900 ml) water	2 cinnamon sticks
4 oz (120 g) sugar	½ teaspoon dried mint flakes
6 oz (170 g) honey	1 teaspoon grated lemon rind
6 whole cloves	nutmeg
8 whole cardamom pods, peeled	

Bring all the ingredients except the nutmeg to the boil in a large saucepan. Simmer, covered, for 15 minutes. Then cool to room temperature.

Once the *sbiten'* has cooled, strain it. Reheat to serve. Grate some fresh nutmeg into each cup.

Serves 4.

Sauerkraut Kvashenaya kapusta

Russian families once required whole cartloads of cabbage to accommodate their yearly sauerkraut-making. Although the process of shredding so many heads of cabbage was laborious, it ensured a constant supply of sauerkraut throughout the winter, to be eaten plain, mixed with other vegetables, or added to the inevitable *shchi*. The sauerkraut was put up in large oaken barrels whose scent permeated the fermenting cabbage. Black-currant or cherry leaves were often layered with the cabbage, further contributing to its final flavour. Unfortunately, neither oaken barrels nor black-currant leaves are as readily available as they once were, so now we must settle for a glazed crock and a slightly more prosaic sauerkraut. Still, it's good! Try adding spices such as caraway, bay leaves, cardamom or peppercorns to vary the flavour.

2 heads white cabbage, about 4 lb (1.8 kg) each	4 tablespoons coarse or pickling salt

The day before you plan to begin making sauerkraut, remove the cabbage to room temperature and let it sit for a day so that the leaves won't be brittle. When ready to make the sauerkraut, remove the outer leaves of the cabbage, then rinse it and cut each head into quarters. Remove the cores and shred the cabbage finely.

Place the shredded cabbage in a large bowl and add the salt, mixing to distribute it evenly. Leave to rest for about 15 minutes. Clean a 25 pint (15 litre) crock with soda and boiling water. Dry with a clean cloth.

Pack the salted cabbage firmly into it, pressing down on it with a wooden spoon. Brine will start to form almost immediately.

Place a clean cloth over the top of the cabbage. On top of the cloth place a plate which just fits inside the rim of the crock. Weight the plate down with a jar filled with water or another heavy weight. The brine should rise about 2 inches above the plate, thus keeping air from reaching the fermenting cabbage.

Leave the crock at room temperature (about 22°C/70°F). Bubbles will form, showing that fermentation is taking place. Each day, remove the cloth and any scum that has appeared on the surface. Rinse the cloth out and then replace it, and the plate and the weight.

If there seems to be a lack of brine at any time (i.e., less than 2 inches above the cabbage), add ½ pint (300 ml) water in which 2½ teaspoons of coarse salt have been dissolved.

The fermentation process will take from 2 to 6 weeks, depending on the room temperature. When the sauerkraut is done, bubbles will stop rising to the surface even though it is still fermenting. Taste the cabbage, and if it is soured enough to your taste, then it is ready and can be refrigerated. It will keep for a month in the refrigerator.

Makes 12¾ pints (7.5 litres).

Note: The right amount of salt is important. Too little salt results in a soft sauerkraut; too much salt prevents fermentation. Uneven distribution of salt may result in the growth of yeast with a pinkish colour.

The top layer of the kraut may turn brown from exposure to air as the cloth is changed, but this layer may be discarded when the kraut is ready to refrigerate and eat.

Sour Cabbage Kislaya kapusta

Sour cabbage differs from sauerkraut in that it sits only long enough to sour, not ferment, and so is easier to prepare. Sour cabbage salad is practically an institution in the Soviet Union, garnishing meals at both lunch and dinner. Here I must break the taboo against mentioning unappetising food in cookery books, for *kislaya kapusta*, as prepared in all too many Soviet cafeterias, can be truly dismal. At its best, the salad is tart and refreshing, but nothing more easily taints the palate than a soggy cabbage salad. One learns early on either to develop a taste for it (a wise idea, since other vegetables are few and far between) or successfully to avoid it. The recipe given here is guaranteed foolproof, however, and makes a salad to put any Soviet café to shame.

2 lb (900 g) white cabbage	2 small bay leaves
1 large carrot, scraped	¼ teaspoon caraway seed
1 large tart apple, peeled and cored	¼ teaspoon dill seed
1 tablespoon salt	thinly sliced onion
8 allspice berries	sugar
8 black peppercorns	vegetable oil

Shred the cabbage, carrot and apple very finely. (This is most easily done in a food processor.) Put the shredded vegetables in a large bowl and sprinkle them with the salt. Leave them to sit for 1 hour, and then squeeze the juice out through a strainer, reserving it. There should be about ¾ pint (450 ml) of expressed juice.

Place a quarter of the shredded vegetables in a 1½ pint (900 ml) jar. Top with half a bay leaf, 2 peppercorns, 2 allspice berries, and a quarter of the caraway and dill seeds. Cover with more shredded vegetables, and continue the process until there are 4 layers.

Pour the reserved juice over the layered cabbage; it should cover it.

Cover the mouth of the jar with muslin and leave it to stand at room temperature for 4 days. Then cover the jar and refrigerate until ready to serve.

To serve, cut a few thin slices of onion. Toss each portion of sour cabbage with some onion, a dash of sugar, and a few drops of vegetable oil.

Serves 8.

Dill Pickles Solyonye ogurtsy

The pickled cucumber is a recurrent character in the cast of Russian foods. These sour pickles are so widespread that the hero Chichikov in Gogol's *Dead Souls* is only mildly surprised to find his hostess's hand reeking of the brine when she proffers it to him in greeting. Actually, the brine is put to as good use as the pickles: for some, it is a sure cure for hangovers; for others, it has a cosmetic effect. I once asked my grandmother, then seventy-two years old, how she kept her skin so wrinkle-free. The secret, she explained, was a daily dose of the fermented brine from the pickle barrel, rubbed into her skin. This treatment explained the unusual smell I'd always associated with my grandmother, but the astringent quality of the brine did seem to work wonders.

Although the cosmetic benefits of these pickles may not be for everyone, I can certainly recommend their gustatory delights. They are tart and crisp, as good as any you'll find at a delicatessen. Just be sure to scrub your hands well after dipping into the barrel, lest you begin to resemble Chichikov's illustrious hostess.

8 lb (3.6 kg) unwaxed pickling cucumbers (preferably small ones)	3 teaspoons coriander seed
	2 teaspoons mustard seed
	8 bay leaves
2 heads of garlic, peeled, the cloves halved (about 18 cloves)	2 fistfuls fresh dill with seeds (about 40 sprigs)
	thick chunk of rye bread (without preservatives)
3 teaspoons whole black peppercorns	1 lb (450 g) pickling salt
2 teaspoons crushed dried hot pepper (or 10 small hot red peppers)	9½ pints (5.5 litres) water

Wash thoroughly a 13 pint (7 litre) crock or barrel. Wash the cucumbers, making sure that none of them have brown spots or bruises. Place half of the dill on the bottom of the crock. Stand the cucumbers on end in the crock as tightly as they will fit, in a single layer.

Dissolve the pickling salt in the water and pour half of it over the cucumbers. Add half of the garlic, peppercorns, hot pepper, coriander seed, mustard seed and bay leaves.

Pack the remaining cucumbers into the crock, standing them on end. Add the rest of the salt water, spices and dill. Place the chunk of rye bread on top. The salt water should completely cover the pickles. Run the blade of a knife down into the crock a few times to make sure there are no pockets of air. If the salt water does not cover the cucumbers, add a little more in the same proportions.

Place a saucer over the pickles, laying it right in the brine, and place a heavy weight on top of the saucer. Then cover the crock loosely with a cloth. Once again, make sure the cucumbers are completely immersed in the brine.

Keep the crock at room temperature, about 22°C/70°F. Every day remove any scum that has formed on top of the brine, each time washing out the cloth, then replacing the saucer, weight and cloth.

Half-sour *(malosol'nye)* pickles will be ready in 3 to 4 days. For fully soured pickles, wait 8 to 9 days. When the pickles are as sour as you like, pack them into jars along with the brine and spices, and refrigerate. They will keep for a couple of months.

Salted Mushrooms Solyonye griby

This excellent method of preserving mushrooms makes even the mildest cultivated mushrooms come alive. For an even more sensational taste, try salting wild forest or field mushrooms.

1 lb (450 g) mushrooms	black peppercorns
2 tablespoons salt	fresh dill
¼ pint (150 ml) hot water	whole cloves
bay leaves	

Take firm, unblemished mushrooms. Rinse them lightly. Place a layer of mushrooms, stems up, in a 3 pint (2 litre) crock. Sprinkle them with salt and desired seasonings. Continue layering the mushrooms (always stems up) with the salt and the seasonings, until the crock is full.

Pour the hot water over all, shaking the jar gently to dissolve the salt. Weight the top layer of mushrooms down with a plate on which something heavy has been placed. Close the jar tightly. Place in a cool, dark place.

After a few days check to see that the mushrooms are immersed in the liquid. If not, add a little more water and salt.

The mushrooms will be ready after 1 month.

Dried Mushrooms Sushonye griby

The best dried mushrooms are those that have been freshly gathered from the woods and fields. To dry them, simply wipe them off with a damp cloth to remove all traces of dirt; do not wash. Remove the stems and, if desired, peel the caps. If the weather is sunny, spread the mushrooms on brown paper and leave them to dry in the sunshine for 2 or 3 days, taking them in at night as soon as it begins to grow damp. The mushrooms should be covered with fine muslin to protect them from insects, and should be occasionally turned. Once they are dry, thread them on twine and hang them in the sun or in a well-ventilated room until they have dried out completely, at which time they may be transferred to jars and stored airtight.

If the weather is not sunny, the mushrooms may be spread on a screen and dried in a 60°C/140°F oven for several hours, until dry.

To reconstitute, soak the dried mushrooms in warm water to cover for at least 30 minutes, then drain and use as directed. The soaking liquid may be added to soups and stews.

Soused Apples Mochonye yabloki

Very Russian, with a taste like wine.

4 lb (1.8 kg) small tart apples	3 pints (1.7 litres) water
oak leaves (or black currant cherry)	4 oz (120 g) honey
	1 tablespoon pickling salt

Wash the apples and layer them with the oak leaves in a 3 pint (1.7 litre) crock.

Bring the water, honey and salt to the boil. Then cool to lukewarm. Pour the liquid over the apples. Place a weight on the top layer of apples to keep them immersed.

Place the crock in a large pan (the apples are likely to ferment very actively at first; the liquid that bubbles out of the crock can then be poured back in to cover the apples). Cover the crock but do not seal tightly.

Check the apples after a few days to make sure they are immersed in the liquid; if not, add more. Store in a cool, dark place for 1 month.

Pickled Aubergines Baklazhan marinovannyi

I first tasted these pickled aubergines in Rostov-on-the-Don. They were a gift from a cheerful old gentleman whose head I remember as being round, smooth and shiny as the aubergines he offered me, though perhaps I am confusing my impressions. This is an unusual pickle which looks lovely when served, as the carrot retains its bright orange colour.

2 aubergines, about 1 lb (450 g) each	4 bay leaves
vegetable oil	3 cloves garlic, slightly crushed
3 large carrots, scraped and grated	16 black peppercorns
6 large cloves garlic, grated	10 allspice berries
1 long stalk of celery	¼ teaspoon mustard seed
1½ pints (900 ml) white wine vinegar (herb-flavoured is nice)	½ teaspoon crushed hot red pepper
	½ teaspoon pickling salt
	¼ pint (150 ml) olive oil

Rinse the aubergines and cut them in half lengthwise. Place them in a baking dish, skin side up. Rub the skins with vegetable oil. Pour 1 in (2.5 cm) of water into the bottom of the pan and then bake the aubergines at 180°C/350°F/Gas 4 for 20 minutes. Set aside to cool.

Meanwhile, grate the carrots and the garlic together.

Bring the vinegar to the boil with the spices. Boil, covered, for 10 minutes. Cool, then stir in the olive oil.

When the aubergines have cooled, scrape out some of the insides, leaving a thick shell of at least 1 in (2.5 cm) on both the bottom and the sides. Stuff each aubergine half with the mixture of grated carrot and garlic.

Cut the celery into 6 very thin strips. Carefully reassemble the aubergines, taking care not to lose any filling. Tie each aubergine with 3 strips of celery, securing them with toothpicks, if necessary.

Turn a scalded 3 pint (1.7 litre) container on its side and slip the aubergines into it, side by side. Turn the container upright and pour the cooled vinegar mixture over the aubergines. Seal.

Leave the aubergines to ripen in a cool, dark place for 3 weeks before eating. Chill well before serving, cut into crosswise slices.

Spiced Pickled Cherries Vishnya marinovannaya

When Peter the Great returned from Holland intent upon westernising his nation, he introduced many innovations, one of which was the practice of serving pickled fruits with meat. Although not all of Peter's measures met with equal delight among the populace, luckily for culinary posterity the Russians took readily to the idea of eating pickled fruits. These cherries provide a lively accompaniment to roast meat or chicken.

2 lb (900 g) sweet cherries	¼ teaspoon mace
1½ pints (900 ml) cider vinegar	½ stick cinnamon
12 oz (340 g) sugar	4 allspice, berries
½ pint (300 ml) water	4 whole cardamom pods,
4 tablespoons kirsch (clear	peeled
cherry brandy)	

Wash the cherries and remove the stems, but do not stone them. Place them in a crock and cover them with the vinegar. Leave them to stand overnight, then drain them, pouring the vinegar into a saucepan.

Boil the vinegar up with the sugar, water, mace, cinnamon, allspice and cardamom. Simmer for 15 minutes. Cool, then stir in the kirsch. Pour the pickling liquid over the cherries and let stand for 3 days.

After 3 days, drain the cherries and boil up the liquid once again. Allow it to cool and then pack the cherries into sterilised preserving jars. Pour the pickling liquid over them and seal the jars. Let sit 1 month before using.

Makes about 3 pints (1.7 litres).

Black-currant Conserve Chornaya smorodina s sakharom

The high vitamin C content of black-currants contributes to their popularity in the citrus-starved Soviet Union, where they are often stirred with sugar and aged for several weeks. I was offered this conserve in homes from Leningrad to Alma-Ata. It is usually prepared in batches large enough to last throughout the winter, and since its sugar content is so high, it needs no refrigeration. Serve this conserve with roast meat for dinner, or in a small jam dish with tea.

    black-currants   sugar

The proportions to use are 1 part black-currants to 2 parts sugar (or less, to taste).

Pick the black-currants over, discarding any damaged ones. Wash them, and then grind them coarsely together with the sugar in a food processor or mincer. Pack into jars and leave for at least 1 month before eating.

Variation: In one variation I tasted, the black-currants are left whole. They are mixed with sugar and then left for at least 3 months before serving, so that the sugar can penetrate them completely.

Kiev Raspberry Jam Malinovoye varen'ye v kievskom manere

As propounded by the Princess in *Anna Karenina*.

    1 lb (450 g) fresh raspberries   1½ lb (700 g) sugar
    1 tablespoon cognac

Place half of the raspberries in a shallow pan. Sprinkle with a little cognac and half of the sugar. Top with the remaining berries and the rest of the cognac and sugar. Refrigerate overnight. The berries should give off quite a bit of juice.

The next day, bring the berries along with their juice to the boil over high heat, then remove the pan from the heat and let it sit for 15 minutes. Bring to the boil again, remove from the heat, and let the berries sit for 15 minutes more. Then bring to the boil for the third time and cook the berries over low heat, skimming any scum that rises to the surface. Cook gently, shaking the pan lightly from time to time, for about 20 minutes, or until the berries are translucent and the syrup thickens.

Leave to cool slightly before pouring into jars so that the berries won't rise to the top. Cover the jars with waxed paper soaked in rum and tie with a cord to fasten; or seal the jars.

Makes 1 pint (600 ml).

Apricot Jam Abrikosovoye varen'ye

A golden jam with bits of whole fruit suspended in it.

1 lb (450 g) fresh apricots	8 fluid oz (225 ml) blanching water
lemon juice	1 tablespoon vodka
1 lb (450 g) sugar	

Blanch the fruits in boiling water to loosen their skins, then peel them. Cut them in half and remove the stones. Place 1 dozen of the stones in a muslin bag and tie it with string. Drop the apricots into cold water acidulated with lemon juice.

In a saucepan bring the sugar and 8 fluid oz (225 ml) of the blanching water to the boil. Boil for a few minutes to make a light syrup. Cool the syrup slightly, then add the halved apricots and the bag of kernels. Bring to the boil over high heat, then remove the pan from the heat and leave it to stand for 15 minutes.

Bring the mixture to a rolling boil again, then once more remove the pan from the heat and leave to stand for 15 minutes.

Bring to the boil for the third time, then pour the mixture into a shallow ceramic or earthenware bowl. Cover the syrupy fruit and leave to stand overnight.

The next day, strain the mixture, catching the liquid in a saucepan. Bring the syrup to the boil, then pour it hot over the fruit, which has been returned to the ceramic bowl. Cover and leave to stand overnight.

The third day, repeat the procedure, straining the fruit and bringing the syrup to the boil. Pour the syrup hot over the fruit once again.

On the fourth day, remove the bag with the kernels. Then bring the entire mixture – both syrup and fruit – to the boil over high heat. Reduce the heat and cook slowly until the fruit is transparent and the syrup has thickened, about 30 minutes.

Remove from the heat; stir in the vodka. Leave the jam to cool slightly until a thin skin forms on the surface, then stir for a few minutes (this prevents the fruit from floating to the top of the jars). Pour into jars and seal.

Makes 1 pint (600 ml) jam.

Rose Petal Jam Varen'ye iz rozovogo tsveta

Making this jam is almost as enjoyable as eating it: the simmering petals fill the air with their fragrance.

8 oz (225 g) rose petals	12 oz (340 g) sugar
2 lemons	¾ pint (450 ml) water

Early in the morning pick fresh, sweet-smelling pink or red roses. Trim the white base of the petals and discard it. Rinse the petals, then drain.

Slice the lemons very thinly. Place them in a pan with the water. Cover and bring to the boil. Simmer for 15 minutes, then remove the lemon slices and discard them.

Bring the lemon water to the boil again and stir in the sugar until dissolved. Then add the rose petals and cook until the leaves are transparent and the liquid syrupy, about 10 minutes. Pour into jars and seal.

Makes two 6 oz (170 g) jars.

Russian Mustard Gorchitsa

Russian mustard is particularly pungent. The name comes from the verb *gorchit'*, 'to have a bitter taste'. The addition of sugar relieves the bitterness, but the piquancy of the mustard remains intact. Use it sparingly!

4 tablespoons powdered dry
    mustard (Coleman's is good)
2 teaspoons water
6 tablespoons boiling water
3 teaspoons freshly squeezed
    lemon juice

1 teaspoon vegetable oil
3 tablespoons sugar
pinch of salt

In a small bowl combine the mustard powder and the 2 teaspoons water to make a paste.

Slowly pour the 6 tablespoons boiling water over the paste and leave to sit for 15 minutes. Then pour the water off.

Stir in the remaining ingredients until the mustard is smooth. Store in the refrigerator.

Prepared Horseradish Khren

In Russian, an 'old geezer' is a *staryi khren* or 'old horseradish' – one who has been through a lot but has not lost his sharp bite. When properly refrigerated, this tangy horseradish will retain *its* bite for several weeks.

6 oz (170 g) piece of
    horseradish root (about half
    of a large root)

4 fluid oz (120 ml) white
    vinegar
½ teaspoon salt

Peel the horseradish root. Grate it coarsely by hand, then place it in the goblet of a liquidiser or food processor along with the vinegar and salt. Grate it very finely until a fairly smooth purée has been formed. Chill at least 2 hours before using.

Makes about 10 oz (280 g) prepared horseradish.

Variations:
1. Beetroot Horseradish: Boil one small beetroot until tender. Peel it

and grate it finely. Stir it into 10 oz (280 g) prepared horseradish. This horseradish has a lovely rose colour.

2. Apple Horseradish: Peel, core and finely grate one large apple. Stir it into 10 oz (280 g) prepared horseradish. This horseradish has a somewhat sweeter and milder taste.

Cranberry-Horseradish Relish Klyukva s khrenom

This relish is a good condiment to serve on the *zakuska* table with cold boiled beef, or if you are not planning a Russian-style meal, it tastes equally good with a pot roast. The Russians love foods which pique the palate – like cranberries with their sour tang and horseradish with its fiery nip.

1 lb (450 g) cranberries	home-made (see p. 170), or
8 oz (225 g) soft brown sugar	use bottled horseradish,
5 oz (150 g) prepared	drained)
horseradish (preferably	juice of 1 lemon

Chop the cranberries medium fine (this is most easily done when they are frozen). Stir in the remaining ingredients and mix well. Place the relish in the refrigerator and chill at least 2 days before serving.

Makes about 1 pint (600 ml).

Home-made Dairy Products Molochnye produkty

One of the triumphs of the Russian kitchen is its imaginative use of dairy products. Even though many of these can now be bought ready-made, they still taste better when prepared at home.

Curd Cheese Tvorog

Tvorog is the name for the dry curds from soured milk so indispensable to Russian baking. It forms the basis for many uniquely Russian dishes, from the glorious Easter *paskha* to the homely *syrniki* or cheese pancakes, but *tvorog* may also be enjoyed on its own, topped with soured cream and sugar as a sweet, or mixed with paprika and caraway seed for a savoury snack. *Tvorog* is not difficult to make at home, but if necessary, bought curd cheese may be substituted.

Method 1 (for the best home-made tvorog)

2 pints (1.2 litres)	2 pints (1.2 litres) double cream
unhomogenised milk	

Heat the milk and the cream together gently and when just warm pour into a glass bowl. Place the bowl in a warm spot (in winter, this could be on a radiator). Leave the mixture to stand, uncovered, for

24 hours,* until a watery liquid appears at the bottom of the bowl. Strain the milk through muslin.

Hang the curds in the muslin over a bowl in the refrigerator or in a cool room; leave to drip for a few more hours until the curds are dry. Transfer to a bowl and cover with plastic wrap.

Method 2 (a quicker and easier version)

1½ pints (900 ml) buttermilk

Place the buttermilk in its unopened carton in a deep pan and fill the pan with water. Bring to the boil and then boil gently for 30 minutes. Remove from the heat but leave the carton of buttermilk in the water. The next morning, open the carton and turn the contents out into a colander. The whey will quickly drain off and approximately ½ lb (225 g) *tvorog* will be left. Store in the refrigerator.

Home-made Soured Cream Smetana

Just as Russian *tvorog* is unique, so is Russian soured cream. The commercially-prepared product we usually buy bears only a superficial resemblance to it. The difference is in both texture and flavour. True *smetana* will not clump when added to hot soups such as *borshch*; nor will it ever overwhelm a dish. Although commercial soured cream may be substituted in most of the recipes in this book, when soured cream is called for as a garnish, try making your own. You will be pleasantly surprised.

1½ pints (900 ml) double cream   2 tablespoons buttermilk

Stir the buttermilk into the double cream. Leave to stand for 24 hours in a warm place. Then stir to blend, and refrigerate.

Home-made Kefir Kefir

Kefir is another well-loved dairy product which the Russians have enjoyed for centuries. For a refreshing drink, serve it ice-cold, plain or flavoured with fruit syrup.

¾ pint (450 ml) single cream   2 tablespoons buttermilk

Heat the single cream to lukewarm, then stir in the buttermilk. Leave to stand for 24 hours in a warm place, then refrigerate. Serve very cold, sweetened or plain.

Baked Milk Varenets

Varenets is as rich and sweet as condensed milk. The Russians consider it a special treat for coffee, and the skin that forms during baking is prized by connoisseurs. *Varenets* may be served either

* Do not let the milk sit out for more than 24 hours or it will take on a bitter taste.

warm from the oven or chilled. Its name comes from the Russian *varit'*, 'to cook', the same root that is found in *samovar*.

> 2 pints (1.2 litres) whole milk

Preheat the oven to 150°C/300°F/Gas 2. Pour the milk into a large, shallow earthenware baking dish. Bake for about 2 hours, or until the milk has turned a deeper colour, occasionally stirring the skin that forms back into the milk. Leave the final skin in place.
Makes 1 pint (600 ml).

Kvass Kvas

In Russia, commercially-brewed beer still has not presented a serious challenge to the well-loved home-made kvass, which ranks second only to vodka as a popular libation. (In a unique nineteenth-century religious sect, it outranked even vodka. The believers were known as *kvasniki*, since they eschewed all drinks except kvass.)

A typical street scene in any Soviet city, large or small, is a kvass lorry parked on a shady corner, surrounded by a crowd of people eager to quench their thirst. More often than not the queues are made up of male workers who seem to be idling away the working day, but sometimes women join the crowd, too, net bags in hand. A kvass lorry looks like the rear end of a petrol tanker. Its long cylindrical tank is usually painted bright yellow, with stencilled red letters proclaiming its contents – *KBAC* – to the passers-by. Even on grey, wintry days the tank shines like a beacon, offering good spirits to those who would imbibe – and there is never a shortage of customers. The lorry is often equipped with its own glasses (cursorily rinsed in cold water after each use), but true *aficionados* bring their own glasses – or jugs – to fill.

The root of the word *kvas* means 'to ferment', and the brew may be made from any number of fruits or vegetables. The most common type of kvass, and the kind sold on street corners, is made from fermented black bread. Special herbs are often added to enliven the brew, and it is said that the best kvass of all is made in Russian Orthodox monasteries, where the secret ingredient is ostensibly a dash of 'religious feeling'.

The recipes below are for three very different kinds of kvass. The first, made from cranberries, has a taste reminiscent of good, dry champagne and may be served as a refreshing summertime drink. The second, a black bread kvass, can also be drunk straight, but I prefer to use it as the base for cold Russian soups like *okroshka* and *botvin'ya*, as the taste for this strong home-made brew is an acquired one. The final recipe is for a beetroot kvass which is not meant to be drunk at all, but to add colour and taste to soups and stews such as *borshch* and *vereshchaka*.

Cranberry kvass Kvas klyukvennyi

1 lb (450 g) cranberries
2¾ pints (1.6 litres) boiling
    water
8 oz (225 g) sugar

½ teaspoon cream of tartar
1 tablespoon active dry yeast
6 raisins

Crush the berries with a potato masher or the back of a wooden spoon. Pour the boiling water over them and then cover the container and leave them to stand undisturbed for 12 hours.

Then strain the berries through muslin, but do not press down on the berries very much in order to extract more juice. To the clear liquid add the sugar, cream of tartar, and the yeast which has been dissolved in a little of the liquid. Stir well to mix. Cover the container, and leave to stand in a warm spot for 8 hours.

The next day, strain the liquid once more through muslin and pour into a large bottle or jar. Add 6 raisins to the bottle. Seal. Leave at room temperature for 8 hours, and then refrigerate until ready to drink.

Makes about 3 pints (1.7 litres).

Black Bread Kvass Kvas sukharnyi domashnii

1½ lb (700 g) stale black bread
1½ tablespoons dried mint
1 small lemon
4 pints (2.3 litres) boiling water

4 oz (120 g) sugar
1 teaspoon cream of tartar
1 tablespoon active dry yeast
8 grains of white rice

Cut the stale bread into cubes. Place them on a baking tray and toast them in a 170°C/325°F/Gas 3 oven for about 20 minutes, or until they are dry. Transfer to a large crock. Sprinkle the mint over the toasted cubes. Cut the lemon into chunks and add it to the bread. Pour the boiling water over all, and cover the crock tightly. Leave to stand for 5 to 6 hours.

Strain the liquid through muslin, pressing down on the bread with the back of a spoon in order to extract as much liquid as possible, but without pushing sediment through. To the strained liquid add the sugar, cream of tartar and the yeast which has been dissolved in a little of the liquid. Stir well to mix. Cover the container, and leave to stand undisturbed for 8 hours.

The next day, strain once more through muslin and pour into a bottle. Add the 8 grains of rice. Seal. Leave to stand for 8 hours more at room temperature. Then strain once more through muslin into a clean bottle and refrigerate until ready to use.

Makes 1½ pints (900 ml).

Beetroot Kvass Svekol'nyi kvas

    4 lb (1.8 kg) beetroot, tops   lukewarm water
      removed

Scrub the beetroot, then peel them and cut them into cubes. Place the cubes in a 6 pint (3.5 litre) crock. Bring water to the boil and leave it to cool to lukewarm. Pour enough water over the beetroot cubes to cover them. Cover the crock and leave the beetroot to stand undisturbed for several days.

After a few days lift the cover and check the liquid. Skim off any scum or mould that has formed. (The fermenting process is very active, so do not be alarmed to find that mould has grown on the liquid.) Repeat this process every 4 to 5 days.

The beetroot kvass will be ready in two weeks. It should give off a sour smell and be a deep red colour. Skim the top of the liquid until it is free of scum, and then strain the liquid through muslin into a clean jar. Store in the refrigerator, or, if desired, freeze.

Makes 3 pints (1.7 litres).

Note: A quicker, though less potent beetroot kvass may be made by *grating* the beetroot and then covering it with warm water. Cover the crock and keep it in a warm place. The kvass will be ready in 3 to 4 days.

Plum Cordial Slivovaya nastoika

In Russia, closely-guarded recipes for fruit liqueurs and brandies have been passed down from generation to generation, and even today Russians delight in regaling their guests with home-made *nalivki* and *nastoiki*. As sage a writer as Chekhov causes one of his characters to claim: 'I can tell you truthfully . . . that home-made brandy is better than any champagne. After the first glass, your sense of smell enlarges, envelops your whole being. It's a great illusion. It seems to you that you're no longer sitting at home in your easy chair, but are somewhere in Australia, astride the softest imaginable ostrich . . .' (*The Siren*). In other words, home-made brandy is potent stuff! This plum cordial is simple to prepare. The only hard part is waiting six weeks to enjoy it.

    2½ lb (1.1 kg) red or purple   1½ lb (700 g) sugar
      plums   2½ pints (1.5 litres) vodka

Cut the plums in half but do not pit them. Place them in a 3 pint (1.7 litre) container. Pour the sugar over the plums, then add the vodka. Cover the container tightly and turn it to distribute the sugar evenly throughout. Let the plums stand in a cool, dark place for 6 weeks, turning the container occasionally if the sugar has settled on the bottom.

Strain the liquid from the plums and bottle it.
Makes about 2½ pints (1.5 litres).

Variation: To make home-made peach brandy, take 2½ lb (1.1 kg) ripe, blemish-free peaches and about 1 lb (450 g) sugar, depending on their sweetness. Blanch the peaches in boiling water to loosen the skins, then peel. Pack the whole peaches into a 5 pint (3 litre) container alternating with half of the sugar. Cover the container loosely and leave to stand for several hours, until the sugar has dissolved and juice is drawn from the peaches. Then add the remaining sugar, stirring to mix it in well. Cover the container loosely again and leave to stand until all the sugar is dissolved. The syrup should cover the peaches, otherwise they will turn brown. Cover the container, but not too tightly, to allow for the release of carbon dioxide. Wrap the container in heavy brown paper and store in a cool, dark place. Test after two months to see if the brandy is ready; it will take from two to three months. The peaches themselves rival the brandy in flavour, and make an excellent topping for ice cream or pound cake.

Dried Fish Vyalenaya ryba

The windows of apartment buildings in the provincial cities of the Soviet Union are often adorned with bunches of fish which have been hung out to dry, adding a homely touch to an otherwise drab urban landscape. The Russians dry all kinds of fish, as long as it is very fresh, but especially prized is the River Don's *rybets* with its delicate flesh. This dried fish makes a perfect summertime picnic when served with boiled potatoes and plenty of beer or *kvas*.

For every 2 lb (900 g) of very fresh fish (cod or haddock, but any may be used):

3 tablespoons salt   1 tablespoon sugar

Rub the salt and the sugar all over the cleaned fish, both inside and out. Leave the fish to sit in a pan for 4 days at room temperature.

Rinse the fish lightly. Then hang it to dry for 2 or 3 days, until it is firm to the touch. (Test for firmness by pressing the flesh with your fingers; this is a sign that the fish is ready.) The fish will have the best flavour if hung in the sun, but if it is rainy or cold, the fish may be wrapped loosely in muslin and set on the radiator. (Turn it occasionally to allow air to circulate.) If the air is not particularly clean, it is best to wrap the fish loosely in muslin even when it is hung outside.

To serve, cut the fish into long, diagonal slices about 1 in (2.5 cm) thick. It is a stunning dish when the slices are reassembled and placed on a platter along with the fish head, surrounded by fresh greens. Store any leftover fish in the refrigerator.

One fish (2 lb/900 g) will serve 4 people.

Toasted Sunflower Seeds Semechki

No picture of the Russian peasant is quite complete unless it also depicts a handful of sunflower seeds. The love of these crisp seeds is near-universal, and even though it is considered gauche to crunch them in public, the floors of public buildings – especially waiting rooms – bear testimony to their popularity. The careful observer can always spot the site of an erstwhile queue from the sunflower hulls strewn over the ground. One of my favourite memories of the Soviet Union is of a tiny girl boarding a train, her hair done up in bright ribbons, proudly clutching her refreshment for the long train ride ahead, a sunflower head almost as big as herself. Most Russians eat the seeds raw, cracking the hulls with their teeth, but they are even better toasted.

| 4 oz (120 g) sunflower seeds in the hull | 1 oz (30 g) butter salt to taste (optional) |

Melt the butter. Toss the seeds in it to coat them well.

Preheat the oven to 170°C/325°F/Gas 3. Turn the seeds out on to a baking tray, separating them. Bake them for 15 to 20 minutes, or until just golden.

Eat the seeds as they are out of your hand, or shell them and salt them, if desired.

Serves 2 as a snack.

Specialities from the Republics

Many non-native dishes have crept into the Russian cuisine and taken hold. In metropolitan Moscow it is no longer unusual to find Georgian-style chicken, Uzbek pilaf, or Estonian cream cake on a restaurant menu. The Russians, with their love for the exotic, have eagerly embraced these new foods and adapted them as festive dishes into their own kitchens.

In all there are fifteen republics which make up the Soviet Union. Three are Slavic: Russia (including Siberia), Ukraine and Byelorussia (White Russia). The Baltic Republics are comprised of three formerly independent nations hugging the coast of the Baltic Sea: Latvia, Lithuania and Estonia. To the south lies the second smallest republic, Moldavia, akin to Romania in both language and culture. The Caucasus Mountains lend their name to the three Caucasian Republics: Georgia, Armenia and Azerbaidzhan. And deep into the steppes and mountains of continental Asia extend the five Central Asian republics: Tadzhikistan, Uzbekistan, Turkmenia, Kirghizia, and Kazakhstan. Within each republic live numerous ethnic groups, each attempting to preserve its own culinary heritage in the face of ever more centralised (and less efficient) food distribution.

The original Russian cuisine is distinguished by the use of dough to enclose fillings in various guises and shapes; by the love of things sour and the abundant use of soured cream; by the variety of salted vegetables and sweetened fruits accompanying meat and fish. Of all the national cuisines, the Ukrainian is closest to the Russian with its inventive soups and robust breads. The Ukraine is, in fact, the breadbasket of the Soviet Union, boasting a rich black soil, the *chernozem*, which yields high-quality grain and vegetables. It is also renowned for its thick dark honey, contributing to the excellence of Ukrainian sweets. And the true home of beetroot soup or *borshch*, so often considered typically Russian, is actually the Ukraine.

Oddly enough, the Russians came to know (and love) Ukrainian cookery through literature. Gogol's tales, written in Russian, are rich with mouth-watering descriptions of Ukrainian eating, vivid enough to stimulate even the most indifferent palate. Nikolai Gogol is rightly considered a master of literature, and perhaps more attention should be paid him in the culinary world as well, for he was reputed to be as excellent a cook as he was a writer. Thanks in large part to Gogol's writings, when the Russians think of the Ukraine they think of abundance: fresh vegetables, savoury stews, thick soups, imaginative pies, fragrant breads, pastries dripping with honey. But even this abundance accounts for only a part of the Ukraine's culinary renown. It is famed as well for its sausages – and what varieties there are! Kazimir Malevich, the founder of the Suprematist school of modern painting, grew up in the Ukraine. In his autobiography, interspersed with details of his evolution as an artist, Malevich indulges in descriptions of Ukrainian life at the turn of the century. As seen through the eyes of a painter, one of the most vivid, even lurid, scenes depicts a market place full of the temptations of a small Ukrainian town.

Oh, the whole glorious town of Konotop glistened with fat! At the market and at the station, behind long rows of tables, sat women called 'lard-sellers' who reeked of garlic. Heaped on the tables were mounds of lard of all different kinds – smoked and unsmoked with a good rind. There were rings of sausage: Cracow-style, stuffed with large chunks of meat and pork fat, blood sausage, and grain sausage with a smell so strong it inflamed a man's glands. There was ham rimmed with fat, *kasha* cooked thick with lamb suet and cut into rounds to resemble buns, and country sausage with gristle. The lard-sellers glistened in their greasy clothes, reflecting the rays of the sun.

I'd buy a ring of sausage for five kopecks and break it into pieces, eating it the way people at the market eat. I didn't even glance at the lamb, which cost only a kopeck and a half per pound, nor at the meat. Pork and fish were the best foods at the market, especially the dried sea-roach at two kopecks a piece, large chunks with fatty red backbone and roe. I liked to eat the pork and the fish with white bread. Or I'd buy a small suckling pig from the lard-seller for forty kopecks – already roasted, with a crisp brown rind stippled with fat. The rind, baked just right, crackled under my teeth. It was easy enough to consume the whole pig in secret from those at home, awaiting me for dinner.

In Konotop, among this Ukrainian fat and garlic, I grew . . .

Of course, such an abundance of fat is perhaps no longer pleasing to our taste. I can recall my own initial aversion to a large chunk of freshly salted lard atop a slice of sour black bread, proudly offered me by a Ukrainian family. Not wanting to refuse their hospitality, I accepted the sandwich. To my great relief the lard was quite palatable, and had I been free of my deeply-instilled preconceptions about cholesterol and animal fats, I might even have found it tasty.

The Ukrainians are not the only people versed in the art of charcuterie. White Russia has long been known for its skilful butchers. Butchers were in especially great demand among the large Jewish population which required kosher cuts of meat. (My own great-grandfather was a butcher in a White Russian village and it was in his shop that the young Marc Chagall played as a child. My family likes to think that the sides of beef and live chickens must have impressed themselves upon the boy's mind, to find later expression as the whimsical chickens and cows in his scenes of village life.) Russians from as far as Rostov-on-the-Don will travel to Minsk in the heart of White Russia in search of the meat reputed to be there; in their own cities the shelves are more often bare.

As one might expect, the people of the Baltic nations leave more of the meat eating to the Ukrainians and White Russians, while they traditionally consume a good deal of fish. Especially prized are the tiny Baltic herring, with a flesh so delectable it is actually sweet. During the summer, city-trapped Leningraders flock to the Baltic coast to enjoy its riches, along with its excellent dairy products produced further inland. Butter and cream are used liberally in Baltic cookery. One favourite dessert common to all three Baltic states is a simple combination of dark rye breadcrumbs mixed with fantastic amounts of fresh sweet cream.

Far to the south lies the tiny landlocked republic of Moldavia. If the Ukraine is the Soviet Union's granary, then surely Moldavia is its cornbasket, for most of the corn produced in the Soviet Union is grown on Moldavia's fertile plains. No wonder, then, that corn is a staple in Moldavia, eaten with the same relish Russians evince for buckwheat. In season the corn is eaten fresh from the cob, but a year-round dish is cornmeal pudding or *mamaliga*, the Moldavian *polenta*. Moldavia also produces some very good wine. When I was in Moldavia I visited a winery in the rolling hills southwest of the capital of Kishinev. At the winery I was greeted as guests are throughout Moldavia – in the special room called *casa mare* reserved for honoured guests. Here, a festive table and an excellent meal were already waiting. In olden days, on the estates of the wealthy, the *casa mare* was sometimes a separate cottage for entertaining guests, hence the name *casa* or 'house' and the expression *a tine casa mare*, 'to live in great style'.

Moldavia, Ukraine, the Baltic republics and Russia are all on the European continent. Travelling 800 miles south and east from Kishinev one crosses the conventional boundary between Europe and Asia, finding oneself in the heart of Transcaucasia, where the Soviet republics of Georgia, Armenia and Azerbaidzhan lie. Here east meets west in a lively mingling of cultures, and the mixing of traditions is evident also in the food. In Baku, the capital of Azerbaidzhan, one might find the inhabitants enjoying refreshing saffron-flavoured *sherbet* or lemonade (there, an ancient drink) as they gaze out on to the oil rigs in the Caspian Sea.

Russians have long considered the people of the Caucasus exotic. The dark-eyed women, the temperamental men who dance daringly and gracefully with unsheathed swords, impressed themselves upon the Russian imagination long ago. And life in the beautiful

Caucasus Range *does* seem exotic and mysterious to the outside observer: ancient vendettas are still acted upon, and people routinely live beyond a hundred years of age (though one wonders why these two facts wouldn't tend to cancel each other out). Watching a wedding celebration in Armenia, I sensed an otherworldliness – in all probability, people had celebrated in just this way centuries before. That day I had travelled to an old monastery in the hills beyond Yerevan, Armenia's capital. The weather was hot and hazy; in the distance the tip of Mt Ararat poked through the clouds, reminding me of Biblical times. The melancholy sound of a reed pipe and other woodwinds carried through the air with haunting insistence. Soon a procession rounded the corner of one of the monastery's narrow streets. It was headed by a finely attired man leading a white lamb by the collar. The lamb wore a red ribbon and its ear had been slashed, marking it for sacrifice. The parade continued through the streets, accompanied by the wailing instruments, and ended up in a shady grove on the banks of a small stream outside the monastery walls. The women in the group began to spread brightly patterned tablecloths on the ground and unpack baskets of wine, cheese, breads and fruit. The mood was gay and anticipatory, enhanced rather than restrained by ritual. Suddenly the leader of the procession drew out a long knife from his belt and with a single flourish cut off the lamb's head, holding it triumphantly on high for all to see. The musicians immediately broke into festive song, and everyone started dancing and passing around goatskins of red wine. Before long I could detect the exquisite smell of skewered lamb grilling on the coals: *shashlyk*, the Armenian contribution to international cuisine. Even now, when I think of Armenia, I can still smell the lamb roasting and see the people dancing in the grass, people full of enthusiasm for life and for good food.

To the Russians, Armenia is not the only exotic southern republic. Georgia is even more so, and it is Georgian cookery that Russians prefer over all other ethnic cuisines. For them it plays the same role French cookery does to many Americans and Europeans – they consider it the height of culinary taste. And a visit to Georgia's capital, Tbilisi, confirms this impression.

The city is dissected by the Kura River, and on the cliffs overlooking the water one can sip strong Turkish coffee and taste the local sweets at an open-air café. Tbilisi's main street is dotted with snack bars, offering the famed Georgian cheesebread, *khachapuri*, and with restaurants serving such excellent appetisers as *lobio* (kidney beans in a plum sauce) and platters of *suluguni*, Georgian cheese served with fresh coriander and spring onions. One of the highlights of the city is its market place, which takes up two entire floors of an old warehouse. Vendors come from all over Georgia to sell their produce, vying with one another to make the most attractive display, hoping to catch the customer's eye and thereby his business. The competition seems greatest among the vendors of *khmeli-suneli*, a characteristically Georgian spice mixture. These vendors are most often older women dressed in bright scarves and shawls. They spoon the spice mixture into high mounds and place themselves decoratively behind. The coriander, dill, pepper and other spices which make up the mixture give off a heady aroma, and the experience of simply standing in the market and breathing in the smells is vivid enough. Most Georgian families hoard the secret of their own private blend of *khmeli-suneli*, and the mixtures at the market range in hue from a deep mossy green to a bright mustard yellow. I returned from the market with five different blends of *khmeli-suneli*, all gifts from the generous Georgian people who pitied this poor American, unaware of the delights of their native spice.

The Georgians are indeed a generous people, and they rival the Russians in hospitality. In Georgia, love and respect for a guest are expressed indirectly through elaborate ritual, and this ritual is enacted around the dining table as toast after toast is raised. Georgian-style toasting is not merely the *pro forma* (albeit sincere) toasting of the Russian meal; it is rather an art in itself, a competition which can – and usually does – go on for hours, each toastmaker trying to outdo the rest with the beauty and expressiveness of his toast. Luckily, the Georgian wine is excellent and, unlike vodka, can be enjoyed glass after glass.

Georgia produces the best wine in the Soviet Union. Especially prized are its aromatic red wines such as 'Kindzmarauli' (reputedly Stalin's favourite) and 'Teliani', the preferred wine of the literati. 'Teliani' in particular has found favour among the great poets of the Soviet period. Zabolotsky is known to have consumed large quantities of the wine, invariably offering it to his guests, and Mandelstam even wrote a poem about it.

Travelling deeper into continental Asia one enters the Central Asian republics, where the mountains and steppes are peopled by literally hundreds of different nationalities. The cookery of these peoples has much more in common with eastern cuisine than with western. Russia first felt the influence of eastern cookery in the thirteenth century when the Mongol hordes came storming across the Asian steppes, carrying with them exotic teas, spices and cooking implements. Later, with Russia's acquisition of Astrakhan in the sixteenth and Siberia in the seventeenth century, eastern influences became even more strongly felt, especially the Tatar influence. To paraphrase Napoleon's famous statement, 'Scratch a Russian and you'll find a Tatar', one might say 'Try Russian food and you'll taste the eastern influence'. Noodles, dried fruits, lemons and jams, so prevalent in Russian cookery, are all of eastern origin.

One of the oldest Central Asian cities is Bukhara, in the republic of Uzbekistan. Bukhara also boasts a lively market place, and the Uzbeks in native garb make it even more colourful than Tbilisi. The market is a gathering place where not only goods but gossip is traded. Turbaned heads tilt together, ear to mouth. The market features row upon row of dried fruits: raisins dark brown and yellow, plump and wizened; apricots, figs, dates and nuts. Some stalls sell balls of hard cheese the size of marbles and as easily popped into the mouth. Since the sights at the market can make one quite hungry, it is best to follow one's nose to a vat of steaming pilaf or *plov*, an Uzbek dish, prepared outdoors in large vats over woodfires, or visit an eastern tea room or *chai-khana*, where customers sit at low tables on pillows and rugs. It is an enchanting experience to sit and chat over a leisurely pot of green tea, sipped from bowls, especially if the tea is served at a teahouse in the town centre overlooking a glassy reflecting pool which mirrors an ornate, carved mosque.

Bukhara lies in the flat steppe of Uzbekistan, and it is not until much further east that mountains begin; yet still one is within the borders of the Soviet Union. In the Altai Mountains bordering China lie the republics of Kazakhstan and Kirghizia, once inhabited by nomadic tribes known for their daring and bravado. The tribes of Kirghizia were also known for their ability to consume large draughts of *koumiss* or fermented mare's milk. Any male visitors to the tribes were expected to down at least one, if not two, of the vessels containing *koumiss*, vessels holding up to three pints apiece. Today this potent beverage is hard to find in the city, but the people of the mountains still swear by it. The casual tourist to Frunze or Alma-Ata is more likely to taste *samsa* (fried meat pies like *pirozhki*) or *lagman* (a meat and noodle stew) than *koumiss*. Or perhaps he will simply enjoy one of the many varieties of apples for which Alma-Ata is famous – the name of the city means 'Father of Apples'.

No book on Russian cuisine could be considered complete without at least mentioning some of the various foods which have influenced its development and which are enjoyed today in the heart of Mother Russia. Here, then, is a random sampling of recipes from the different republics.

Siberian Dumplings Sibirskie pel'meni

Almost every national cuisine boasts its own version of boiled dumplings wrapped around pockets of seasoned meat. No doubt many English kitchens are already familiar with won ton, kreplach and tortellini. *Pel'meni* are the Siberian version, now popular throughout the Soviet Union. Moscow alone has several *pel'mennayas*, cafés specialising in these dumplings. *Pel'meni* are practical for the harsh Siberian winter. Prepared in large quantities, they can be buried in the snow where they keep for months on end, ready to boil up at a moment's notice.

Siberians swear by a mustard and vinegar sauce for *pel'meni*: place a spoonful of hot mustard on the edge of each plate and mix it with concentrated vinegar to taste. Muscovites prefer a milder garnish, slathering butter and soured cream on the dumplings in lavish amounts. *Pel'meni* are most often served steaming hot, mounded high on a platter, but they may also be boiled in chicken broth and eaten with the soup.

When making *pel'meni*, it's wise to make a lot. As one Russian saying goes, 'You can never have too many *pel'meni*.' And once you've tasted these wonderful dumplings, you're bound to agree.

Dough	1 teaspoon salt
12 oz (340 g) plain flour	4 tablespoons warm water
3 whole eggs	

Mix together the flour and the salt in a medium-sized bowl. Make a well in the centre and pour in the eggs and water. Toss the mixture together and then knead by hand until the dough holds together. Form the dough into a ball and place it on greaseproof paper or a floured surface. Cover the dough with an overturned bowl and leave to rest at room temperature for 1 hour.

Filling	6 oz (170 g) melted butter
1½ lb (700 g) minced beef and	hot mustard
pork, mixed	strong vinegar
1 medium onion	soured cream
1 teaspoon salt	
freshly ground pepper to taste	

In a food processor or mincer mince the beef, pork, onion, salt and pepper very finely, until there is a smooth mass with no lumps. Set aside for the flavours to blend while the dough is resting.

Divide the dough into four pieces. Working with one piece at a time, roll the dough out on a floured board as thinly as possible (¹⁄₁₆ in (1.15 mm) thick or less) and with a biscuit cutter or a glass cut out 2 in (5 cm) rounds. Place a heaped teaspoon of the meat filling on each round. Bring one edge of the round over to meet the other and seal the edges tightly, forming a half-moon. Then take the two pointed edges and bring them together in the centre of the half moon, along its straight edge. Lift these edges slightly so that a round ball is formed. Make sure that the edges are securely pressed together in the centre. As each ball is formed, place it on a clean tea towel.

If you are not going to boil the *pel'meni* right away, cover them with a tea towel so that they don't dry out. When ready to serve them, bring a large pan of salted water to the boil. Add a teaspoon of vegetable oil to the water to keep the dumplings from sticking to one another. When the water has reached a rolling boil, drop in the *pel'meni* and boil them gently for 5 minutes, or until they rise to the top of the water. Make sure not to crowd them in the pan; they may be cooked in several batches.

Drain the *pel'meni* and immediately pour the melted butter over them. Bring them to table piled high on a platter and let each person choose his own garnish: mustard and vinegar, or soured cream and more butter.

Makes 8 to 10 dozen *pel'meni*, or enough for 6 servings.

Variations:

1. To serve the *pel'meni* in chicken broth, boil them as directed above in salted water. When they are done, transfer them to hot chicken broth and serve each bowlful with a generous dollop of soured cream.

2. A delicious way to eat any leftover *pel'meni* is to fry them in butter until golden brown. Serve with the above garnishes.

3. In Central Asia *pel'meni* are made with a filling of fresh greens. Mix together spring onion, fresh coriander, sorrel and spinach in desired proportions. Chop the greens finely and season them with salt and pepper. Place a generous teaspoonful of the chopped vegetables on each round of dough. Shape the *pel'meni* as directed above and boil in salted water. Serve with plenty of melted butter.

Ukrainian Steamed Cabbage Soufflé Nakiplyak iz kapusty

A festive, delicious way with cabbage.

1 head of white cabbage, about 2 lb (900 g), with large outer leaves intact	1 teaspoon sugar
	1¼ teaspoons salt
	freshly ground white pepper to taste
¼ pint (150 ml) milk	dash of cayenne
2 oz (60 g) butter	1 teaspoon marjoram
1 large onion, finely chopped	3 egg yolks
2 oz (60 g) fine dry breadcrumbs	5 egg whites

Core the cabbage, peel off the large outer leaves and blanch them in boiling water for 5 minutes to soften. Drain and set aside.

Cut the cabbage into chunks and place it in a large pan. Pour the milk over the cabbage and simmer, covered, for about 30 minutes or until tender. Drain the cabbage and chop it finely.

Meanwhile, sauté the chopped onion in the butter. In a large bowl mix together the chopped cabbage, sautéed onions (along with all the butter from the frying pan), the breadcrumbs, seasonings and egg yolks.

Beat the egg whites until stiff but not dry. Fold them into the cabbage mixture.

Spread a large, clean linen tea towel on a table. On the towel arrange the blanched cabbage leaves in an overlapping pattern, making a circle large enough to contain the soufflé filling. Pile the filling in the centre, making sure first that there are no openings in the cabbage leaf circle that the filling could seep out of. Carefully fold the leaves up to cover the filling. Then bring the ends of the tea towel together in the centre and tie them securely with kitchen string.

Place the towel-wrapped cabbage in a colander to retain its round shape. Place the colander in a large, deep pan over a few inches of water. If the pan lid will not fit over the colander, don't worry, use foil to cover the pan, sealing it tightly.

Bring the water to the boil and simmer the cabbage for 50 minutes. Remove the cabbage from the colander and untie the string. Open the tea towel and place a plate over the cabbage leaves. Invert the plate to turn out the soufflé and peel off the towel from the top.

To serve, cut the soufflé into wedges.

Serves 8.

Braised Chicken with Prunes Kuritsa, tushonaya s chernoslivom

The original recipe for this Ukrainian dish calls for prunes which have been dried over a smoky wood fire, imparting a dusky flavour to the chicken. The commercially-processed prunes substituted here yield a subtler taste, but one which is equally delightful.

1 chicken (2½–3 lb/1.1–1.4 kg), cut up	½ pint (150 ml) rich chicken stock
salt, pepper to taste	¼ pint (150 ml) dry white wine
2 oz (60 g) butter	½ lb (225 g) prunes
2 tablespoons olive oil	½ pint (300 ml) water
2 large carrots, scraped and chopped	1 tablespoon freshly squeezed lemon juice
2 large onions, sliced	1 tablespoon flour
4 small cloves garlic, crushed	2 teaspoons sugar
4 sprigs parsley	
2 bay leaves	
2 slices of lemon, seeded	

Season the chicken with salt and pepper to taste. In a large, heavy frying pan heat 1 oz (30 g) butter together with the olive oil. Add the chicken pieces and fry them until golden, about 15 minutes. When the chicken has browned, transfer it to a plate and keep warm.

Add the carrots, onions and garlic to the frying pan, and cook them over medium heat until soft but not brown, about 8 minutes. Return the chicken pieces to the pan, skin side up. Place the parsley, bay leaves and lemon slices on top of the chicken. Pour in the chicken stock and dry white wine all at once. Cover the pan; bring to the boil, then simmer for about 30 minutes, until the chicken is tender.

While the chicken is simmering, prepare the prunes. In a saucepan combine the prunes, water and lemon juice. Bring to the boil, uncovered, and simmer until the prunes are plump and tender, about 15 minutes. Drain and set aside.

When the chicken is done, transfer it with a slotted spoon to a platter and keep it warm. Strain the broth from the frying pan into a bowl, pressing down hard on the vegetables with the back of a spoon to extract all their juice. Set aside.

In the frying pan melt the remaining butter. Add the flour and stir to make a roux. Cook for about 3 minutes or until the flour browns slightly. Gradually add the reserved broth, stirring constantly, and bring to the boil. Simmer until slightly thickened, then stir in the sugar. Test for seasoning. When the sauce is done, return the chicken and the prunes to it, and heat through.

Serve the chicken on a large platter, garnished with the prunes and about half of the sauce. Pass the remaining sauce in a sauceboat.

Serves 4.

Ukrainian Pork Stew Vereshchaka

This Ukrainian peasant stew comes from a very old recipe making use of the best local products – pork, beetroot and rye bread. In some households it is prepared just before Lent and served over *blini* during Butter Week celebrations. But no matter what the time of year, *vereshchaka* is delicious, its rich burgundy colour a feast for the eyes alone.

3 thick bacon rashers
2 onions, coarsely chopped
1 lb (450 g) boneless pork loin,
    cut into strips
salt, pepper to taste
¾ pint (450 ml) beetroot kvass
    (see p. 175)

4 oz (120 g) fresh rye
    breadcrumbs, crusts
    removed
fresh parsley or dill

In a heavy pan fry the bacon until slightly crisp. Remove it from the fat and set aside.

Fry the chopped onion in the bacon drippings until golden. Then add the strips of pork, turning to brown them on all sides. Add salt and pepper to taste.

Crumble the bacon into the pan, then pour in the beetroot kvass. Cover and bring to the boil. Simmer, covered, for 30 minutes, then stir in the rye breadcrumbs and simmer for 30 minutes more.

Transfer the stew to a serving bowl and garnish with snipped dill or parsley. Serve with boiled potatoes.

Serves 4.

Note: If no beetroot kvass is on hand, ¾ pint (450 ml) beef stock may be poured over 2 grated beetroot in a saucepan. Bring to the boil, then remove the pan from the heat and leave to stand for 1 hour. Strain and add to the stew in place of the kvass. This makes quite an acceptable substitute, though the flavour of the stew will not be as rich.

Ukrainian Dumplings Vareniki

These excellent Ukrainian dumplings were purportedly the writer Gogol's favourite food, and he was quite a connoisseur. In true Russian philosophical style, he is said to have mused on occasion over the inconceivability of life without his beloved *vareniki*. Others who have lived in the Ukraine are likely to share Gogol's sentiments: the painter Malevich, long after his Ukrainian childhood had passed, still fondly recalled boiled *vareniki* with cherries, covered with soured cream and dark Ukrainian honey.

Vareniki are a very adaptable food, changing with the seasons. They are perhaps most glorious in mid-summer when served stuffed with fresh berries, cherries, or plums. In autumn, field mushrooms are likely to replace the summertime fruits, while the heavier demands of a cold winter season call for *kasha* and sauerkraut. Ukrainians serve the most popular *vareniki* of all – filled with curd cheese (*tvorog*) all year round. They make a savoury main course or a slightly sweetened dessert.

12 oz (340 g) plain flour	2 egg yolks
½ teaspoon salt	½ pint (300 ml) water

Place the flour and salt in a bowl and make a well in the centre. Add the egg yolks and water, gradually, and work with your hands until a fairly stiff dough is formed, adding more water if necessary. Knead the dough on a lightly floured surface, then place under an overturned bowl and leave to rest for 1 hour.

Roll the dough out very thinly to ¹⁄₁₆ in (1.15 mm) thick or less. Cut into 4 in (10 cm) rounds. Place the desired filling on each round, shape into half-moons, crimping the edges with a fork to seal. Place on a tea towel and cover with another towel until ready to boil.

Bring a large pot of salted water to the boil, drop in the *vareniki* and boil gently until they rise to the surface, about 5 minutes. Remove with a slotted spoon and serve immediately.

Tvorog filling

1 lb (450 g) *tvorog* (see p. 171) or curd cheese	2 tablespoons soured cream
	3 oz (85 g) sugar (optional)
2 egg yolks	1 teaspoon grated lemon rind (optional)
pinch of salt	

Mix together well all of the above ingredients, adding the sugar and lemon rind if sweet dessert *vareniki* are desired. Place ½ teaspoon on each round of dough. Serve these *vareniki* with plenty of melted butter and soured cream, and, if desired, browned breadcrumbs.

Cherry filling

2 lb (900 g) sour cherries	1½ oz (45 g) cornflour
10 oz (280 g) sugar	1 oz (30 g) plain flour

Stone the cherries and mix them with 2 oz (60 g) sugar.* Leave in a warm spot (ideally in the sun) for several hours, stirring occasionally.

The cherries will produce about ¼ pint (150 ml) of juice. Add enough water to make ¾ pint (450 ml). Pour into a saucepan and stir in the remaining sugar. Dissolve the cornflour in a little of the liquid. Bring the syrup to the boil and then stir in the dissolved cornflour, mixing well. Simmer for 5 minutes. Keep warm over low heat.

Dredge the cherries in 1 oz (30 g) plain flour. Place 2 cherries on each round of dough. Seal. Boil as directed above. Serve with the cherry sauce or with buckwheat honey. These are very sweet!

Makes about 8 to 10 dozen dumplings.

Ukrainian Sweet Braid Bulka

Honey often figures as a temptation in Nikolai Gogol's Ukrainian tales. In one tale, *Viy*, some young seminarists visit a market place where they are tempted by a stunning array of home-baked goods. The peasant women cajole them to buy bread, one offering her special poppy-seed buns, another claiming that *her* loaf has been sweetened with real honey. The recipe below is for a typical Ukrainian sweet loaf, one which even the strictest seminarist cannot resist.

1 tablespoon dried yeast	1 teaspoon salt
4 tablespoons warm water	grated rind of 1 lemon
pinch of sugar	1½ lb (700 g) plain flour
¼ pint (150 ml) milk	
4 oz (120 g) butter	
3 eggs, beaten	1 egg yolk
6 oz (170 g) honey	1 tablespoon water
¼ pint (150 ml) soured cream	blanched sliced almonds

Dissolve the yeast and the sugar in the warm water until bubbly.

Scald the milk; stir in the butter, cut into small pieces, and let it cool to lukewarm. Then add the milk mixture to the yeast, along with the eggs, honey, soured cream, salt and lemon rind. Stir in the flour, 4 oz (120 g) at a time, adding enough to make a soft dough.

Turn the dough out on to a floured board and knead until smooth and elastic, about 10 minutes. Place the dough in a greased bowl, turning it to grease the top. Cover and leave to rise in a warm place

---

* Canned sour cherries may be used if no fresh ones are available. Use two 1 lb (450 g) cans of cherries. Drain the liquid and reserve it to add to the juice produced by the cherries. Proceed as directed above.

until doubled in bulk, about 2 hours. Knock back the dough and let rise again until doubled, about 1 hour.

Turn the dough out on to a floured board and divide it in half. Divide each half into three balls of equal size. Roll each ball out between your palms into a rope about 12 in (30 cm) long. Braid three ropes together and place the loaf on a greased baking tray. Repeat with the remaining dough.

Cover the loaves and leave them to rise until doubled, about 40 minutes.

Preheat the oven to 190°C/375°F/Gas 5. Brush the loaves with a glaze made by beating the egg yolk with the water. Sprinkle the almonds over the tops of the loaves.

Bake for 35 minutes, or until nicely browned on top.

Makes 2 loaves.

Ukrainian Honey Cake Medivnyk

The famous Ukrainian *myod* or honey lends its name to this excellent cake, rich with dates and nuts. *Medivnyk* is traditional for Christmas but is baked throughout the year because it is so popular. Hawkers set up their rickety stands in the streets of Kiev, selling slices of *medivnyk* by the gram weight. In the summer the stands are often surrounded by swarms of honeybees, bewitched by the heavy smell of honey in the air, but the hawkers are expert at selling their luscious cake without ever getting stung.

4 oz (120 g) butter
8 oz (225 g) Barbados sugar
12 oz (340 g) dark honey
  (preferably buckwheat
  honey)
4 eggs, separated
10 oz (280 g) plain flour
2 teaspoons bicarbonate of
  soda
1 teaspoon baking powder

pinch of salt
grated rind of 1 orange
8 fluid oz (225 ml) soured
  cream
1 teaspoon cinnamon
½ teaspoon nutmeg
3 oz (85 g) currants
4 oz (120 g) chopped walnuts
6 oz (170 g) chopped pitted
  dates

Cream the butter and the sugar together until light and fluffy, then beat in the honey. Separate the eggs and beat in the yolks one at a time, mixing well after each addition. Stir in the flour, bicarbonate of soda, baking powder and salt. Mix well. Add the grated orange rind and soured cream, beating until the batter is smooth. Then stir in the cinnamon, nutmeg, currants, walnuts and dates. Whip the 4 egg whites until stiff but not dry and fold them into the batter.

Preheat the oven to 150°C/300°F/Gas 2. Prepare a 10 in (25 cm) savarin tin by greasing it and then lining the bottom and sides with brown paper. Grease the paper. Pour the batter into the pan, spreading it evenly.

Bake the cake for 1 hour and 15 minutes, or until a cake tester comes out clean. Remove the outer part of the pan and let the cake cool (upright) in the tube section. When completely cool, remove the cake from the pan.

Wrap the cake in foil and leave it to age at room temperature for 2 days before serving. (It may be eaten sooner, but the flavour won't be as rich.)

Note: Buckwheat honey, if available, is really the best choice for this cake. The light honey will not give it as distinctive a taste.

Prunes Stuffed with Cheese Chernosliv, farshirovannyi tvorogom

A lovely Byelorussian dessert, as served at the 'Minsk' restaurant in Moscow.

½ lb (225 g) prunes	2 oz (60 g) sugar
½ lb (225 g) *tvorog* (see p. 171) or curd cheese	1 oz (30 g) chopped walnuts
	2 tablespoons plum brandy

Pour boiling water over the prunes and soak them, covered, until they are swollen. Drain. If the prunes have not been stoned, carefully remove the stones with a sharp knife, leaving the prunes as intact as possible. Dry them on kitchen paper.

Mix the sugar with the *tvorog*. With an icing bag, fill the prunes with the sweetened *tvorog*.

Place the prunes in a lightly greased baking dish. Preheat the oven to 180°C/350°F/Gas 4. Sprinkle the walnuts over the prunes, then bake them for 20 minutes. Remove from the oven and sprinkle with the plum brandy, flaming it if desired. Serve hot.

Serves 6.

Estonian Potato Salad Rossol'ye

Here is one more potato salad to round out your repertoire, this one tarter and heartier than its Russian cousin.

2 boiling potatoes (1 lb/450 g)	4 tablespoons reserved juice from the pickled beetroot
1 large sweet onion, chopped	2 tablespoons cider vinegar
1 large tart apple, cored and chopped, but not peeled	2 teaspoons dry mustard
2 large dill pickles, chopped	1 teaspoon sugar
8 oz (225 g) jar of pickled beetroot, juice reserved and beetroot chopped	¼ pint (150 ml) soured cream
	½ teaspoon salt
½ lb (225 g) ham, chopped	freshly ground white pepper
1 salt herring, cleaned, soaked, and chopped	2 hard-boiled eggs, sieved
milk or buttermilk	parsley

The night before making the salad, soak the salt herring in milk or buttermilk to cover. The next day rinse it, remove the backbone, and then chop it coarsely.

Boil the potatoes in salted water until tender. While still warm, peel them and chop them coarsely. Put them in a large bowl.

Add the chopped onion, apple, pickles, beetroot, ham and herring. Mix well.

Make the dressing. Mix the dry mustard with the vinegar until smooth. Stir in the reserved beetroot juice. Add the sugar, soured cream, salt, and pepper to taste. Mix well.

Pour the dressing over the salad and toss until all the ingredients are coated. Cover the bowl with foil and leave at room temperature for 1 hour, then chill in the refrigerator for at least 6 hours, or overnight, before serving.

Just before serving, mound the salad on a large platter and garnish with the sieved hard-boiled eggs. Strew some parsley around the base of the salad.

Serves 8 to 10; more if served as *zakuska*.

Latvian Apple Pudding Yablochnaya zapekanka

Rye flour is not just for bread, as proved by this delicious cake-like pudding. Variations of this dessert are found throughout the Baltic states.

4 medium apples, cored and diced	5 oz (150 g) plain flour
	3 oz (85 g) rye flour
2 oz (60 g) unsalted butter	1 teaspoon baking soda
8 oz (225 g) sugar	½ teaspoon baking powder
1 egg, well beaten	pinch of salt
1 teaspoon vanilla essence	2 oz (60 g) chopped nuts

Lightly grease and flour a round 9 in (22.5 cm) baking dish. Preheat the oven to 180°C/350°F/Gas 4.

Melt the butter in a large skillet. Remove the pan from the heat and stir in the sugar until well blended. Then stir in the prepared apples. Set aside.

In a medium bowl mix together the plain flour, rye flour, baking soda, powder, and salt.

Beat the egg until frothy and stir in the vanilla essence. Beat the egg into the apple mixture which should have cooled somewhat.

Stir in the dry ingredients, mixing well. Finally, stir in the nuts. Turn the batter into the prepared baking dish. Bake the pudding at 180°C/350°F/Gas 4 for 35 to 40 minutes, until a tester comes out clean.

Serve with fresh sweet cream, if desired.

Serves 8 to 10.

Cornmeal Pudding (Mamaliga) Mamalyga

Traditionally, Moldavian cornmeal pudding is cooked slowly over a low fire and stirred with a wooden spoon reserved especially for this dish. *Mamalyga* lovers also insist that the cooled pudding should never be cut with a knife, but with string, so as not to destroy its texture.

5 oz (150 g) yellow cornmeal	1 pint (600 ml) boiling water
1½ teaspoons salt	1½ oz (45 g) butter
½ pint (300 ml) cold water	

In a large saucepan combine the cornmeal and salt. Pour the cold water over the cornmeal and stir until well mixed. Add the boiling water, stirring constantly, and bring the mixture to the boil. Stir in the butter. Cook over low heat until slightly thickened, then cover and simmer for 12 to 14 minutes. Serve immediately, topped with butter, grated cheese, or gravy.
   Serves 4.

Variations:
1. Add 4 oz (120 g) feta cheese to the hot cornmeal and spread the mixture in a greased ovenproof casserole. Top with ¼ pint (150 ml) soured cream and bake uncovered at 190°C/375°F/Gas 5 for 15 minutes.
2. To make *mamalyga* a meal in itself, prepare it as in the variation above, and top each portion (there will be 4) with a freshly poached egg.
3. Pour the hot cornmeal into a greased 9 in (22.5 cm) square baking dish and leave to harden. Chill. The next day cut into squares and fry in butter over low heat until golden on both sides. Serve with syrup or jam. (This is a good use for leftover pudding as well.)
4. To make *mamalyga* dumplings: shape cold *mamalyga* into balls and with your finger make an indentation in each ball. Stuff with chopped cooked ham, crumbled bacon, chopped hard-boiled egg or chopped cooked mushrooms. Seal with more *mamalyga* and dredge with flour. Deep fry in hot oil (182°C/360°F) until golden, about 5 minutes.
5. Cheese dumplings are made by taking 8 oz (225 g) cold *mamalyga* and adding to it 2 oz (60 g) grated cheese. Form into balls. Take some plain *mamalyga* and mould a thin layer of it around each cheese ball. Dredge with flour and deep fry as directed above.

Moldavian Stuffed Peppers Perets, farshirovannyi v moldavskom stile

The Moldavians love peppers, which grow in abundance in their small republic. In the recipe below, two kinds of peppers – green bell and red hot – are joined in a lively combination. After chopping some hot red pepper for the filling, there is no need to waste the rest. Instead, do as the Moldavians do: place the pepper in a glass, cover it with vodka, and leave it to stand for 24 hours. Then remove the pepper and transfer the vodka to a jar, which should be stored in the refrigerator. The next time you feel a cold coming on, drink about 6 ounces of this fiery vodka before bedtime – by morning all your ills will be gone!

4 large bell peppers	salt, freshly ground black
½ a small head of white	pepper, and fresh dill to
cabbage	taste
1 large onion	¼ teaspoon minced hot red
3 medium carrots	pepper (or more, to taste)
5 tablespoons olive oil	¼ lb (120 g) Brynza cheese
4 tablespoons parsley, finely	
chopped	

Slice the tops off the bell peppers about 1 in (2.5 cm) down from the top. Scrape the insides clean of seeds and membrane. Parboil the peppers in salted water for 3 to 4 minutes, then set them aside on kitchen paper to drain. They should still be firm.

Shred the cabbage, onion and carrots finely. (The shredding disc on a food processor is ideal for this.) Place the vegetables in a large frying pan, in which the olive oil has already been heated. Toss them well to coat with the oil. Add the parsley, salt, pepper, dill and red pepper. Cook, stirring occasionally, for 5 to 7 minutes, or until the vegetables are soft but not mushy.

Preheat the oven to 180°C/350°F/Gas 4. Place the drained peppers upright in a deep casserole. Spoon the vegetable mixture into the cavities, packing it firmly. Pour about ¼ in (6 mm) of water into the bottom of the casserole. Top each stuffed pepper with a portion of grated cheese.

Cover the casserole and bake for 30 minutes. Then remove the lid and put the peppers under the grill for a few minutes, until they are browned and bubbly.

Serves 4.

Note: If Brynza cheese is unavailable, substitute 4 oz (120 g) of feta or another sharp cheese.

Tatar Meat Pies Peremech

These succulent meat pies are Tatar in origin, very much like the
Kazakh *belyashi* enjoyed throughout Russia. This recipe was given to
me by a dear Tatar friend, Zainab, whose house is hung with heavy
Oriental carpets and whose kitchen never fails to produce delectable
surprises. These *peremech*, typical for a Tatar meal, should be eaten
right from the frying pan, juicy and hot.

Dough	6 tablespoons single cream
2 eggs, beaten	pinch salt
4 fluid oz (120 ml) soured	pinch sugar
cream	10 oz (280 g) plain flour

Beat the eggs until light, then beat in the soured cream, single
cream, salt, sugar and flour. Knead until smooth and elastic. Wrap
the dough in waxed paper and refrigerate overnight before using.

Filling	1 onion
1 lb (450 g) boneless lean beef	1 clove garlic
chuck	1 teaspoon salt

In a food processor or mincer, mince all the above ingredients
together finely.

Prepare the meat pies: working with one-quarter of the dough at a
time (leave the rest in the refrigerator), roll out each piece into a 12 in
(30 cm) rope. Cut each rope into 6 pieces, then roll the pieces into
balls between the palms of your hands. Flatten the balls slightly, and
on a floured surface roll each ball out into a round 3½–4 in (9–10 cm)
in diameter.

Spread 1 tablespoon of meat mixture on each round, leaving 1 in
(2.5 cm) around the edges.

To shape the meat pies, gather the dough in little pleats all the
way around the patty, using an upward, folding motion. The result
should be a round, flat pastry with a hole the size of a five pence
piece in the middle. As each patty is made, place it on a linen cloth
and cover with another cloth so that the pastries do not dry out.

Pour vegetable oil into a large frying pan to a depth of ½ in
(12 mm). Heat it, and once it is hot add the *peremech*, a few at a time,
hole side down. Cook the meat pies, turning once, for about fifteen
minutes or until golden brown.

Makes 2 dozen meat pies.

Crimean Meat Pies　Chebureki

Chebureki are native to the Crimea. This recipe comes from the town of Simferopol, where the pies are a source of passion and pride. *Chebureki* should always be eaten with the hand – never with knife and fork – so that the first bite sends a spurt of hot juice right into the mouth.

12 oz (340 g) plain flour	1 teaspoon salt
1 generous tablespoon vegetable oil	8 fluid oz (225 ml) water

Mix together the flour and salt, then stir in the oil. Add the water to make a soft dough. Turn the dough out on to a floured board and knead it until smooth and elastic. Wrap in plastic wrap and refrigerate for at least 2 days before using.

Filling	1¼ teaspoons salt
6 oz (170 g) beef	freshly ground black pepper to
4 oz (120 g) well-larded or fatty	taste
lamb	6 tablespoons water
1 clove garlic	vegetable oil for frying
1 small onion	
12 sprigs of parsley, leaves only	

In a mincer or food processor mince together the beef, lamb, garlic, onion and parsley, till the mixture is fine and smooth. Stir in the salt, pepper and water. Set aside.

Cut the dough into 16 equal pieces. On a floured board roll each piece out thinly to a circle 6–8 in (15–20 cm) in diameter. (The thinner the dough, the crisper the pies will be.)

Spread a generous tablespoon of the filling on half of each circle, then fold the other half over the filling to enclose it, forming a half-moon. Seal the edges well with the tines of a fork.

Heat ½ in (12 mm) of oil in a large frying pan. Fry the *chebureki* two at a time until golden, turning once. Serve immediately.

Serves 4.

Circassian Chicken　Kuritsa po-cherkesski

The Circassian people, renowned for their beauty and bravery, inhabit the mountainous regions of the Caucasus. Legend has it that this chicken was named after a beautiful Circassian peasant girl, said to have ground the nuts by hand in preparing this dish for her lover, a prince of some kind who would come to her at midnight. Unfortunately, the legend ends there. We'll never know whether the girl's devoted cookery made a princess out of her, but Circassian Chicken is certainly an excellent dish.

2 whole chicken breasts
    (2½ lb/1.1 kg)
1½ pints (900 ml) cold water
1 bay leaf
1 onion, quartered
1 carrot, scraped and cut in half
½ teaspoon tarragon
6 black peppercorns
1¼ teaspoons salt
2 sprigs parsley
4 oz (120 g) walnut halves
4 oz (120 g) hazel-nuts
2 tablespoons olive oil

1 small onion, finely chopped
1 clove garlic, crushed
2 slices white bread, crusts
    removed
4 tablespoons double cream
¼ teaspoon paprika
freshly ground white pepper to
    taste
dash of cayenne
8 fluid oz (225 ml) of the
    chicken stock
soft-leaved lettuce, parsley,
    walnut halves

Put the chicken breasts in a stockpot, pour the cold water over them, and add the bay leaf, onion, carrot, tarragon, peppercorns, 1 teaspoon salt and parsley. Simmer for 45 minutes, or until the chicken is tender. Remove the chicken and strain the broth. Return the broth to the pot and cook it over high heat until it is reduced by half.

Remove the skin from the chicken breasts, bone them, and cut the flesh into strips.

Pour boiling water over the walnut halves and slip off the thin skins. (This is a tedious process, but a necessary one, because the skins will make the sauce taste bitter. The hazel-nuts do not need to be peeled.) Then place the walnuts on a baking tray in a low oven to dry out.

When the walnuts have dried out grind them together with the hazel-nuts in a food processor or nut grinder.

In a large frying pan sauté the onion and garlic in the olive oil until golden. Soak the bread in the double cream, then add it to the sautéed onions without squeezing the liquid from it. Stir in the ground nuts, paprika, ¼ teaspoon salt, pepper, cayenne and 8 fluid oz (225 ml) of the reserved chicken stock. Mix well. Cool to room temperature.

Spread a serving platter with leaves of lettuce. Place a layer of the chicken strips in the centre of the platter, the strips radiating out like the spokes of a wheel. Cover the chicken with a layer of the nut sauce, then top with another layer of chicken, this one also radiating out from the centre and overlapping the bottom layer.

Top the chicken with more nut sauce and continue in this manner until all of the meat has been used, reserving enough sauce to decorate the top of the mound. Spread the remaining sauce over the top, piling it somewhat higher in the middle, and garnish with chopped parsley and walnut halves.

Serve at room temperature or very slightly chilled. The chicken may be prepared a day ahead of time and chilled, covered, in the refrigerator overnight, but it must be brought almost to room temperature before serving, otherwise its flavour will not come through.

Serves 6.

Armenian Flat Bread   Lavash

Lavash has been baked for centuries in Armenia. The raw, flat rounds of dough are traditionally slapped on to the sides of a hot cylindrical oven or *tonir*, where they bake in less than 5 minutes, but nowadays the bread is more often baked in large, modern ovens. *Lavash* is an excellent crisp bread to serve with cheese or soup.

4 oz (120 g) strong plain flour	4 teaspoons vegetable oil
4 oz (120 g) wholemeal flour	¼ pint (150 ml) milk
2 teaspoons salt	sesame seeds or poppy seeds

Mix the flours and the salt together in a bowl. Drizzle the oil over the flour, and with the palms of your hands, rub the oil into the flour until it is well incorporated. Make a well in the centre and pour in the milk. Mix with your hands to form a dough.

Turn the dough out on to a floured board and knead it for 5 to 10 minutes, until smooth and pliable. Cover the dough with an overturned bowl and leave to sit at room temperature for at least 30 minutes. (It may be refrigerated at this point, if necessary.)

Cut the dough into 8 pieces. Taking one piece at a time, knead the dough and press it into a round on a floured board. With a rolling pin, roll out the round until the dough is 8 in (20 cm) in diameter. Sprinkle it generously with sesame or poppy seeds, then roll it out once more with the rolling pin (it will have contracted a little), pressing the seeds firmly into the dough.

Preheat the oven to 200°C/400°F/Gas 6. As the rounds are finished, place them on large baking trays. Bake for 10 to 12 minutes, or until lightly browned on top. Do not overbake. Cool on racks before serving.

Makes 8 pieces of bread.

Note: Unbaked rounds of *lavash* may be frozen between sheets of greaseproof paper. As needed, unwrap and bake as directed.

Variation: Lavash may also be used as a soft sandwich bread to wrap around meat or cheese: Moisten the rounds of baked bread on both sides under cold running water, until they are moist but not soggy. Wrap them in a damp towel and leave to stand until soft, about 45 minutes.

Caucasian Skewered Lamb   Shashlyk

Shashlyk is the skewered, grilled lamb made throughout the Caucasus and Central Asia. Its name comes from the word *shashka* or sword, since *shashlyk* once was the fare of mountain tribesmen who roasted meat on their swords over open fires. The aroma of roasting lamb is one hard to resist. In Solzhenitsyn's *Cancer Ward*, when Oleg is finally released from the hospital, he is given an allowance of five roubles a day. But once tempted by the irresistible odour of grilling *shashlyk* from a kerbside brazier, Oleg cannot help but relinquish three of his precious roubles for a skewer of meat. The meat is grilled to perfection – still rosy, not charred.

To grill *shashlyk* to perfection at home, simply put it over hot coals and serve it rare. *Tkemali* or sour plum sauce is a traditional accompaniment.

2 lb (900 g) boneless shoulder or leg of lamb	freshly ground black pepper to taste
¾ pint (450 ml) pomegranate juice	1 bay leaf, crushed
4 tablespoons olive oil	1 teaspoon crushed thyme
1 teaspoon salt	2 cloves garlic, crushed

Cut the lamb into 2 in (5 cm) cubes. Mix together the remaining ingredients, and marinate the lamb overnight in the mixture. The next day, place the meat on skewers, alternating if desired with cubes of aubergine which have been salted and drained.

Grill over hot coals for about 10 minutes. Serve with pilaf and *tkemali* sauce.

Serves 4 to 6.

Variation: To make *Shashlyk Karsky*, buy a whole rack of lamb and cut it into large serving-sized pieces, about 3 in (7.5 cm) × 5 in (12.5 cm). Alternate the lamb on skewers with fresh lamb kidneys. Grill as directed above.

Sour Plum Sauce Sous tkemali

¾ lb (340 g) fresh sour plums	1 tablespoon chopped fresh basil
6 tablespoons pomegranate juice	salt, hot pepper sauce to taste
3 small cloves garlic	
1 tablespoon chopped fresh coriander (cilantro)	

Bring the plums to the boil with water and simmer them until soft, about 6 to 8 minutes. Drain the plums; then peel and stone them.

Mash the plums in a bowl and then stir in the remaining ingredients. Transfer the mixture to a saucepan. Bring to the boil and simmer uncovered for 20 to 25 minutes.

Serve at room temperature. This sauce is best when made one day ahead of serving time and allowed to mellow overnight.

Caucasian Skewered Beef Basturma

Like the more familiar *shashlyk*, *basturma* is a grilled speciality from
the Caucasus, made with beef instead of lamb. The meat is left to
season overnight in a highly spiced marinade, then cooked quickly
over hot coals. An outstanding summer meal.

2 lb (900 g) boneless beef
    sirloin, cut into 2 in (5 cm)
    cubes
1 large onion, grated
1 teaspoon salt
3 black peppercorns, crushed
2 cloves garlic, crushed
2 tablespoons chopped fresh
    coriander

1 tablespoon chopped fresh
    basil
½ pint (300 ml) olive oil
6 fluid oz (170 ml) freshly
    squeezed lemon juice

fresh tomatoes, spring onions

Place the meat cubes in a large bowl. (They should be at room
temperature.)
   Mix together thoroughly the grated onion, salt, crushed peppercorns and garlic, and the chopped herbs. Combine the olive oil and
lemon juice and stir the onion mixture in. Pour over the meat.
   Marinate overnight or preferably for 24 hours. Grill over hot coals
for about 10 minutes, turning once. The meat should still be pink
inside.
   Serve garnished with sliced or quartered tomatoes and spring
onions. A simple rice pilaf makes a nice accompaniment to this
meal.
   Serves 4 to 6.

Azerbaidzhan Lamb Patties Lyulya-kebab

Yet another grilled treat from the Caucasus.

2 lb (900 g) boneless lamb
    shoulder, with some fat left
    on
2 large onions
2 tablespoons freshly squeezed
    lemon juice
1 teaspoon salt (or more, to
    taste)

freshly ground black pepper
cayenne
basil

spring onions, tomatoes,
    lemon wedges

In a food processor or mincer, mince the lamb and the onions
together finely. Then stir in the lemon juice and add salt, pepper,
cayenne and basil to taste.
   Shape the mixture into sausages about 4 in (10 cm) long and 2 in
(5 cm) wide. Chill them for 2 hours.
   Prepare coals in a grill. When they are hot, skewer the lamb
patties, pressing the meat firmly with your hands to make sure it

adheres to the skewers. Grill over hot coals for about 10 minutes, turning to brown all sides. The lamb should still be pink inside.

Serve the patties garnished with fresh spring onions, tomatoes and lemon wedges on a bed of fresh greens.

Serves 4 to 6.

Variation: Wrap the patties in softened *lavash* (Armenian flat bread – see p. 198) and serve them as sandwiches.

Georgian Cheese Pie Khachapuri

In Tbilisi, many restaurants cater to the Georgians' love for this rich cheese pie. In fact, some of the restaurants even approximate western fast-food shops, and the poor quality of the *khachapuri* there is only to be expected. It is far wiser to visit a café such as the one on Tbilisi's main thoroughfare, which can be reached only by descending a steep flight of stairs into a subterranean room. In spite of its windowless location, the café shimmers with an abundance of gilded mirrors and polished marble walls and floors. The *khachapuri* there are served hot from the oven, and they are a good 8 inches in diameter – more than enough for even the heartiest eater. The pies may be ordered plain or with an egg baked on top, as in the variation below.

Khachapuri is a versatile bread. Serve it with salad for supper or wrap it hot in layers of newspaper and foil to take along on a picnic. And if you have the patience, shape the *khachapuri* into bite-sized pieces and serve them as a striking hors d'œuvre.

Dough
6 fluid oz (170 ml) milk
1½ tablespoons dried yeast
½ teaspoon honey
3 oz (85 g) butter, at room temperature
¼ teaspoon ground coriander

1½ teaspoons salt
8 oz (225 g) flour

Filling
1½ lb (700 g) Munster cheese
1 egg
1 oz (30 g) butter

Heat the milk to lukewarm. Dissolve the yeast and honey in 4 tablespoons of the milk. Set aside for 10 minutes. Then stir in the remaining milk. Add the butter, coriander, salt and flour, mixing well.

Turn the dough out on to a floured board and knead until smooth and elastic, about 10 minutes. Place it in a greased bowl, turning to grease the top. Cover and allow to rise in a warm place until doubled in bulk, 1½ to 2 hours.

Meanwhile, prepare the filling: in a food processor or liquidiser grate the cheese. Beat in the egg and the butter until a smooth, fluffy purée has been formed. (You may have to do this in several batches.) Set aside.

When the dough has doubled in bulk, knock it back and then

leave it to rise again until doubled, about 45 minutes. Knock back and divide the dough into 6 equal pieces. Let it rest for 10 minutes.

On a floured board roll each piece of dough out to a circle 8 in (20 cm) in diameter. Grease six 4 in (10 cm) cake or pie tins. Put one 8 in (20 cm) round of dough in each tin.

Divide the cheese mixture into six equal parts. Spread the filling on each circle of dough, heaping it higher in the centre. Then begin folding the edges of the dough in towards the middle, moving in a clockwise direction, allowing each fold of dough to overlap the previous one, until the cheese mixture is completely enclosed in the pleated dough. Grasp the excess dough in the centre of the pie and twist it into a topknot to seal.

Preheat the oven to 190°C/375°F/Gas 5. Let the pies rest for 10 minutes, then bake them for 35 to 40 minutes, until browned. Slip the *khachapuri* out of the tins and serve them immediately.

Serves 6.

Variation: To make *khachapuri* with egg, follow the instructions above for shaping the pies, only instead of making a tall topknot, flatten the knot so that the surface of the pie is relatively level. Bake the pies as directed. When they are done, crack one raw egg on to the top of each pie. Return to the oven and continue baking for another 5 minutes or so, just until the eggs are set. Serve at once.

Chicken Satsivi

1 small chicken (2½ lb/1 kg)	2 tablespoons coriander seed
1 bayleaf	1 teaspoon *khmeli suneli*
1 large carrot	(optional)
2 sprigs parsley	cayenne to taste
2½ pints (1 litre) cold water	1 teaspoon ground black
salt to taste	pepper
4 tablespoons chicken	¼ teaspoon cinnamon
fat/butter	2 tablespoons minced fresh
3 large onions	parsley
10 small whole heads garlic	2 tablespoons minced fresh dill
4 oz (120 g) walnuts	2 teaspoons vinegar

Place chicken, bay leaf, carrot, parsley sprigs, water and salt to taste in a large stock pot. Bring to the boil, skimming any froth that rises to the surface. Simmer, covered, for 1 hour, then remove the chicken to a large sieve and let it drain. Reserve the broth, measuring out 1½ pints (850 ml). Preheat oven to 210°C/425°F/Gas 7. Place the chicken on a baking sheet and roast until skin is glazed. Set aside to cool, then bone and separate the meat into good sized chunks.

In a large frying pan melt 4 tablespoons butter – chop the onions and sauté in fat till soft and transparent. Meanwhile peel the garlic and grind in a mincer or magimix. Grind the walnuts. Finely crush the coriander seed. When the onions are ready add the garlic, nuts and coriander then stir in the remaining spices and herbs. Stir in the vinegar and blend well. In a steady stream add the reserved chicken broth. Simmer the mixture for 10 minutes then add the chicken pieces. Simmer 5 minutes more.

Remove the *satsivi* from the heat and transfer to a serving dish. Chill well before serving. Garnish with minced fresh coriander, if desired.

Serves 8.

Chicken Tabaka Tsyplyata tabaka

For garlic-lovers, a Georgian classic.

4 poussins (1 lb/450 g each)	*Sauce*
2 oz (60 g) butter	¼ pint (150 ml) rich beef stock
2 tablespoons olive oil	6 large cloves garlic, crushed
12 large cloves garlic, crushed	
salt, freshly ground black	
pepper to taste	

First make the sauce. Pound the 6 cloves of garlic in a mortar to make a paste. Gradually add enough hot rich beef stock (approximately ¼ pint/150 ml) to make a thin sauce. Let the sauce sit at room temperature while the chicken is being prepared.

Prepare the poussins. Pat them dry and turn them breast-side down on a large cutting board. With a sharp knife, cut along both sides of the backbone down its entire length to free it. Then turn the poussin over and break the backbone away from the keel bone which holds the two sides of the breast together. Remove the backbone and the keel bone, along with any adhering white cartilage.

Next, push back the chicken skin to reveal the thigh joint. With a sharp knife, make a cut halfway through the joint so that it can be straightened out. Then, using the knife, make a small slit on each side of the breast just below the ribcage. Push the tips of the drumsticks through these slits, one on each side, so that the knobby ends of the drumsticks protrude on the skin side.

Place the prepared poussins between sheets of greaseproof paper and pound lightly with a meat pounder to flatten slightly. Remove the greaseproof paper and salt the poussins liberally. Dust with pepper, and rub with the crushed garlic.

In one or two large frying pans heat the butter and oil over medium high heat. Place the poussins, skin side up, in the pans and immediately reduce the heat. Cook for 1 minute, then turn the poussins so that the skin side is down.

Place a heavy frying pan over the chicken pieces (if using a 12 in (30 cm) frying pan for the chicken, top it with a 10 in (25 cm) one) and weight it down with a heavy can or a bowl filled with water so that the poussins are flattened still more. Cook the poussins over medium low heat for 15 minutes, then turn them, weighting them down once more. Cook for 10 minutes more.

Transfer the poussins to a platter and serve them at once with the garlic sauce. *Tkemali* (Plum) Sauce (see p. 199) also makes a good accompaniment to the chicken.

Serves 4.

Note: Chicken Tabaka is meant to be eaten with the fingers. It is a good idea to provide finger bowls of warm lemon-scented water, so the diners can unabashedly dig in.

Chicken Chakhokhbili   Chakhokhbili iz kur

A young girl's future was once determined by her skill in preparing chicken by this old Georgian method. When she came of marriageable age, each Georgian girl was given a whole chicken and told to prepare *chakhokhbili* from it. Only if she could cut the chicken up into seventeen precise pieces and make this succulent dish was she considered ready for matrimony.

Fortunately, times have changed. Here, for modern ease of preparation, the chicken is divided into only eight pieces, but the beauty and taste of the dish have not been lost. It is well suited for dinner parties, as it must be prepared a day ahead and reheated before serving.

a 3 lb (1.4 kg) chicken, cut up into eight pieces	4 large cloves garlic, minced
2 teaspoons salt	4 tomatoes, peeled, seeded, and cut into eighths
¼ teaspoon ground thyme	6 tablespoons minced parsley
freshly ground black pepper to taste	1 lemon, cut into thin slices (about 10 slices)
1½ oz (45 g) butter	4 bay leaves
3 large onions, cut into slices	4 tablespoons dry white wine

Mix the salt with the thyme and pepper. Season the chicken pieces all over. Set aside while preparing the vegetables. Slice the onions, mince the garlic and parsley, peel, seed and cut the tomatoes. Cut the lemon into thin slices.

Brown the chicken in a large frying pan in the butter. Lightly grease a baking dish large enough to hold all of the chicken in a single layer. Place half of the onion slices on the bottom of the baking dish, and top them with the browned chicken.

Strew the remaining onion slices, as well as the garlic, tomatoes, parsley and lemon over the chicken. Tuck in the bay leaves. Pour the wine over all.

Preheat the oven to 180°C/350°F/Gas 4. Cover the chicken and bake it for 1 hour.

Leave the chicken to cool to room temperature, and then refrigerate it overnight before serving. Reheat to serve.

Serves 4 generously.

Georgian Kidney Beans Lobio

Lobio means 'bean' in Georgia, where the legumes are put to imaginative use. Here are two traditional ways of preparing kidney beans, one with a sweet plum sauce, the other with plenty of herbs.

Savoury Kidney Beans Lobio

6 oz (170 g) dried kidney beans
¼ teaspoon salt
1 clove garlic, halved
¼ teaspoon crushed hot red pepper
½ teaspoon crushed basil
½ teaspoon crushed mint
2 tablespoons red wine vinegar

1 medium onion, finely chopped
2 small tomatoes, peeled, seeded and chopped
2 tablespoons fresh coriander (cilantro), chopped

1 clove garlic, minced
1 teaspoon salt
freshly ground black pepper to taste
¼ teaspoon crushed hot red pepper
¼ teaspoon crushed basil
¼ teaspoon crushed mint
3 tablespoons chopped parsley
2 tablespoons red wine vinegar
2 tablespoons olive oil

¼ lb (120 g) crumbled feta cheese

Soak the beans in water to cover overnight. The next day, bring to the boil with ¼ teaspoon salt, 1 clove garlic, ¼ teaspoon red pepper, ½ teaspoon each basil and mint and 2 tablespoons vinegar. Simmer until just tender, about 1 hour. Drain.

While the beans are still warm, stir in the remaining ingredients, except for the cheese. Leave to stand at room temperature until cool, then stir in the feta cheese. Refrigerate for several hours or overnight before serving.

Serves 6 to 8.

Kidney Beans with Plum Sauce Lobio tkemali

6 oz (170 g) small dried kidney beans
1 clove garlic, halved
¼ teaspoon salt
¼ teaspoon crushed hot red pepper
1 bay leaf
2 tablespoons red wine vinegar

1 clove garlic, minced

¼ teaspoon crushed hot red pepper
½ teaspoon salt
freshly ground black pepper to taste
2 teaspoons chopped fresh coriander (cilantro)
2 tablespoons red wine vinegar
4 oz (120 g) plum jam

Soak the beans overnight in ample water to cover. The next day, bring them to the boil with 1 clove garlic, ¼ teaspoon red pepper, ¼ teaspoon salt, the bay leaf and 2 tablespoons vinegar. Simmer until just tender, about 1 hour. Drain.

While the beans are still warm, stir in the remaining ingredients.

Leave to stand at room temperature until cool. Then refrigerate several hours or overnight before serving.

Serves 6.

Georgian Cauliflower Tsvetnaya kapusta s yaitsom

An innovative approach to cauliflower.

1 small cauliflower (1 lb/450 g),
  separated into flowerets
4 oz (120 g) butter
2 small onions, finely chopped
4 tablespoons minced parsley

2 tablespoons minced fresh
  coriander (cilantro)
2 large eggs, beaten
salt, freshly ground white
  pepper to taste

Steam the cauliflower over boiling water for 10 minutes. Drain. Meanwhile, in a large frying pan sauté the onion in 2 oz (60 g) butter until golden. Add the remaining butter and stir in the cauliflowerets, turning them to coat with the butter. Cook, covered, for 10 minutes more, until tender.

Stir in the parsley, coriander and the beaten egg. Toss to coat, cooking only until the egg is done. Season to taste.

Serves 4.

Uzbek Pilaf Uzbekskii plov

Plov is what we know as pilaf, an eastern dish, really, but very popular in Russia as well. I first tasted *plov* in Bukhara, where vast quantities of the rice are kept steaming all day in iron cauldrons hung over outdoor fires. For one rouble a bowl is heaped high with rice and vegetables, either pumpkin and marrow, or carrots and onion with just a hint of saffron, as in the recipe below. *Plov* is perfect for entertaining, as it is simple to prepare and it feeds a crowd. Serve it liberally strewn with sliced raw onion, with wedges of hot flat bread on the side.

2 lb (900 g) boneless shoulder
  or leg of lamb, with some
  fat*
2 tablespoons olive oil
2 large onions, cut into
  julienne strips (¾ lb/340 g)
3 carrots, in julienne strips
  (½ lb/225 g)
1¼ lb (570 g) uncooked long
  grain rice

1¾ pints (1 litre) boiling water
1 teaspoon crushed dried red
  pepper *or* ½ teaspoon
  adzhika (see below) to taste
3 teaspoons salt
⅛ teaspoon saffron
freshly ground black pepper to
  taste

raw onion, sliced paper thin

* If the lamb is extremely lean, ask the butcher to give you some fat. It lends great flavour to this dish.

Cut the lamb into chunks. Heat the olive oil in a large casserole. Stir in the lamb and brown it on all sides. Remove to a platter and keep warm.

Stir the onions and carrot into the fat remaining in the pan, adding a little more olive oil if necessary. Cook over medium heat for 10 to 15 minutes, until the vegetables are tender but not brown. Then return the lamb to the pot and stir in the rice. Cook, stirring, for 5 minutes, or until the rice begins to turn golden. Pour in the boiling water, stirring to mix well. Add the red pepper, salt, saffron, and black pepper. Cover the pan; cook over low heat for 20 minutes, until the rice is done.

Serve liberally garnished with paper-thin slices of raw onion.

Serves 6 to 8.

Note: To make *adzhika* grind together equal amounts of red bell peppers, cleaned and seeded, and hot red peppers, including seeds. Add crushed garlic to taste. Store in a covered container in the refrigerator.

Kazakh Lamb and Noodle Stew Lagman

A combination of vegetables and lamb, *lagman* is a cross between a soup and a stew.

2 lb (900 g) boneless lamb, cut into 1 in (2.5 cm) chunks	½ teaspoon dried hot red pepper
4 tablespoons olive oil	1½ pints (900 ml) beef stock
2 onions	salt, freshly ground black pepper to taste
4 large cloves garlic	
1 large carrot, scraped	*Noodles*
1 small green pepper	6 oz (170 g) plain flour
1 medium red pepper (225 g)	½ teaspoon salt
½ lb aubergine	7 tablespoons (approx.) water
4 tablespoons tomato purée	½ oz (15 g) melted butter
4–5 tablespoons cider vinegar	spring onions

Brown the lamb in the olive oil; transfer the meat to a dish and keep warm.

Chop the onions, garlic, carrot, green pepper, red pepper and aubergine (do not peel the aubergine). To the oil remaining in the pot add the onions, garlic and carrot. Cook over medium heat for 10 minutes. Then add the chopped peppers and aubergine. Cook 5 minutes longer. Stir in the tomato purée, vinegar, beef stock and seasonings. Return the lamb to the pot. Cover and simmer for 1½ hours.

Meanwhile, make the noodles. Mix together the flour and the salt. Make a well in the centre and pour in enough water to make a firm dough. Knead for a few minutes. Cover the dough with an up-turned bowl and leave to rest for 1 hour.

Roll the dough out paper thin. Cut into long strips for noodles. Boil the noodles in salted water until tender, then toss with the melted butter.

Place a portion of noodles in each soup plate, then pour some of the lamb mixture over. Garnish each serving with chopped spring onion.

Serves 6.

Sitting Around the Samovar

'A house is beautiful not because of its walls,
but because of its cakes.'
– Old Russian saying

Picture a brass urn with wooden handles, its high patina reflecting the warmth of a cosy room. The face of this urn, emblazoned with medals and etched with the likeness of the Tsar, tapers down to an ornate spigot. This is the samovar, the symbol of Russian hospitality at its best.

The samovar is integral to Russian entertaining. When I picture it, I see it in an opulent setting, one of imperial Russia. The chairs are high-backed and adorned with antimacassars. The light of a late-afternoon wintry day slants through leaded glass windows. The ladies are dressed in full skirts, their necklines either high or daringly low. The table is spread with a starched white cloth and laden with crystal dishes of tempting confections – jams, biscuits, cakes, nuts. The samovar is carried in, steaming, catching the fading light in the room and focusing everyone's attention.

The samovar was never restricted to the homes of the wealthy, however. Even the lowliest peasant hut housed a samovar – perhaps tinplated instead of brass, or perhaps not made in Tula, the city renowned throughout Russia for its finely crafted samovars. Still, the samovar always occupied a place of honour at the table next to the hostess. Even today, in Soviet Russia, samovars can be found, but more often than not electric ones have replaced the original charcoal-heated urns.

In Russian *samovar* means 'self-cooker'. Contrary to popular belief, tea itself is not made in the samovar; the samovar serves only to heat water and keep it hot. Nor is the samovar strictly a Russian discovery. The idea was first introduced to Russia by the invading Mongol hordes in the thirteenth century, hence the samovar's exotic appearance and resemblance to the Mongolian hot pot. But the tea-loving Russians found it too efficient to be ignored, and by the late eighteenth century the samovar had been adapted to everyday use and become an essential part of Russian life. It was always kept burning, ready to refresh guests with a cup of hot tea.

The samovar works on a simple principle. Within the central body is a wide tube. The tube is filled with hot coals or charcoal, and water is poured into the body of the urn surrounding it. The coals efficiently heat the water, the only drawback being the smoke they produce. In the summertime the samovar was always heated outdoors to avoid smoking up the house. In the winter it was too cold to carry it outside, so most families used a pipe extension which fitted on to the large Russian stove and carried the soot and fumes out through the stove's chimney. But many poor peasant families had only a makeshift hole in the roof of their cottage through which the smoke lazily drifted out, much of it, however, remaining in the cottage and settling in a thick layer below the ceiling. Cottages with only a roof hole were known as *chornye izby* or black cottages, while those fitted with a chimney extension were called *belye*, or white.

Once the water boils the samovar is brought to table. The tea is brewed separately and made into a strong concentrate or *zavarka*. This *zavarka* is brewed in a tiny teapot which is kept warm on top of the samovar. To make tea, a small amount of the concentrate is poured into each cup, and the cup is then filled with hot water from the samovar's ornate spigot. In this way the strength of the tea can be adjusted according to taste.

The hostess traditionally presided over the samovar, pouring the tea into porcelain cups for the ladies and into glasses for the men. The glasses were inserted into *podstakanniki*, metal or often filigreed silver holders, so that the tea could be held comfortably. Noble families often had their own *podstakanniki* designs. Children were permitted – in fact, encouraged – to drink tea from their saucers, so as not to burn their lips. Today tea is usually served in glasses at restaurants and cafés, in cups at home. Children still drink from their saucers.

My Russian friends were rather horrified to learn that I drink my tea 'straight'. (Actually I prefer a slice of lemon in it, but since lemon is so hard to come by in the Soviet Union today, I stopped asking for it, having learned my lesson my first week in Moscow when I stopped at a café for some tea. The menu offered two types: Plain Tea or Tea with Lemon. I was surprised to see lemon on the menu and assumed that the food situation must be better than I'd heard. When the waitress came for my order, I requested the tea with lemon. She looked at me with disbelief, then with disdain. 'Lemon?' she repeated scornfully. 'Next you'll be asking for a slice of orange in your tea!' When she plopped the tea down in front of me, it was plain, but she was kind enough to suggest adding sugar to it.) The Russians love sugar in their tea. They say it brings out the flavour of the leaves. In fact, just how the sugar is used is expressed by three Russian idioms used only in conjunction with tea:

pit' chai vnakladku: to drink tea with sugar in it;
pit' chai vpriglyadku: to drink tea without any sugar at all;
pit' chai vprikusku: to drink tea with a cube of sugar clenched between the teeth.

This third method was a favourite among peasants and no doubt largely responsible for their high incidence of tooth decay. Even today many Russians swear by a cube of sugar between the teeth for the greatest satisfaction from a cup of tea.

Another very Russian way of drinking tea is with jam, and the jam in the Soviet Union is marvellous – very thick, with whole pieces of fruit suspended in it. The jam is served alongside the tea on tiny, flat, crystal jam dishes called *rozetki*. It can either be eaten right from the dish or spooned into the tea itself, giving the brew a fruity aroma and taste.

Often a slice of apple replaces the lemon in tea – a popular choice, because not only are the Russians fond of apples, but the autumnal fragrance of the fruit brings to mind the great Russian poet, Pushkin, whose favourite season was autumn and who captured its essence in his poetry. (Russians love their poets even more than their tea!) The apple slice is an attempt to recapture that essence in tea.

If one should catch cold in Omsk or Tomsk one is advised to drink plenty of tea with raspberry jam. Or else add a teaspoon of red wine to the tea – it relaxes as it helps the cold symptoms disappear.

An old Hanukkah custom among Russian Jews is to serve flaming tea, a festive and delicious drink. A cube of sugar is saturated in brandy, then placed in a teaspoon with a little more brandy. The teaspoon is then balanced across the rim of a full cup of tea. A lighted candle is passed around to ignite the cubes, and they are dropped, flaming, into the tea.

The Russians drink mainly black tea, the best of which is grown on the mountain slopes of Georgia and Azerbaidzhan. In Central Asia, however, green tea predominates. It is said to be refreshing even on the hottest of desert days. Most of the tea in the Soviet Union is sold loose, or in packets, but occasionally one encounters *plitochnyi chai* or brick tea. This tea is made of inferior leaves which have been pressed into bricks, often with a design imprinted on the surface. Brick tea is the standard brew of Siberian exiles, who sometimes use so much of it that it produces a narcotic effect, helping them to endure their hardship.

Tea drinking is still a favourite pastime in the Soviet Union. Most cities and towns have tea rooms (and most of the tea rooms are less than imaginatively named either 'Samovar' or 'Russian Tea'). Often they are decorated in the old style with brightly painted ceilings and embroidered tablecloths. Typically the tea rooms contain one or two huge samovars, standing several feet tall. On top of the samovars perch tea cosies made in the round shape of Russian peasant women with disarming faces. Behind the samovars stand the real thing – rotund, matronly women dispensing the tea. After sitting down with one's tea, one can choose from a variety of sweets displayed on the tables.

Making a good cup of tea is an art in itself, a task not to be undertaken lightly. It is essential to start with leaves of high quality. Loose tea will not lose its flavour if stored in a tightly sealed container away from moisture and strong-smelling foods. The steps to follow in making a perfect cup of tea in the Russian manner are as follows:

Bring a kettle of water to the boil – but just barely. The kettle should not whistle away and there should not be much steam.

While the water is heating, rinse the teapot with very hot water and then keep it warm in a low oven or under a cosy. It should not be allowed to cool off. It is important, too, that the teapot be porcelain or ceramic, as metal imparts an off taste to the tea.

Sprinkle the loose tea into the warm teapot, using not less than 1 teaspoon tea for each cup of water, plus 1 teaspoon for the pot.

Pour in the just-boiled water to half full. Close the lid of the teapot, and then cover the entire pot with a clean linen towel or napkin. Let the tea steep for 4 to 5 minutes. Then fill the pot with water and immediately pour the tea into cups.

If making a *zavarka* – the concentrate – instead of a pot of regular-strength tea, use 1 heaped teaspoon tea for every ¼ pint (150 ml) water. Cover and let steep for 5 minutes. Do not add any more water to the pot.

Following are some recipes which traditionally grace the Russian tea table. For inveterate coffee drinkers, these desserts will taste just as good with a cup of coffee, although the experience won't be quite as Russian.

Russian Tea Biscuits Pechen'ye chainoye

The Russians have a notoriously sweet tooth, and even a cup of tea must be accompanied by jam at the very least. Happily, this craving for sweets has produced a wonderful variety of tea biscuits and cakes, such as the biscuits below, simple to prepare and rich with butter.

2 oz (60 g) unsalted butter	pinch of salt
4 oz (120 g) sugar	½ teaspoon baking powder
1 egg	¼ teaspoon mace
½ teaspoon vanilla essence	⅛ teaspoon ground coriander
4 oz (120 g) plain flour	candied orange peel

Preheat the oven to 190°C/375°F/Gas 5. Cream the butter and sugar together until light and fluffy. Beat in the egg and the vanilla essence.

Sift together the dry ingredients and add them to the butter mixture, mixing well.

Drop by scant teaspoonfuls on to lightly greased and floured baking trays. Top each biscuit with a piece of candied orange peel, pressing down lightly to flatten the biscuit.

Bake for 8 to 10 minutes, until lightly browned.

Makes 3 dozen small biscuits.

Meringue Tea Biscuits Pechen'ye chainoye s meringoi

A plain tea biscuit made fancy with meringue, jam and nuts.

3 oz (85 g) unsalted butter	3 oz (85 g) tart apricot jam
4 oz (120 g) sugar	1 egg white
1 egg yolk	2 oz (60 g) sugar
½ teaspoon vanilla essence	¾ teaspoon cinnamon
1 tablespoon single cream	2 oz (60 g) finely chopped
4 oz (120 g) plain flour	pecans
1 teaspoon baking powder	

Cream the butter with the sugar until light and fluffy. Beat in the egg yolk, vanilla essence and cream. Sift together the flour and baking powder, then stir them into the butter mixture, blending well. Form the dough into a ball. Wrap in greaseproof paper and chill in the refrigerator for at least 1 hour.

When the dough is firm, roll it out on a floured board to ¼ in (6 mm) thick. (Since the dough will be somewhat sticky, make sure the board and rolling pin are well floured.) Cut into rounds with a 2 in (5 cm) biscuit cutter. Place the rounds on a lightly greased baking tray, about 1 in (2.5 cm) apart.

Preheat the oven to 180°C/350°F/Gas 4. Spread each round with a thin layer of apricot jam, and then top with meringue.

To make the meringue: beat the egg white until stiff, gradually beating in the sugar, 1 tablespoon at a time. Whip in the cinnamon; fold in the nuts.

Spread the meringue over the jam, leaving an outer rim of dough visible around the edge of the biscuits. Bake for 12 to 15 minutes, until browned. Let cool on the baking tray for about 3 minutes, then transfer to wire racks to cool. These biscuits are best when very fresh.

Makes 2 dozen biscuits.

Souvorov Biscuits Pechen'ye suvorovskoye

Aleksandr Souvorov was a great Russian military commander who found fame during the Russo-Turkish Wars. Exactly how these dainty biscuits came to be named after him has been lost to history, but we do know that the recipe is an old one, dating back to his time.

8 oz (225 g) plain flour	pinch of salt
4 oz (120 g) unsalted butter	3 oz (85 g) thick jam (raspberry
2 oz (60 g) sugar	or apricot)
¼ pint (150 ml) double cream	icing sugar

Cut the butter into the flour. Add the sugar, cream and salt. Form the mixture into a ball and wrap in greaseproof paper. Chill for at least 1 hour in the refrigerator.

On a floured board roll out the dough ⅛ in (3 mm) thick. Using a flower-shaped biscuit cutter (or other decorative shape), cut out the dough into biscuits about 1½ in (3.5 cm) in diameter. Place on ungreased baking trays.

Preheat the oven to 190°C/375°F/Gas 5. Bake the biscuits for 10 to 12 minutes, until golden around the edges. Remove from the baking trays and cool on wire racks.

To assemble, sandwich two biscuits together with a layer of thick jam in between, putting the two flat sides together. Dust with icing sugar before serving.

Makes 5 dozen small biscuits.

Almond Rings Kol'tso mindal'noye

These crisp biscuits were a mainstay of my diet in the Soviet Union. I used to frequent a bakery where a cup of tea or juice could be had along with an assortment of baked goods. The first time I entered the shop I came face to face with a surly saleswoman who slapped the biscuits down on the counter so hard that they crumbled. I wisely decided to take this only as a sign of their freshness, and continued to frequent the shop, each time asking for the same two almond rings. Before long the saleswoman and I were great friends, and she always set aside the biscuits with the most almonds for me.

Even though I make these almond rings at home now sometimes, I still feel nostalgia for that saleswoman and her bakery in Rostov.

8 oz (225 g) butter
6 oz (170 g) sugar
2 small eggs
8 oz (225 g) plain flour

2 egg yolks, lightly beaten
4 oz (120 g) finely chopped
   almonds

Cream the butter and 4 oz (120 g) sugar until light and fluffy. Beat in the eggs, and then stir in the flour. Mix well. Form into a ball and refrigerate the dough for 1 to 2 hours, until firm.

Preheat the oven to 190°C/375°F/Gas 5. On a floured pastry board roll out the dough to ½ in (12 mm) thick. Cut out rounds with a 4 in (10 cm) cutter, preferably a fluted one. Then take a 1 in (2.5 cm) round cutter and cut a hole out of the centre of each round.

Transfer the biscuits to a greased baking tray and brush them with the lightly beaten egg yolks, then sprinkle them with a mixture of the chopped almonds and the remaining sugar.

Bake for 12 to 15 minutes, until golden.

Makes 18 large biscuits.

Hazel-nut Rusks Sukhariki

Crisp and slightly sweet, these rusks are lovely on the afternoon tea table or with morning coffee.

2 eggs
6 oz (170 g) sugar
4 oz (120 g) flour

5 oz (150 g) hazel-nuts,
   coarsely chopped

Beat the eggs and the sugar until light and fluffy. Dredge the nuts with the flour; blend them into the egg mixture.

Preheat the oven to 150°C/300°F/Gas 2. Grease an 8 in (20 cm) loaf tin. Pour the batter into the tin and bake at 150°C/300°F for 50 minutes.

Turn the loaf out of the tin and wrap it in a moist tea towel. Leave to stand for 4 hours. Then cut it into slices about ⅓ in (8 mm) thick.

Preheat the oven to 130°C/250°F/Gas ½. Place the slices on a baking tray and bake them until lightly browned and crisp, about 3 hours.

Makes 2 dozen rusks.

Curd Cheese Tartlets Vatrushki

These wonderful tartlets always disappear fast. Though they may be made larger (Gogol's Chichikov feasted on *vatrushki* 'at least as big as a dinner plate, if not larger'), I find the diminutive size perfect for eating with the fingers. A classic accompaniment to *borshch*, these tartlets can also inspire a tea or *zakuska* table.

Dough
8 oz (225 g) plain flour
1 oz (30 g) sugar
½ teaspoon salt
4 oz (120 g) butter
2 egg yolks
scant 6 fluid oz (170 ml) soured cream

Filling
1½ lb (700g) *tvorog* (see p. 171) or curd cheese

3 egg yolks
¼ teaspoon salt
3 oz (85 g) sugar
3 oz (85 g) soured cream
2 oz (60 g) raisins

Glaze
1 egg yolk
1 tablespoon cold water

To make the dough mix together the flour, sugar and salt. Cut in the butter. Work in the yolks and soured cream. (The mixture will be slightly sticky.) Wrap the dough in greaseproof paper and chill for at least 30 minutes before using.

To prepare the filling, beat the egg yolks into the cheese. Stir in the salt, sugar, soured cream and raisins, blending well. Chill.

Roll the dough out on a floured board to ⅛ in (3 mm) thick. With a biscuit cutter, cut out 4 in (10 cm) rounds. On each round place 2 heaped tablespoons of filling, spreading it to within 1 in (2.5 cm) of the edges.

Bring the edges of the dough up around the filling in gentle folds, leaving the filling exposed and making a narrow border of dough. Place on a greased baking tray.

Preheat the oven to 190°C/375°F/Gas 5. Brush the tartlets with the egg yolk which has been mixed with the cold water. Bake for 25 minutes until the filling is puffed and the dough golden.

Makes 20 tartlets.

Note: If the *vatrushki* are to be served as an accompaniment to *borshch*, cut down on the sugar and omit the raisins.

Walnut Crescents Rogaliki

Rogaliki or 'little horns' are a speciality of southern Russia and the Ukraine. This recipe was given to me by a motherly woman named Margarita, who throughout my stay in the Soviet Union kept trying to fatten me up with goodies from her kitchen, such as these excellent pastries stuffed with sugar and nuts.

Pastry	*Filling*
8 oz (225 g) plain flour	2 egg whites
1 tablespoon dried yeast	pinch of salt
7 oz (200 g) unsalted butter, cut into small pieces	6 oz (170 g) walnut pieces
2 egg yolks	6 oz (170 g) sugar
8 fluid oz (scant) soured cream	

In a medium-sized bowl mix together the flour and the yeast. Cut in the butter until the mixture resembles coarse meal. Stir in the egg yolks and soured cream, and with your fingers mix just until the dough holds together. (The less you work this dough, the more tender it will be.) The dough will be sticky. Shape into a ball, wrap in waxed greaseproof paper, and refrigerate for at least 2 hours.

Meanwhile, prepare the filling. In a frying pan sauté the walnuts over low heat for about 5 minutes to release their flavour, being careful not to burn them. Then grind them coarsely along with the sugar.

Beat the egg whites with the salt until stiff but not dry. Fold in the nut mixture.

Preheat the oven to 180°C/350°F/Gas 4. Divide the dough into 3 parts. With a floured rolling pin, on a well-floured board, roll out each part into a circle ⅛ in (3 mm) thick. Cut 10 pie-shaped wedges out of each circle. Spread the wedges with the filling and then roll them up like croissants, starting at the wide end.

Place the *rogaliki* point-side down on a lightly greased baking tray, turning the edges in slightly to form crescents. Bake for 15 to 20 minutes, until puffed and golden.

Makes 30 pastries.

Variation: Spread the dough with thick jam instead of the nut filling. Proceed as directed above.

Raisin Buns Bulka s izyumom

A superb choice for morning coffee or tea.

1 tablespoon dried yeast	grated rind of 1 lemon
4 tablespoons warm water	2 eggs, well beaten
2 oz (60 g) sugar	11 oz (310 g) plain flour
1 teaspoon salt	8 oz (225 g) cream cheese, at
2 oz (60 g) unsalted butter, at	room temperature
room temperature	9 oz (250 g) stoned raisins
about ½ pint (300 ml) single	
cream	1 oz (30 g) melted butter

Dissolve the yeast in the warm water. Heat 4 fluid oz (120 ml) single cream to just below boiling, then pour it over a mixture of the sugar, salt and butter in a mixing bowl, stirring until the butter melts. Cool to lukewarm.

Stir in the yeast, lemon rind, eggs and enough flour to make a soft dough. Cover the bowl and chill the dough in the refrigerator for 3 to 4 hours, or until it is workable. (The dough may be left overnight in the refrigerator.)

Meanwhile, beat the cream cheese until smooth. Stir in enough remaining single cream, to make a light but firm filling. Beat out any lumps, then stir in the raisins.

Roll the dough out on a floured board to ⅛ in (3 mm) thick. Cut it into squares. Place a heaped tablespoon of the cream cheese filling in the middle of each square. Bring the edges together in the centre and pinch to seal. (If it is more convenient, the buns may be put in the refrigerator and chilled overnight to be baked fresh in the morning; or they may be baked now.)

Grease a large baking tray. Place the buns on it and brush them with the melted butter. Let them rise until doubled, covered. Preheat the oven to 200°C/400°F/Gas 6. Bake the buns for 12 minutes or until lightly browned. These buns are best when still slightly warm.

Makes 2 dozen.

Sweet Boiled Buns Bubliki

In the 1920s Soviet Russia instituted its New Economic Policy (NEP), permitting a certain degree of private enterprise. A new breed of Soviet citizen, the wily entrepreneur, emerged, wheedling the public to buy wares often of dubious quality. Many less sophisticated sellers also took to the streets in an attempt to peddle their goods, and for a while the cities were once again full of all manner of colourful hawkers.

One of the most popular products of this era were the *bubliki*, or buns, sold hot from portable ovens and immortalised in a contemporary song, 'Bublichki', in which a young girl bewails her father's drunkenness and the fact that she must eke out her livelihood hawking buns on the street.

The well-loved *bubliki* are actually none other than water buns, or bagels, boiled until puffy and then baked to a golden finish in the oven. The recipe presented here is a less common version of these popular buns. A sweet, enriched dough is boiled in flavoured milk before baking, resulting in a light and dainty bun perfect for breakfast or tea.

2 oz (60 g) unsalted butter	¼ teaspoon mace
4 oz (120 g) sugar	1½ pints (900 ml) milk
3 egg yolks	2 teaspoons vanilla essence
6 oz (170 g) plain flour	
1½ teaspoons baking powder	1 egg yolk, beaten
pinch of salt	sugar crystals

Cream the butter and sugar. Beat in the egg yolks. Stir in the baking powder, mace and enough flour to make a firm dough. Divide the dough into 12 pieces. Shape each piece into a ring 2 in (5 cm) in diameter.

In a deep pan bring the milk and vanilla essence to the boil. Drop in the rings of dough, a few at a time, and cook them in the boiling milk, until they rise to the surface, which will take only a minute.

With a slotted spoon, transfer the rings to a baking tray and brush them with the beaten egg yolk, then sprinkle with large crystal sugar.

Preheat the oven to 150°C/300°F/Gas 2. Bake the *bubliki* until they are puffed and brown, about 30 minutes. Transfer to racks to cool.

Makes 1 dozen buns.

Lemon Cake Limonnyi tort

A tart lemon filling is sandwiched between the layers of this wonderfully fragrant loaf. Thinly sliced and served with a cold fruit soufflé, it makes an excellent ending to a light meal.

1 tablespoon dried yeast	*Glaze*
4 tablespoons warm milk	2 oz (60 g) icing sugar
1 tablespoon sugar	1 tablespoon hot water
9½ oz (265 g) flour	¼ teaspoon vanilla essence
1 egg	
8 oz (225 g) butter, cut into small pieces, at room temperature	curls of lemon rind
	tiny raspberries or strawberries

Filling
1 whole lemon
8 oz (225 g) sugar

220 SITTING AROUND THE SAMOVAR

Dissolve the yeast in the milk; gradually add 1 tablespoon sugar and ½ oz (15 g) flour. Cover; leave to sit in a warm place for 1 hour, until bubbly.

Stir in the egg, butter and remaining flour. The dough will be *very* soft. Place it in a greased bowl and leave to rise until doubled in bulk, about 1½ hours. While the dough is rising, prepare the filling. Cut the whole lemon into eighths and remove any pips. Then, in a food processor or mincer, grind the lemon, including the rind. Stir in the 8 oz (225 g) sugar and set aside.

Generously grease a large baking tray. When the dough has risen, knock it back. Then take two-thirds of the dough and press or roll it out into a circle 7 in (17.5 cm) in diameter, flouring it lightly from time to time to make it more manageable, if necessary. Place the circle of dough on the baking tray. Pinch the edges of the circle up all the way around, making a rim high enough to contain the lemon filling. Pour in the filling.

Press or roll the remaining dough into a circle 6 in (15 cm) in diameter which will fit over the lemon filling, covering it completely and meeting the outer rim of the larger circle. Pinch the edges of the top and bottom layers of dough together to seal.

Preheat the oven to 190°C/375°F/Gas 5. Leave the cake to rise for about 20 minutes, then bake it for 25 minutes, or until nicely browned.

Remove the cake from the oven. While it is still warm swirl the glaze over it, which has been made by combining the icing sugar, hot water and vanilla essence. After about 20 minutes carefully transfer the cake to a rack to continue cooling. Serve at room temperature, decorated with tiny berries along the seam of the cake and lemon curls on top.

Serves about 12.

Note: In spite of the yeast, this is a rather flat cake, about 1 in (2.5 cm) high.

Apple Cake with Chocolate Glaze Yablochnyi pirog

My friend Sonya, an excellent cook, gave me this recipe for an apple cake which has been made for generations in her family. I first tasted it when we returned to her small Moscow apartment after a day of cross-country skiing in the countryside. The weather was bitterly cold, and as soon as we'd taken off our wet clothes Sonya brewed a fresh pot of tea and offered this delightful cake along with it.

¾ lb (340 g) apples, pared,
   cored, and thinly sliced
3 eggs
8 oz (225 g) sugar
4 oz (120 g) plain flour
¼ teaspoon salt
1 teaspoon bicarbonate of soda
1½ teaspoons freshly squeezed
   lemon juice
½ teaspoon cinnamon

Glaze
2 oz (60 g) butter
2 tablespoons milk
2 oz (60 g) icing sugar, sifted
2 tablespoons unsweetened
   cocoa powder

chopped walnuts (optional)

Preheat the oven to 190°C/350°F/Gas 4. Grease and lightly flour a 9 in (22.5 cm) springform tin.

Beat the eggs with the sugar. Stir in the flour and the salt. Dissolve the bicarbonate of soda in the lemon juice and add it to the batter. Stir in the cinnamon, mixing well. Finally, stir in the apples.

Pour the batter into the prepared tin and bake for 1 hour, until browned, or until a cake tester comes out clean.

Prepare the glaze 5 minutes before the cake is removed from the oven. Melt the butter over low heat in a small saucepan. Stir in the milk, icing sugar and cocoa powder. Bring the mixture just to the boil, then remove the sides of the tin and spread the glaze over the top of the cake while the cake is still hot.

Decorate the top of the cake with chopped walnuts, if desired.

Cool to room temperature before serving.

Serves 10.

Cranberry-Apple Roll Rulet s klyukvoi

Here is a very Russian dessert.

Pastry
6 oz (170 g) butter, at room
   temperature
6 oz (170 g) cream cheese, at
   room temperature
1 egg yolk
6 oz (170 g) plain flour
¼ teaspoon salt

Filling
¼ lb (120 g) cranberries

4 oz (120 g) (scant) sugar
1½ oz (45 g) honey
1 tablespoon water
grated peel of ½ lemon
1 tablespoon flour
¼ teaspoon cinnamon
2 large tart apples, pared,
   cored and finely chopped

1 egg yolk, beaten

Cream the butter and cream cheese together. Beat in the egg yolk. With your hands work the flour and salt into the butter mixture until a soft dough has been formed. Shape into a ball, wrap in greaseproof paper, and chill for at least 30 minutes before rolling out.

Make the filling: place the cranberries, sugar, honey, water, lemon peel, flour and cinnamon in a heavy saucepan. Bring to the boil and cook, stirring, until the cranberries burst, about 10 minutes. Remove from the heat and stir in the apples.

Roll the dough out and trim it to a 9 in (22.5 cm) × 18 in (45 cm) rectangle. Leaving a 3 in (7.5 cm) wide strip down the centre of the dough, cut 3 in (7.5 cm) long strips radiating out from the centre down both sides of the dough. (Use a fluted pastry cutter if you have one.) Thus there will be a 3 in (7.5 cm) wide centre strip with approximately 12 fluted ribbons on either side of it.

Spread the filling along the centre strip. Then, alternating sides, fold in the fluted strips at an angle, each one overlapping the next, so that the filling is completely covered.

Transfer the roll to a greased baking tray using two spatulas. Brush with the beaten egg yolk.

Preheat the oven to 190°C/375°F/Gas 5. Bake the roll for approximately 1 hour, if necessary covering it with foil towards the end of the baking so that it doesn't brown too much. Transfer the baked roll to a rack while still slightly warm. Serve at room temperature.

Serves about 10.

Note: This pastry will also make 1 dozen *pirozhki*.

Apricot Tart Abrikosovyi pirog

Butter, soured cream, jam and nuts join forces once again in this excellent tart.

8 oz (225 g) plain flour	2 egg yolks, lightly beaten
4 oz (120 g) butter	1 tablespoon soured cream
⅛ teaspoon salt	12 oz (340 g) thick apricot jam
4 oz (120 g) sugar	2 oz (60 g) sliced blanched
¾ teaspoon baking powder	almonds
1 tablespoon freshly squeezed	
lemon juice	1 egg yolk, beaten
grated rind of ½ lemon	

Cut the butter into the flour, then add the salt, sugar and baking powder. Stir in the lemon juice, rind, egg yolks and soured cream, mixing well to form a soft, sticky dough. Set aside one-third of the dough for the lattice top.

Lightly grease a baking tray and place a greased 9½ in (24 cm) flan ring on it, or use a false-bottomed tart tin. Pat the larger piece of dough evenly into the flan ring, covering the bottom and sides.

Spread the jam over the top of the dough, then sprinkle the almonds over the jam.

Press out the remaining piece of dough and either cut or mould it into pieces to make a lattice crust. Brush the top of the tart with the beaten egg yolk.

Preheat the oven to 180°C/350°F/Gas 4. Bake the tart for 25 minutes, or until golden. Cool to room temperature before serving.

Serves 6 to 8.

Poppy Seed Torte Makovyi tort

A delicate torte, which separates into three ribboned layers upon baking.

4 oz (120 g) poppy seed	6 oz (170 g) potato flour
8 egg yolks	6 bitter almonds, ground
8 fluid oz (225 ml) double	3 oz (85 g) semi-sweet
cream	chocolate, grated
4 oz (120 g) icing sugar, sifted	6 egg whites, beaten

Pour ½ pint (300 ml) boiling water over the poppy seeds to scald them. Leave to soak for 1 hour, then strain through muslin. Set aside to drain well.

Beat the egg yolks until light and lemon coloured, then beat in the cream. Gradually add the sugar and potato flour, continuing to beat well. Stir in the ground almonds and grated chocolate, and finally stir in the drained poppy seeds.

Beat the egg whites until stiff but not dry. Fold them into the cake batter. The mixture will be quite loose.

Preheat the oven to 170°C/325°F/Gas 3. Grease and dust with fine breadcrumbs a 10 in (25 cm) springform tin. Pour the cake mixture into the pan and bake for 45 minutes.

Cool the torte completely before removing the outer ring of the pan. Dust the top of the torte with powdered sugar and decorate with chocolate curls.

Serves 10.

Russian Caramel Torte Tort 'Tyanuchki'

A favourite of the Russian expatriots living in Scandinavia, this fabulous torte is so popular that Finland's largest confectionery firm, Fazer, produces it commercially. The name comes from its topping, *tyanuchki*, an old-fashioned white fudge which is left to cook for long hours until thick and caramel-coloured. So sleek is this topping, it looks like liquid marble. Serve the torte in small portions. It is very, very rich.

3 oz (85 g) unsalted butter	*Topping*
generous 6 oz (170 g) sugar	4 fluid oz (125 ml) double
3 eggs, separated	cream
3 boiled potatoes (1½ lb (700 g);	3 oz (85 g) sugar
to yield 1 lb (450 g) mashed)	3 tablespoons corn syrup
6 oz (170 g) blanched almonds	1 oz (30 g) unsalted butter
6 bitter almonds	½ teaspoon vanilla essence
pinch of salt	apricot jam

Cream the butter and sugar. Beat in the egg yolks. Grind the blanched almonds together with the bitter almonds. Mash the potatoes and leave them to cool slightly. Add the almonds, potatoes and salt to the butter mixture, beating well until there are no lumps left in the batter (this will take some work). Beat the egg whites until stiff but not dry and fold them in to the batter.

Preheat the oven to 180°C/350°F/Gas 4. Grease and flour two 8 in (20 cm) round cake tins; cover the bottoms of the tins with rounds of greaseproof paper and grease the greaseproof paper. Pour the batter into the pans and bake for 1 hour, until a cake tester comes out clean.

Prepare the topping while the cake is baking. In a heavy saucepan combine the cream, sugar and corn syrup. Cook over medium heat, stirring, until the sugar has dissolved. Then cook slowly for 50 minutes until the mixture is thick and caramel-coloured (a sugar thermometer will register 104°C/220°F). Off the heat, stir in the butter and vanilla essence. Cool slightly.

Turn the cake layers out on to a rack and leave to cool. Then spread a thin layer of jam between the layers and assemble them. Pour the caramel topping over all, letting it drip down the sides and then smoothing it with a spatula until the cake is entirely coated. Decorate with sliced almonds, if desired.

Refrigerate for 24 hours before serving.

Serves 10 to 12.

Variation: Prepare only the topping and serve it warm over fresh cranberries or pears.

'Mother-in-Law' Torte 'Svekrukha'

This festive torte, reserved for special occasions in Russia, has a creamy ivory filling sandwiched between four crisp cake layers topped with a chocolate glaze. The recipe was given to me by my cousin Roma, who works as a pathologist, but whose real vocation is baking. He regularly turns out flaky *pirogi* with wild mushroom stuffing and *pirozhki* filled with chopped cabbage and eggs. This torte is Roma's speciality. It was his mother who passed the recipe on to him, so Roma's wife Raya dubbed the cake 'Mother-in-Law' Torte. It is a favourite with children, as evidenced by the clamorous cries of Roma's own two children when the torte appears on the table.

Cake Layers

7 oz (200 g) unsalted butter	4 oz (120 g) walnuts, ground
2½ oz (75 g) sugar	2 tablespoons soured cream
½ teaspoon salt	8 oz (225 g) plain flour

Melt the butter, then pour it into a mixing bowl. Stir in the sugar, salt, ground walnuts and soured cream, mixing well. Then stir in the flour until it is well blended. The dough will be loose.

Preheat the oven to 180°C/350°F/Gas 4. Spread two baking trays with foil and grease the foil.

Divide the dough into 4 parts. On the foil, pat out 4 rounds, each ¼ in (6 mm) thick and 8 in (20 cm) in diameter. Bake the rounds for about 15 minutes, until browned around the edges.

Cool the rounds before removing them from the foil, since they are very fragile.

Buttercream Filling	1 oz (30 g) walnuts, heated
2 oz (60 g) unsalted butter	slightly in a frying pan to
2 oz (60 g) sugar	release their flavour, then
½ teaspoon vanilla essence	finely chopped
1 small egg, slightly beaten	1 tablespoon cognac
4 tablespoons soured cream	

Cream the butter and the sugar until light. Gradually stir in the vanilla essence, egg and soured cream. Add the finely chopped nuts and the cognac, beating well. This filling will be very loose, so chill it for at least 10 minutes in the refrigerator before speading it on the cake layers.

Spread the buttercream filling between the cooled cake layers. Prepare the glaze:

Chocolate Glaze	1 scant teaspoon unsweetened
2 tablespoons milk	cocoa powder
2 oz (60 g) sugar	½ oz (15 g) unsalted butter

Pour the milk into a small saucepan. Mix together the sugar and cocoa powder and add them to the milk. Bring to the boil and simmer for 10 minutes, stirring constantly. Remove from the heat and stir in the butter. Immediately spread the glaze over the top layer of the torte.

Place the torte in the refrigerator and chill for several hours before serving.

Serves 12.

Glacéed Apricots Zasakharennye abrikosy

Perfect for eating with the fingers or for decorating lavish tortes.

8 oz (225 g) sugar	dash of salt
4 fluid oz (120 ml) hot water	4 oz (120 g) dried apricot halves
pinch of cream of tartar	

Combine the sugar, water, cream of tartar and salt in a heavy saucepan. Bring to the boil, stirring until the sugar dissolves, and cook until the mixture registers 143°C/290°F on a sugar thermometer – the hard-crack stage.

Immediately remove the syrup from the heat and dip the apricots into it, one at a time. This is most easily done by grasping the edge of each apricot half with a pair of tweezers.

As each apricot is dipped, place it on a lightly buttered drying rack

or marble slab to harden. If the syrup should become too thick, heat
it gently until it loosens again.

Makes about 2 dozen candies.

Note: These apricots must be prepared in dry weather, otherwise the
sugar coating will not harden.

Almond Caramels Makagigi

These chewy caramels come from Ukrainian kitchens, but their
name suggests a Turkish origin.

2 oz (60 g) sugar	6 oz (170 g) blanched almonds,
4 oz (120 g) butter	coarsely chopped
4 oz (120 g) honey (preferably	
buckwheat)	

In a large frying pan melt the sugar and cook it over low heat, stirring
constantly, until it has caramelised (turned light golden brown). Be
very careful not to let the sugar burn.

Stir in the butter and the honey and cook the mixture at the barest
simmer for 5 to 8 minutes, stirring constantly, until a bit of the
mixture dropped into a glass of iced water holds a pliable ball (hard
ball stage on a sugar thermometer).

Stir in the almonds and drop by teaspoonfuls on to a buttered
marble slab or well-buttered greaseproof paper. Cool.

Makes 3 dozen caramels.

Apple Confections Pastila

Pastila are a cross between confectionery and meringue biscuits.
They are light, airy puffs with a delicate apple flavour, the adorn-
ment of elegant tea tables since the mid-nineteenth century.

3 large, tart green apples	¼ teaspoon cinnamon
(1¼ lb/570 g)	2 egg whites, stiffly beaten
1 teaspoon fresh lemon juice	yellow food colouring
8 oz (225 g) sugar	(optional)
¼ teaspoon (scant) almond	
essence	

Steam the apples whole and unpeeled over boiling water until
tender, about 25 to 30 minutes. It's all right if the apples fall apart.
Put them through a vegetable mill. Stir in the lemon juice, sugar,
almond essence and cinnamon.

Beat the egg whites until stiff but not dry. Stir them into the apple
mixture along with 16 drops of yellow food colouring if a pale yellow
tint is desired. Beat the mixture at high speed with an electric mixer
for at least 5 minutes, until fluffy, or for 10 to 15 minutes by hand.

Preheat the oven to 65°C/150°F/Gas ⅛. Spread a sheet of foil on a baking sheet. Grease it lightly and then dust with flour. Drop the apple foam by tablespoons on to the foil.

Bake for about 6 hours in a slow oven, until the confections are dry. Then transfer them to a wire rack to cool.

Makes about 5 dozen confections.

Note: The *pastila* look especially lovely when served in fluted paper cups displayed on an epergne.

Index

A NEW, MORE SENSIBLE AND HEALTHIER WAY
OF EATING FOR THE ENTIRE FAMILY

MARY BERRY
Feed your family the healthier way!

Mary Berry takes the mystery out of healthy eating
and shows you how to change your family's diet without
them even noticing. She indicates the foods that really
are good for your family, as well as simple, economical
recipes that will have them asking for more.

FEED YOUR FAMILY THE HEALTHIER WAY contains
an easy guide to selecting and preparing more
nutritious foods, helpful hints for introducing natural
foods like brown rice and wholemeal flour into your
family's diet and 175 delicious recipes for everything
from breakfast to puddings. Mary Berry makes good
eating easy.

COOKERY/HEALTH   0 7221 1641 1   £2.95

Also by Mary Berry in Sphere Books:
FAST CAKES
FRUIT FARE
FAST STARTERS, SOUPS &
SALADS
FAST SUPPERS
FAST DESSERTS
NEW FREEZER COOKBOOK
KITCHEN WISDOM

A selection of bestsellers from SPHERE

FICTION

THE GLORY GAME	Janet Dailey	£3.50 ☐
NIGHT WARRIORS	Graham Masterton	£2.95 ☐
THE DAMNATION GAME	Clive Barker	£3.50 ☐
SECRETS	Danielle Steel	£2.95 ☐
KING OF THE GOLDEN VALLEY	Alan Scholefield	£2.95 ☐

FILM & TV TIE-IN

SEX WITH PAULA YATES	Paula Yates	£2.95 ☐
RAW DEAL	Walter Wager	£2.50 ☐
INSIDE STORY	Jack Ramsay	£2.50 ☐
SHORT CIRCUIT	Colin Wedgelock	£2.50 ☐
MONA LISA	John Luther Novak	£2.50 ☐

NON-FICTION

THE MAUL AND THE PEAR TREE	T. A. Critchley & P. D. James	£3.50 ☐
DUKE: THE LIFE AND TIMES OF JOHN WAYNE	Donald Shepherd & Robert Slatzer	£3.95 ☐
WHITEHALL: TRAGEDY & FARCE	Clive Ponting	£4.95 ☐
GODDESS: THE SECRET LIVES OF MARILYN MONROE	Anthony Summers	£3.95 ☐
1945: THE WORLD WE FOUGHT FOR	Robert Kee	£4.95 ☐

All Sphere books are available at your local bookshop or newsagent, or can be ordered direct from the publisher. Just tick the titles you want and fill in the form below.

Name _____

Address _____

_____

Write to Sphere Books, Cash Sales Department, P.O. Box 11, Falmouth, Cornwall TR10 9EN.

Please enclose a cheque or postal order to the value of the cover price plus:

UK: 60p for the first book, 25p for the second book and 15p for each additional book ordered to a maximum charge of £1.90.

OVERSEAS & EIRE: £1.25 for the first book, 75p for the second book and 28p for each subsequent title ordered.

BFPO: 60p for the first book, 25p for the second book plus 15p per copy for the next 7 books, thereafter 9p per book.

Sphere Books reserve the right to show new retail prices on covers which may differ from those previously advertised in the text or elsewhere, and to increase postal rates in accordance with the PO.